BIRDS IN MEDIEVAL ENGLISH POETRY

Nature and Environment in the Middle Ages

ISSN: 2399-3804 (Print)
ISSN: 2399-3812 (Online)

Series Editor
Michael D.J. Bintley

Editorial Board
Jennifer Neville
Aleks Pluskowski
Gillian Rudd

Questions of nature, the environment and sustainability are increasingly important areas of scholarly enquiry in various fields. This exciting new series aims to provide a forum for new work throughout the medieval period broadly defined (c.400–1500), covering literature, history, archaeology and other allied disciplines in the humanities. Topics may range from studies of landscape to interaction with humans, from representations of 'nature' in art to ecology, ecotheory, ecofeminism and ecocriticism; monographs and collections of essays are equally welcome.

Proposals or enquiries may be sent directly to the series editor or to the publisher at the addresses given below.

Dr Michael D.J. Bintley, Department of English and Humanities, School of Arts, Birkbeck, University of London, 43 Gordon Square, London, WC1H 0PD

Boydell & Brewer, PO Box 9, Woodbridge, Suffolk, IP12 3DF

Previously published:

1: *The Natural World in the Exeter Book Riddles*, Corinne Dale
2: *Birds in Medieval English Poetry: Metaphors, Realities, Transformations*, Michael J. Warren
3: *Restoring Creation: The Natural World in the Anglo-Saxon Saints' Lives of Cuthbert and Guthlac*, Britton Elliott Brooks

BIRDS IN MEDIEVAL ENGLISH POETRY

Metaphors, Realities, Transformations

Michael J. Warren

D. S. BREWER

© Michael J. Warren 2018

All Rights Reserved. Except as permitted under current legislation no part of this work may be photocopied, stored in a retrieval system, published, performed in public, adapted, broadcast, transmitted, recorded or reproduced in any form or by any means, without the prior permission of the copyright owner

The right of Michael J. Warren to be identified as the author of this work has been asserted in accordance with sections 77 and 78 of the Copyright, Designs and Patents Act 1988

First published 2018
D. S. Brewer, Cambridge
Paperback edition 2021

ISBN 978 1 84384 508 9 hardback
ISBN 978 1 84384 591 1 paperback

D. S. Brewer is an imprint of Boydell & Brewer Ltd
PO Box 9, Woodbridge, Suffolk IP12 3DF, UK
and of Boydell & Brewer Inc.
668 Mt Hope Avenue, Rochester, NY 14620–2731, USA
website: www.boydellandbrewer.com

A catalogue record for this book is available
from the British Library

The publisher has no responsibility for the continued existence or accuracy of URLs for external or third-party internet websites referred to in this book, and does not guarantee that any content on such websites is, or will remain, accurate or appropriate

CONTENTS

List of Illustrations	vi
Acknowledgements	vii
List of Abbreviations	viii
Introduction	1
1 Native Foreigners: Migrating Seabirds and the Pelagic Soul in *The Seafarer*	25
2 Avian Pedagogies: Wondering with Birds in the Exeter Book Riddles	65
3 A Bird's Worth: Mis-Representing Owls in *The Owl and the Nightingale*	103
4 'Kek Kek': Translating Birds in *The Parliament of Fowls*	147
5 Birds' Form: Enabling Desire and Identities in *Confessio Amantis*	179
Epilogue	219
Glossary: Old and Middle English Bird Names	225
Bibliography	237
Index	255

ILLUSTRATIONS

Plate 1 **Common tern** *Sterna hirundo*
þær him stearn oncwæð / isigfeþera 'there the tern answered them, icy-feathered' (*The Seafarer*, 23b–24a)   24

Plate 2 **Barnacle goose** *Branta leucopsis*
þa ic of fæðmum cwom / brimes ond beames on blacum hrægle; / sume wæron white hyrste mine 'when I came out of the embrace of water and wood in a black garment, some of my wear was white' (Exeter Book Riddle 10, 6b–8)   64

Plate 3 **Little owl** *Athene noctua*
Þu wenest þat ich ne miʒte iso / Vor ich bi daie noʒt ne flo 'You think that I cannot see because I do not fly by day' (*The Owl and the Nightingale*, 371–2)   102

Plate 4 **Turtle dove** *Streptopelia turtur*
'I am a seed-foul, oon the unworthieste' (*The Parliament of Fowls*, 512)   146

Plate 5 **Lapwing** *Vanellus vanellus*
A lappewincke mad he was, / And thus he hoppeth on the gras ('Tale of Tereus', *Confessio Amantis*, V.6041–2)   178

Plate 6 Tereus, Philomela and Procne transformed into birds in a depiction from the *Ovide moralisé*, Paris, BnF, MS Arsenal 5069, f. 91r.   180

Plates 1-5: photographs by Brian Lawrence, reproduced by kind permission.

ACKNOWLEDGEMENTS

The origins of this book stretch back nearly two decades. From the beginning, Ruth Kennedy has been an inspirational teacher and friend whose influence has been vital to the survival and completion of this project. I owe gratitude as well to other members of the English department at Royal Holloway for their generous support and time: particularly Catherine Nall, but also Alastair Bennett, Jennifer Neville, Corinne Dale and Neville Mogford.

I am most fortunate to have received invaluable advice from numerous scholars in my field over the last few years, in particular, Robert Stanton, Carolynn Van Dyke, Gillian Rudd, Jonathan Hsy and Heide Estes. Two of my chapters have been published in shortened forms in *Studies in the Age of Chaucer*, 38 (2016), 109–32, and *English Studies*, 98:8 (2017), 825–45. I am grateful to the editors and publishers of these journals for permission to reproduce this material, and to the anonymous peer reviewers who helped make those articles what they are. I thank, too, the readers for Boydell and Brewer whose comments helped shape the content further, and the Boydell team themselves, especially Caroline Palmer, who first saw potential in the manuscript and has suffered persistent inquiries since then.

Beyond academic circles, my gratitude goes to the committee of New Networks for Nature for their encouragement and for providing me with an important platform for sharing my research to a wider audience. I must thank Jeremy Mynott most of all, whose friendship and advice is much appreciated.

Finally, my love and deep thanks go to family members, especially my parents for encouraging me to love birds and literature so many years ago, Brian Lawrence (whose beautiful photographs illustrate this book), and Ginny, my wife and fellow birder, for her tolerance, expertise in translating obscure Latin texts, and her unstinting encouragement.

ABBREVIATIONS

ASE	*Anglo-Saxon England*
ASPR	G. P. Krapp and E. V. K. Dobbie, eds, *The Anglo-Saxon Poetic Records*, 6 vols (London: Routledge and Kegan Paul, 1931–1953)
BnF	Bibliothèque nationale de France
Bosworth-Toller	J. Bosworth, *An Anglo-Saxon Dictionary Based on the Manuscript Collection of the Late Joseph Bosworth*, ed. by T. Northcote Toller (1888–98; repr. London: Oxford University Press, 1954), and T. Northcote Toller, *An Anglo-Saxon Dictionary Based on the Manuscript Collection of the Late Joseph Bosworth, Supplement* (1921; repr. Oxford: Oxford University Press, 1955)
BWP	Stanley Cramp, gen. ed., *Birds of the Western Palearctic*, 9 vols (Oxford: Oxford University Press, 1977–94)
CR	*Chaucer Review*
CSASE	Cambridge Studies in Anglo-Saxon England
EETS OS	Early English Text Society, Original Series
ES	*English Studies*
Etym.	Isidore of Seville, *The Etymologies of Isidore of Seville*, ed. by Stephen A. Barney and others (Cambridge: Cambridge University Press, 2009)
HA	Aristotle, *The History of Animals*, in *The Complete Works of Aristotle*, ed. by Jonathan Barnes, 2 vols (Princeton, NJ and Chichester: Princeton University Press, 1984), vol. 1

Abbreviations

HN	Pliny, *Natural History*, ed. by H. Rackham, 10 vols (Cambridge, MA: Harvard University Press, 1938–62)
Lat.	Latin
MÆ	*Medium Ævum*
ME	Middle English
MED	Hans Kurath and Robert E. Lewis, eds, *Middle English Dictionary* (Ann Arbor, MI: University of Michigan Press, 1999)
MLat.	Medieval Latin
MLR	*Modern Language Review*
OE	Old English
RES	*Review of English Studies*
Riverside Chaucer	Larry D. Benson, general ed., *The Riverside Chaucer*, 3rd edn (Oxford: Oxford University Press, 1988)
SAC	*Studies in the Age of Chaucer*
Trevisa	Bartholomaeus Anglicus, *On the Properties of Things: John Trevisa's Translation of Bartholomaeus Anglicus, De proprietatibus rerum*, ed. by M. C. Seymour and others, 3 vols (Oxford: Clarendon Press, 1975), vol. 1
Wright-Wülcker	Thomas Wright and Richard Paul Wülcker, *Anglo-Saxon and Old English Vocabularies*, 2 vols (London: Trübner and Co., 1884), vol. 1

The following abbreviations from *Riverside Chaucer* (p. 779) are also used: 'Chaucer's Words Unto Adam' (*Adam*); Book of the Duchess (*BD*); Boece (*Bo*); House of Fame (*HF*); Manciple's Tale (*MancT*); 'Complaint of Mars' (*Mars*); Merchant's Tale (*MerT*); Nun's Priest's Tale (*NPT*); Squire's Tale (*SqT*); Troilus and Criseyde (*Tr*).

Introduction

IF THE VOCABULARY of medieval English is anything to go by, birds were a conspicuous and abundant presence in the lives of medieval people. In Old English alone, one might talk of a *fughel-dæg* 'bird-day'; of being a *fugel-bana* 'bird-killer' gone *fugelung* 'fowling' with a *fugel-net* 'bird-net' somewhere *fugel-wylle* 'abounding in birds'; or of a *fugel-hælsere* 'bird-diviner' observing *fugel-cynn* 'bird-kind'; or perhaps of *feðer-cræt* 'feather-embroidering' or a *feðer-bed*.[1] Raucously and richly vocal, feathered and flying, birds impressed and enriched, sustained and enabled the bodily and cognitive experiences of daily living. As much as their mammalian fellows, birds were participants in rural and urban living in a time, as one historian goes so far as to say, in which 'animals and humans shared space, food, famines, work, and weather conditions more intensely' than any other historical age except human prehistory.[2] As the Old English terms above suggest, birds were often of practical interest. The most proximate, everyday species were domestic poultry: chickens were an important and protected resource, enjoyed by almost every social stratum, and geese, a more labour-intensive poultry species, not only provided meat and eggs, but their feathers, plucked from living or dead birds, were a crucial resource for arrows and quills.[3] Tamed birds of prey were highly prized among the nobility,

---

[1] See Bosworth-Toller, s.v. (n.) *fugel* through to (n.) *fuhlas*, and MED, s.v. (n.) *brid*, senses 1–2, 3a and 5, (n.) *briddere*, and (n.) *foul*, senses 1–10.

[2] Esther Pascua, 'From Forest to Farm and Town: Domestic Animals from ca. 1000 to ca. 1450', in *A Cultural History of Animals in the Medieval Age*, ed. by Brigitte Resl (Oxford and New York, NY: Berg, 2007), pp. 81–102 (81).

[3] For discussion of the importance of poultry in the later Middle Ages, including their roles in large-scale economic and social processes, see Philip Slavin, 'Chicken Husbandry in Late-Medieval Eastern England: c. 1250–1400', *Anthropozoologica*, 44:2 (2009), 35–56, and 'Goose Management and Reading in Late Medieval Eastern England, c. 1250–1400', *Agricultural History Review*, 58:1 (2010), 1–29.

nurtured and flown by falconers who knew intimately the birds' idiosyncratic habits and moulting patterns. All these birds could occupy less prosaic roles, too. Raptors had powerful semiotic value as emblems on escutcheons, or through the projection of 'shared' courtly values in literary realms, and even the humble chicken could, in cockerel form, function as a symbol of Christian light and hope, or the hen feature as an encrypted marvel in an Old English riddle, or a reminder of God's divine wisdom in bestiary sources.[4]

Recent interest in human-nonhuman relations has emphasised this eclecticism of animal meaning in pre-modern living, but particularly nonhuman physicality, reminding us that these creatures existed within a network of relations and interactions with human subjects who were well acquainted with the origins and husbandries of those natural sources that provided foods and technologies. Observations like these risk over-speculation, but they do remind us that the nonhuman in most, if not all, medieval human lives was evident and palpable. As Susan Crane states in one of the most recent and significant literary studies on this subject, 'medieval writers ... had no animal experience, however physically immediate, that they did not apprehend cognitively as it unfolded. Conversely, there is no thinking ... that can entirely forget the living creature'.[5] In the main, traditional or popular perceptions of the nonhuman in medieval experiences have emphasised the two extremes of nonhuman significance – creatures exist to serve a subjugated purpose as food or worker, or live an abstracted existence in the realm of instructive allegory which little heeds actual birds and animals. It was possible, though, for nonhuman subjects to occupy positions variously and contrarily along a spectrum of representation and

---

[4] The best example of medieval falconry knowledge is Frederick II's *De arte venandi cum avibus*, which reveals an intimate understanding of birds' habits; see Frederick II, *The Art of Falconry*, ed. and trans. by Casey A. Wood and F. Marjorie Fyfe (Boston, MA: Charles T. Branford, 1955). For the bestiary cockerel and hen, see *Bestiary: Being an English Version of the Bodleian Library, Oxford, MS 764*, trans. by Richard Barber (Woodbridge: Boydell Press, 1992), pp. 172–3 and 174–5, respectively. For the hen riddle, see Exeter Book Riddle 13 (and 42) in ASPR, vol. 3.

[5] Susan Crane, *Animal Encounters: Contacts and Concepts in Medieval Britain* (Philadelphia, PA: University of Pennsylvania Press, 2013), p. 1.

significance, which could, and did, include and attend closely to interactions with creatures that were literal, physical and haptic, without being simply utilitarian.

Such thinking is typical of the wide and overlapping range of interdisciplinary approaches currently making their mark, which aim not only to emphasise the inherent value of the nonhuman, but to explore with greater sensitivity and clarity the multiplex ways in which the natural world was perceived, experienced and depicted.[6] Literary studies seek nonhuman material traces in textual representations, teasing out the potential revelations of nonhuman presence and relation in the layers of linguistic detail. More specifically, medievalists are confronted with the task of seeking how writers represent the nonhuman within orthodox frameworks that typically point out a desirable categorical difference between human and animal, and remind us that – to take one iteration of a popular concept – 'from animals people may learn what behaviour should be imitated, what avoided, what may wisely be borrowed from them, and what should rightly be avoided'.[7] I engage here with the breadth of these ecologies to attempt a full exploration of how and why birds mattered in a range of poetic texts from across the Middle Ages.[8]

---

[6] The flourishing of such studies in recent years has made the aims and principles of ecocriticism and animals studies familiar, so I refrain from more than a cursory summary in this introduction. For further discussion, see Crane, *Animal Encounters*, pp. 4–5; Karl Steel, *How To Make a Human: Animals and Violence in the Middle Ages* (Columbus, OH: Ohio State University, 2011), pp. 4–23; and Gillian Rudd, *Greenery: Ecocritical Readings of Late Medieval English Literature* (Manchester: Manchester University Press, 2007), pp. 4–10.

[7] Peter Damien, *De bono religiosi status et variorum animantium tropologia*, 2, cited in and trans. by John Boswell, *Christianity, Social Tolerance, and Homosexuality* (Chicago, IL: University of Chicago Press, 1980), pp. 304–5.

[8] Like all scholars in these fields, I am faced with terms which do not adequately represent the heterogeneity of the natural world. 'Animal', e.g., for medieval and modern writers, both distinguishes and integrates other creatures from and with the human category. Likewise, 'nonhuman' risks an unintended assumption that all that is not human holds inferior status. For the sake of clarity and ease, however, I use 'nonhuman' consistently throughout this study. For further discussion of this semantic difficulty, see Steel, *How To Make a Human*, pp. 19–20.

It is surely no surprise that domestic birds, most immediately present and relevant to human experiences, feature prominently in cultural representations. At the other end of the scale are the fantastical species belonging to the *Physiologus* and bestiary traditions: the phoenix, for example, or the alerion, caladrius, cinnamologus, hercinia or griffin. Birds of all sorts abound in medieval literature and art, treated and envisaged richly and widely, at times familiar co-inhabitants, at others exotic and improbable. The birds at the heart of this study, however, are those whose flights largely occur beyond the domesticated space of household, farmstead and myth, beyond clipped wings, lures or cages.[9] In the chapters that follow, I am largely preoccupied with the wild, native British species that were recognisable and nameable in real-world engagements, and which feature as one of the most ubiquitous nonhuman groups to appear in the various poetic traditions of the Middle Ages. Historians of ornithology have tended to overlook possible pre-modern contributions, side-lining medieval interests in, and understandings of, birds as under-developed or neglected in an age that had yet to discover the rigours of empiricism that came with the early modern era; there was at best an 'indifference' to birds in a 'retrograde' age 'not orientated towards facts'.[10] Modern scholars, following on from the apparent priorities of medieval writers, concern

---

[9] By and large, interest in birds per se has focused on tamed or fictional birds. See, e.g, Susan Crane, 'For the Birds', *SAC*, 29 (2007), 23–41; Donna Beth Ellard, 'Going Interspecies, Going Interlingual, and Flying Away with the *Phoenix*', *Exemplaria*, 23:3 (2011), 268–92; and Lesley Kordecki, *Ecofeminist Subjectivities: Chaucer's Talking Birds* (New York, NY: Palgrave Macmillan, 2011), pp. 121–41. One precursor to my study is chapter two in Dorothy Yamamoto, *The Boundaries of the Human in Medieval English Literature* (Oxford: Oxford University Press, 2000), pp. 34–55. See also Heide Estes, who does comment on how several of the Exeter Book Riddles describe birds to reflect 'the varied qualities of birds and the close observations humans have made of them'; Heide Estes, *Anglo-Saxon Literary Landscapes: Ecotheory and the Environmental Imagination* (Amsterdam: Amsterdam University Press, 2017), p. 135.

[10] The first two citations here are from J. H. Gurney, *Early Annals of Ornithology* (London: H. F. & G. Witherby, 1921), p. 14; the last is from H. R. Hays, *Birds, Beasts and Men* (London: J. M. Dent and Sons, 1973), p. 38. Popular expressions of this sentiment reveal the same assumptions: 'people knew little about birds, and cared even less'; Stephen Moss, *A Bird in the Bush: A Social History of Birdwatching* (London: Aurum, 2004), p. 29.

themselves 'not, of course, with birds as they are in nature but as they exist in the mind', as moralised symbols of Christian virtues and vices, as correlatives to lyric emotions.[11] This book contends that the sources available to us insist on a more complex history, in which the multitude of native birds observable in England's habitats registered meaningfully in human experiences. Critical responses hint at these possibilities when they acknowledge 'correct observations' and the 'purely avian detail' of nearly all the poems I address, but have yet to fully explore the implications of such details.[12] I propose that those sensibilities capable of responding to one harsh winter's 'destruction of birds' alongside the 'mortality of men, disease among animals, both wild and domestic', of describing a migratory finch irruption, or depicting both common and lesser-seen species in manuscript margins (as demonstrated on the cover of this book), hint at diverse, interpenetrating orientations towards the natural world in which natural and cultural histories overlap, reciprocate and interweave.[13] There is, in short, evidence for a medieval ornithology that deserves fuller, more serious attention. Moreover, this ornithology can affect our understanding of how birds function in fictional and cultural contexts. This premise is at the heart of this book: in the case of the texts I explore, spanning the tenth to the fourteenth century, real contacts with birds contribute richly to the poems' avian interests, and recommend the diversity of ways in which birds could appeal to medieval thought.

---

[11] Beryl Rowland, *Birds with Human Souls: A Guide to Bird Symbolism* (Knoxville, TN: University of Tennessee University Press, 1978), p. viii.

[12] Henry Barrett Hinckley, 'Science and Folklore in *The Owl and the Nightingale*', *Modern Language Association*, 47:2 (1932), 303–14 (p. 314), and Kathryn Hume, *The Owl and the Nightingale: The Poem and Its Critics* (Toronto and Buffalo, NY: University of Buffalo Press, 1975), p. 91.

[13] For the avian mortality in 1111, see *The Chronicle of John of Worcester, Volume III: The Annals from 1067–1140*, ed. and trans. by P. McGurk (Oxford: Clarendon Press, 1998), p. 127; for Matthew Paris's famous description and image of a crossbill irruption in 1251, see Suzanne Lewis, *The Art of Matthew Paris in* Chronica Majora (Berkeley and Los Angeles, CA: University of California Press, 1987), p. 297; for an impressive range of naturalistically depicted British species in illuminations, see Janet Backhouse, *Medieval Birds in the Sherborne Missal* (London: British Library, 2001), and Cambridge, Fitzwilliam Museum, MS 2-1954.

Avian quiddities hold a strong sway, too, in modern philosophical enquiries into the nonhuman, and suggest a useful comparison to medieval interests as an indication of the transhistorical fascination with birds. The anthropologist Andrew Whitehouse has pinpointed birdsong in the current age – or rather a lack of birdsong – not only as foregrounding 'anxieties that stem from the ambiguities implicit in the Anthropocene's formulation of human relations with other species', but as a precise and important example to which human cultures respond in their participations with the 'lines, knots and texture of the meshwork' of living forms and worlds.[14] Whitehouse's words echo those of two co-authors that have become household names in animal studies disciplines; for Gilles Deleuze and Félix Guattari, birds embody specific, illuminating examples of the intimate and fundamental connections across and between all things (what they term 'refrains').[15] In their anthropological and philosophical speculations about the refrain's functions ('amorous, professional or social, liturgical or cosmic') the bird comes first in their list of instances: 'Bird song: the bird sings to mark its territory'.[16] Throughout their discussion they return to birds to illustrate their meaning, not through metaphor, but with real living birds: the stagemaker's courtship displays, the chaffinch's non-mimicking song, the wren's territorial behaviours. Perhaps most familiar of all are Claude Lévi-Strauss's remarks on birds' totemic roles in human cultural structures. On the subject of assigning proper names to nonhumans, he ponders, 'why should it … particularly be birds that profit from this liberal attitude?'[17] He postulates elsewhere:

> Birds … can be permitted to resemble men for the very reason that they are so different. They are feathered, winged, oviparous and they

---

[14] Andrew Whitehouse, 'Listening to Birds in the Anthropocene: The Anxious Semiotics of Sound in a Human-Dominated World', *Environmental Humanities*, 6 (2015), 53–71 (pp. 53 [abstract] and 60).

[15] Gilles Deleuze and Félix Guattari, *A Thousand Plateaus*, trans. by Brian Massumi (London and New York, NY: Bloomsbury Academic, 2013), p. 363.

[16] Ibid.

[17] Claude Lévi-Strauss, *The Savage Mind*, trans. by George Weidenfeld and Nicolson Ltd (London: Weidenfeld and Nicolson, 1966), p. 204. Originally *La Pensée sauvage* (Paris: Librairie Plon, 1962), p. 270.

are also physically separated from human society by the element in which it is their privilege to move. As a result of this fact, they form a community which is independent of our own but, precisely because of this independence, appears to us like freedom; they build themselves homes in which they live a family life and nurture their young; they often engage in social relations with other members of their species; and they communicate with them by acoustic means recalling articulate language.

Consequently, everything objective conspires to make us think of the bird world as a metaphorical human society: is it not after all literally parallel to it on another level?[18]

None of these modern paradigms, I think, would have been incomprehensible to medieval thinkers. Lévi-Strauss's assertions, particularly, resound with the sorts of parallels between avian and human orders that are prevalent in medieval literary forms such as the dream vision, in which birds' peculiar unlike-likeness makes them suitable metaphors because they can be assimilated and distanced at once. Birds are distinctly unhuman, well removed anatomically from humankind, and yet there is an enduring inclination to identify bird society as 'homologous to that in which we live'.[19] On the one hand, medieval paradigms involving the nonhuman operate as they do for Lévi-Strauss – 'by *means* of a creature, and not the creature itself'.[20] Indeed, this comparison draws attention to the fact that certain forms of medieval literature often require us to read overtly 'by means', particularly when it comes to that much favoured mode, the allegory. The medieval penchant for allegory and exegesis, for thinking of one thing in terms of another, presents a central problem for scholars attempting to write about real birds and animals in texts that require us to read non-literally. It is, as Onno Oerlemans recognises, 'the mode that best reflects the deep conflict in how we have thought about the relationship between humans and animals'.[21] In conventional terms, allegory makes it 'inconsequential to determine whether the fabulous stories connected with the animals are true,

---

[18] Lévi-Strauss, *Savage Mind*, p. 204.
[19] Ibid.
[20] Ibid., p. 149 (italics mine).
[21] Onno Oerlemans, 'The Animal in Allegory: From Chaucer to Gray', *Interdisciplinary Studies in Literature and Environment*, 20:2 (2013), 296–317 (p. 300).

but ... essential to discover and determine the religious significance they confirm'.²² Augustine's words echo clearly in the bestiary materials, those chief medieval texts for allegorical animals. Birds are one of the best represented nonhuman classes of all in allegory, particularly as the stock figures in late medieval dream visions and debate poems in which those avian characteristics that Lévi-Strauss lists are specifically employed to establish bird-human parallels.²³

Like other scholars who have recently begun to tackle the philosophical and textual difficulties inherent in these treatments, though, I aim to show how these acts of figuration are sometimes more complicated than has previously been acknowledged. The avian aspects that Lévi-Strauss marks as 'so different' are, for him, central to what makes birds such potent metaphors for human societies; because they are separated from us so distinctively in various ways, we can more objectively identify the parallels that birds offer (unlike mammals, presumably, which, because of their closer species proximity, are less obviously 'literally parallel to ... [us] on another level'). Although the differences that put birds at a remove do suggest 'something like freedom', they are ultimately part of reinforcing similarities – the associations that work by 'means' of a nonhuman creature transfigured into totemic concept. Medieval discourses involving birds embrace this same paradox, but other approaches are also evident which engage literal qualities in further ways, and can encourage less orthodox interpretations. How might we respond, for example, to the well-known seabirds in *The Wanderer*? Like *The Seafarer*, this poem is often assumed to be allegorical to some degree, with a journey that ought to be read in figurative terms. Like the wanderer's journey itself, though, literal and metaphorical elements involving birds are not so easily

---

22   'Psalm 102', in *Saint Augustine: Exposition of Psalms*, trans. by A. Cleveland Coxe, Nicene and Post-Nicene Fathers, First Series, 8, ed. by Philip Schaff (Grand Rapids, MI: Eerdmans, 1956), p. 497.
23   See, e.g., besides the debate poems addressed in this book, *The Thrush and the Nightingale, The Clerk and the Nightingale,* Clanvowe's *Cuckoo and the Nightingale,* and Dunbar's *Merle and the Nightingale*. All poems available in John Conlee, *Middle English Debate Poetry* (East Lansing, MI: Colleagues Press, 1991). See also William Langland's extended treatment of birds' nest building as a model for human endeavour in *Piers Plowman* (Passus XI.344–61).

distinguishable. The seabirds do seem to function in some sort of metaphorical relation to the wanderer himself, conveying something of his misery and desolation. But they are also undeniably physical birds which the wanderer momentarily confuses with his hallucinogenic visions of lost kinsmen. These birds do not respond, they are not allocated the faculty of human speech or idealised. They simply attend to themselves, *baþian brimfuglas, brædan feþra* 'seabirds bathing, spreading feathers'.[24]

The Wanderer's seabirds are a more unusual occurrence. Many birds in medieval poems are not depicted in clearly realistic terms at all, but stylised at the other end of the spectrum in full-blown formal allegory. In the fourteenth-century 'Bird with Four Feathers', for instance, the speaker happens upon a lone bird with no flight feathers. In the first place, she only ever had 'Fedres fowre' (41), two on each wing, which explicitly signify youth, beauty, strength and riches (45–6).[25] Here we have a talking, Christian bird, who cites biblical exempla with all the skill of a pulpit preacher –.precisely the sort of characteristic representation that leads us to believe that, 'as far as nature itself goes', the anonymous writer of this poem 'does not seem to draw his inspiration from the fields'.[26] But a more sensitive analysis might also query why birds' voices are so often paralleled with human speech in medieval poems, or how the bird apparently has privileged access to some mystic divinity evident in '*Parce*' (12), a word and concept that is 'bale and bote of gostly sore' (236), upon which the narrator 'thought me wele' (235). The Latin refrain in the poem (*Parce michi, Domine*) is beyond any real bird's knowledge or capabilities, but it is also unfamiliar to the human narrator, which suggests some correlation between

---

[24] Unless otherwise noted, all OE quotations are from ASPR. Translations of OE are my own.

[25] Text from Susanna Greer Fein, ed., *Moral Love Songs and Laments*, TEAMS Middle English Text Series (Kalamazoo, MI: Medieval Institute Publications, 1998). Cf. the use of a bird–woman pairing in 'A Bird in Bishopswood'; Ruth Kennedy, '"A Bird in Bishopswood": Some Newly-Discovered Lines of Alliterative Verse from the Late Fourteenth Century', in *Medieval Literature and Antiquities: Studies in Honour of Basil Cottle*, ed. by Myra Stokes and T. L. Burton (Cambridge: D. S. Brewer, 1987), pp. 71–87.

[26] Beryl Rowland, *Blind Beasts: Chaucer's Animal World* (Kent, OH: Kent State University Press, 1971), p. 15.

esoteric Latin and inscrutable birdsong, both of which may provide access to desirable, otherworldly knowledges. Moreover, both these poems might encourage us to think more carefully about how 'briddes wise' specifically (to adopt Chaucer's phrase) are relevant, even in forms like allegory.[27] How are the concerns of a forlorn, wave-bound traveller shared with, and expressed by, preening seabirds? How do the translation interests between Latin and vernacular English implied in the 'Bird with Four Feathers' raise queries about possible translations between other 'languages' too, and how might poets engage with these possibilities?

In the readings I offer in this book, medieval poets embrace the sophisticated potential of such moments so that metaphors and realities fuse and collide when observed avian behaviours or utterances enhance and undercut literary figurative procedures. Three chapters, in fact, address birds in poems – *The Seafarer*, *The Owl and the Nightingale* and *The Parliament of Fowls* – whose textual histories are characterised by long-standing debates about their allegorical statuses, and in the last of these the avian 'community which is independent of our own' is so pointedly different that allegory falters because those differences struggle to sustain the illusion of similarity. *The Parliament of Fowls* will concern me most directly and fully with the difficulties of allegory, but all the poems in some way confront metaphorical representation. Moments of distancing do not simply put assimilation in relief, as they do for Lévi-Strauss (who clearly understands that birds 'literally' exist, but for whom this is not an obstacle or complication to metaphor). Instead, the poems contemplate, exploit and interrogate the tricky differences or incompatibilities revealed by the presence of real birds or real avian attributes. The interaction between like and unlike, in other words, pays serious attention to the 'creature itself', not just the 'means', generating responses and understandings that are variously profound, comic, affective and unsettling. Alterity is directed towards nuanced purposes that complicate various forms of transfiguration: from mysterious to intelligible, indistinct to classified, and in

---

[27] *Mars* (23). Cf. *Tr* (II.921). All quotations from Chaucer's works are from *Riverside Chaucer*. Translations of all ME, where provided, are my own.

Gower's 'Tale of Tereus' the tangled relations between distance and proximity are highlighted in further ways still when correlation is pushed beyond metaphor into fully reified bird-human bodies.

In their own ways, the poets represented in this study are sensitive to the same remarkable avian intelligences and skills that have fascinated modern researchers and thinkers. Comparisons with modern theorising, moreover, help to clarify why the bird, as category or species, might be especially appealing. In one respect, the arguments presented in this book function as a general contribution to recent interests in ecological themes and complexities in medieval culture. The chapters can be thought of as explorations of the nonhuman animal in English poetic texts which happen to focus on birds. More crucially, however, I contend that birds' suitability to the complex and sometimes contradictory procedures of figurative imagining presents unique interests and crystallises focuses on specific medieval concerns. Birds provoke the same reactions in medieval thinkers and writers that move modern philosophers to exclaim: 'How different are these two kinds of bipeds, birds and humans, whose bodies and evolutions are so remote from each other! The more intriguing then some of the feats of intelligence and ingenuity performed by birds; of all the mammals only humans are capable of anything remotely like them.'[28]

Like Alphonso Lingis, medieval writers pondering the bird must have been struck by birds' bipedality. Even if they do not philosophise explicitly on this shared avian-human physical characteristic, it would have been evident to some, in the later Middle Ages at least, through contact with Aristotle's texts.[29] Birds' two-footedness would have surely resonated with the commonplace medieval image of bipedal heaven-facing man and quadrupedal earth-facing

---

[28] Alphonso Lingis, 'Understanding Avian Intelligence', in *Knowing Animals*, ed. by Laurence Simmons and Philip Armstrong (Leiden and Boston, MA: Brill, 2007), pp. 43–56 (43).

[29] See, e.g., *Progression of Animals*, I.704b5. See Aristotle, *The Progression of Animals*, in *The Complete Works of Aristotle*, ed. by Jonathan Barnes, 2 vols (Princeton, NJ and Chichester: Princeton University Press, 1984), vol. 1. All references to Aristotle are to this edition.

beast (often invoked to defend human, rational superiority).³⁰ Birds, in this way, set themselves apart from mankind's anatomically closest relatives. There is a sense in which birds, like humans, achieve an elevated status separating them from other nonhuman creatures, and consequently this aligns them – conveniently, but also uncomfortably – with human privileges. Medieval encyclopaedic discussions of birds certainly recognised the literal manner in which birds were elevated; they are 'of þe eire', the 'foules of heuene' who physically occupy a space that even mankind is denied in his earthly time.³¹ Birds, of course, were classed as *animalia*, but their unique aerial skills also emancipated them from the lowly beasts, earned them 'special mencioun … in þe texte of þe bible ouþir in þe glose'.³² Their strange mobility and corporeality that seems incorporeal in flight must surely have registered with the conventional hierarchy in which humans are poised midway between animals and angels, as recalled in artistic representations in which angels are typically depicted with birds' wings, or in the traditional bird-soul metaphor. It is not difficult to recognise how birds presented themselves as illuminating, curious parallels when, as David Wallace puts it, the 'perilous art' of aligning 'bawdy bodies and stargazing intelligences' was an unavoidable predicament of the human condition.³³ Birds model this art, crossing the boundaries that limit terrestrial existence and troubling those that are necessary, at other times, to maintaining self-perceptions of human sovereignty.

Fugel-cynn or *briddes*, then, were outliers in medieval conceptions: on the one hand, base and subject to human dominion like any other creature; on the other, aligned (ostensibly at least) with human abilities and privileges. In Trevisa's translation of '*the standard medieval encyclopaedia*' – Bartholomaeus Anglicus's *De*

---

30 See, e.g., Boethius's *De consolatione philosophiae* (in Chaucer's *Bo*, V.v.16–9) and *Etym.*, XI.i.5.
31 Trevisa, XII.i (p. 596).
32 Ibid. In some depictions of Noah's ark, the birds are assigned a space between humans and the other animals, seemingly as an indication of their elevated nonhuman status. See, e.g., Paris, BnF, MS français 938, f. 86r.
33 David Wallace, *Geoffrey Chaucer: A New Introduction* (Oxford: Oxford University Press, 2017), p. 35.

proprietatibus rerum – birds' troublesome kind is suggested from the start.[34] Bartholomaeus places birds according to their environment (air, weather, wind) in book twelve, which is entirely devoted to birds, but also in book eighteen, under animals and in book nineteen, under colours. These category models show an Aristotelian influence, but they also reflect the boundless essences of birds, which are at once animals, but equally pertain to other, very unanimal-like qualities. The range of 'condiciouns and propirtees' by which we may know birds (again deriving from Aristotle) also hints at the vexing challenge of defining birdness: according to substance and complexion, habitat, by feet or bill shape, by manner of hunting and eating.[35]

Birds not only defy categories, but in doing so they display transformative abilities that at once distinguish them, and provide them with the means of persistent escape from these laboursome human efforts to classify. There is an in-betweenness apparent in their very substance 'þat beþ bytwene þe tweye elementis þat beþ most heuy and most liȝt'.[36] These are creatures who 'haueþ lasse of wordlich heuynesse and more of liȝtnesse of eire þan bestis', who do not share the same regrettable earthliness as humans because they 'beþ deschargid of weiȝte of fleische and fleþ most hiȝe', and 'in here composicioun and makynge eire and water haþ most maistrie'.[37] This definition according to difference from other creatures is repeated: as Bartholomaeus concludes his opening summary, 'it nediþ onliche to knowe þat among oþir kynde of beestis generalliche foules ben more pure and liȝt and noble of substaunce and swift of meuynge and scharp of siȝt'.[38] As will be evident in some of the chapters to come, birds, in flight and in bodily matter, exist and move between substances and territories, embodying the core sense of movement and change at the etymological root of Old English

---

[34] A. S. G. Edwards, 'Bartholomaeus Anglicus' *De Proprietatibus Rerum* and Medieval English Literature', *Archiv für das Studium der neueren Sprachen und Literaturen*, 222 (1985), 121–8 (p. 121) [italics original].
[35] Trevisa, XII.i (p. 596).
[36] Ibid.
[37] Ibid., pp. 596–7.
[38] Ibid., pp. 601–2.

cynd and Middle English *nature* (Lat. *natura*).³⁹ Bartholomaeus's gull ('þat hatte *larus*'), for instance, 'woneþ somtyme in watris and somtyme in londe ... boþe in ryuere and in londes and now swymmeþ as a fissche and now fleeþ as a bridde'.⁴⁰ *Larus*'s curious shape-shifting recalls certain metamorphosing birds that we will encounter below – in the Old English riddles, for instance, or the Ovidian transformations that occur in Gower's *Confessio Amantis*.

Like other encyclopaedic treatments of the natural world, Bartholomaeus borrows from the hugely influential authority of Isidore of Seville, whose etymologically-centred claims about birds proliferate right across the Middle Ages. Bartholomaeus's comments on the curious misfit properties of birds strongly echo a general aspect of the class that Isidore identifies and which is consistently repeated, often verbatim, by his imitators. In an observation that anticipates something of Jacques Derrida's consternation at the term 'animal' which masks the prolific 'heterogeneous multiplicity of the living', Isidore notes that 'There is a single word for birds, but various kinds, for just as they differ among themselves in appearance, so do they differ also in the diversity of their natures'.⁴¹ Of all the world's *unrimu cynn* 'countless species' (*The Panther*, 2a), birds are the most prolific and various. No other group of animals in Isidore is characterised in this way: animals (*De animalibus*) are apparently much easier to subdivide (livestock [*pecus*], beasts of burden [*iumenta*]).⁴² The prolific diversity of birds creates and perpetuates the avian enigma. Birds' diversity is a central theme throughout Bartholomaeus's description. Like Isidore, who begins his chapters on birds by outlining specific examples of avian difference, Bartholomaeus's vocabulary is peppered with 'somme ... and somme' (Lat. *alia*): birds have 'dyuers complexioun ... dyuers

---

[39] Both terms derive from Proto-Indo-European *gen*, meaning 'to beget', and thus convey the senses of development or process. See Joseph T. Shipley, *The Origins of English Words: A Discursive Dictionary of Indo-European Roots* (Baltimore, MD: Johns Hopkins University Press, 1984), s.v. *gn*, *gen*.

[40] Trevisa, XII.xxiv (p. 633).

[41] Jacques Derrida, *The Animal That Therefore I Am*, trans. by David Wills, ed. by Marie-Louise Mallet (New York, NY: Fordham University Press, 2008), p. 31, and *Etym.*, XII.vii.1, respectively.

[42] *Etym.*, XII.i.1–8.

Introduction

manere of place', 'dyuers maner of doynge', 'dyuers disposicioun of membres'.[43]

Among all this diversity there are two avian abilities that are especially prominent. Perhaps most alluring is the enduring medieval belief (in scholastic milieux, anyway) that birds' flight – with its associated accoutrements and contiguities: feathers, wings, air – engages these creatures in transformative evasions that literally leave no traces by which we might purchase more tangible, evidential understandings of avian being. For Isidore, the very name for these creatures in Latin reveals their defining characteristic: 'They are called birds (*avis*) because they do not have set paths (*via*), but travel by means of pathless (*avia*) ways'.[44] It is not simply flight, but a secretive flight known only to birds themselves. Bartholomaeus elaborates: birds are 'as it were "without waye" … for here wayes in þe eyre be not distinguyd in certayne', and 'anone aftir þe fliȝt þe eire closiþ itself and leueþ noo signe neiþir tokene of here passage'.[45] It is quite impossible (because birds fly and can disappear without 'signe neiþir tokene') for mankind 'to penetrate all the wildernesses of India and Ethiopia and Scythia, so as to know the kinds of birds and their differentiating characteristics'.[46]

Isidore's interest in the multiplicity and great variation of birds also addresses that other familiar aspect of birds' brilliance, the voice. It is, after all, birds' songs and calls that give many species their names (some non-bird creatures also have well-known onomatopoeic calls, of course [sheep, cow, dog], but birds are especially marked in so frequently being named after these utterances). As with their appearances and natures, so birds' vocal abilities are marvellously diverse: 'Many bird names are evidently constructed from the sound of their calls, such as the crane (*grus*), the crow (*corvus*), the swan (*cygnus),* the peacock (*pavo*), the kite (*milvus*), the screech owl (*ulula*), the cuckoo (*cuculus*), the jackdaw (*graculus*), et

---

[43] Trevisa, XII.i (pp. 598, 599, and 601). 'Dyuers' does describe other nonhuman creatures (see book eighteen), but nowhere near as frequently as it does birds.
[44] *Etym.*, XII.vii.3. Cf. Hrabanus Maurus, *De rerum naturis*, VIII.vi, and Alexander Neckam, *De naturis rerum*, I.xxiii.
[45] Trevisa, XII.i (p. 596).
[46] *Etym.*, XII.i.2.

cetera. The variety of their calls taught people what they might be called.'[47] From an etymological perspective, many birds' voices produce another form of in-betweenness; their onomatopoeic titles preserve the distinctive sounds of their own vocal utterances, making their names both the product of contrived, assigned human signifiers, and of their own natural voices. Onomatopoeic bird names circumnavigate onomastic procedures to some extent because the sounds that are ultimately fixed in approximating human signs do at least derive from the creature itself in the first place; their names are less wholly or obviously the product of human-created and -assigned terms that announce or clarify the cultural uses or suggestions of nonhuman creatures. When Isidore claims that 'Cranes (*grus*) took their name from their particular call, for they whoop with such a sound', the semantic deconstruction that attends his typical analysis of other non-onomatopoeic terms is less complete because the name signifies naturally as well as artificially.[48] Unlike *sorex* (shrew), for instance ('named because it gnaws and cuts things off like a saw [*serra*]'), *grus* cannot be assigned specific linguistic meaning; its value exists only in its culturally specific approximation of the actual bird call.[49] *Grus* itself remains indeterminable, the inscrutable property of the bird.

This instability and curiosity of avian vocals in the linguistic context was clearly of interest to medieval writers. Birdsong generally is a stock motif in dream visions and romances, often because their voices can be usefully paralleled with human speech. As a measure of their relevance to medieval grammars, the variety and skill of birds' songs and calls is often engaged and celebrated in school texts. Birds occupy much space in the popular Latin animal-sound word lists (*voces animantium* 'the voices of animate things'), for instance, and are given their own platform in one versified list of this sort devoted almost entirely to birds' calls.[50] In the same context, the

---

[47] *Etym.*, XII.vii.9.
[48] *Etym.*, XII.vii.14. For natural and artificial categories of voice, see Trevisa, XIX, vol. 2, p. 131.
[49] *Etym.*, XII.iii.2.
[50] 'De cantibus avium' is recorded in three continental MSS from the late Anglo–Saxon period (earliest tenth century). See Franciscus Buecheler and Alexander

Introduction

legacy of Philomela and the famous vocal abilities of the nightingale appear in poems about the diversity and virtuosity of this nonpareil species.[51] More disconcertingly, though, avian voices raised serious queries relating to the definition of voice (*vox*) in some grammatical discourses, precisely because birds are not human, but appear, at least, to have all the 'acoustic means recalling articulate [human] language', particularly those species that are capable of mimicry.[52] For some theologians and grammarians this situation called for necessary, unequivocal differentiation: bird sound is arguably discrete in a linguistic or musical sense, but it needed to be assigned inarticulate status for the sake of the privileged human voice. Difference under these circumstances served as a device for more clearly perceiving, and confirming, metaphorical congruence; birds' voices only *seem* like human voices, but do not actually have the same rational, divinely-gifted properties. For others, however, like the poets represented in the chapters to follow, differences are established in more intricate ways which can still expose the artificiality of metaphorical parallels, but not in ways that dispense with the avian components or reduce them to insignificance. Strange vocal correlations between birds and humans could be fertile grounds for comic exploitation and philosophical engagement that explore, rather than fix, the boundaries between species.

I identify flight and voice as especially important here because their prominence in medieval discourses involving birds means that they feature, separately or together, as elements of the effects achieved in all the poems I will address. The voice, particularly, is confronted as a distinctive avian facet that encourages fascinated comparison between birds and humans. It appears to greater and lesser degrees in four of my chapters to establish both humorous and poignant interspecies affinities, prompting the sorts of

---

Riese, eds, *Anthologia Latina: sive poesis latinae supplementum*, 2 vols, 2nd edn (Leipzig: B. G. Teubneri, 1894), vol. 1, part 1, pp. 218–19.

[51] See 'De filomela' (with its persistent refrain 'Vox, filomela' [1]), surviving in eight MSS, and the same-titled 'De filomela', extant in seven MSS. For the texts and details of MSS, see Buecheler and Riese, *Anthologia Latina*, pp. 130–1 and 246–50, respectively.

[52] Lévi-Strauss, *Savage Mind*, p. 204.

questions I raised about the 'Bird with Four Feathers'. In all aspects, though, birds embody, perform and represent transformation, variously and wondrously: in their colours, moults, migrations, flights, oviparous reproduction, songs and displays. Medieval writers marvelled at how birds' prolific diversity of kind and appearance, and their distant, untraceable directions that do not seem directions at all, make these aerial shape-shifters masters of evasion, misdirection and resistance, always moving above, across and beyond. They enjoyed and worried about how birds' voices could be so uniquely human-like among nonhuman creatures, capable of complex modulations. The full breadth of these transformations, it seems to me, are key to the rich set of nuances and tensions between like and unlike in avian-human comparisons. Their unique capabilities summon parallels, but their mysteries also position metaphorical relation at the point of disintegration more keenly than perhaps any other nonhuman creature, where a space is re-opened (or remains open) to iterate ultimate and uncategorised difference, all the while refusing to provide alternative indications for safe classification. In the poems I examine, birds are compelling agents and actors that not only invite comment on bird kind itself, but also on how avian specifics are repeatedly and intricately pertinent to various forms of identity and to a range of deeply significant religious and secular medieval trans-actions and trans-forms. Real avian transformations are crucial to the potentialities, effects and limitations of human imaginative, and literal, transformations that pursue through comparison something enduringly profound and revealing in birds' astonishing abilities.

In Chapter One I begin with perhaps the most influential of all transformations to the medieval mind – the arduous heaven-bound journey of all Christians that played out in numerous forms in medieval thought and practice: as pilgrimage, as life-long psychological preparation, as spiritual ascension on death, as psychosomatic experience at Judgement. *The Seafarer*, one of numerous overtly and didactically religious poems in the tenth-century Exeter manuscript, engages with this popular theme through a narrative that is at once metaphorical and literal; it involves an ascetic peregrination of the yearning spirit, but also the tactile and physical endurance

Introduction

of a solitary, desolate voice navigating the *atol yþa gewealc* 'terrible tossing of waves' (6a). Into this maritime portrayal of pious transcendence comes an equally abiding image, the soaring bird. Chapter One, then, takes as its starting point the enduring association of salvific aim or achievement, and a bird's most characteristic and noticeable property. The key envy of birds which makes them dynamic movers between elements and between spheres enables these creatures to occupy an in-betweenness that has made them commonplace figures of the fleeing or liberated human soul across cultures and centuries, including Anglo-Saxon England. Whilst the six species named in lines 19b–25a of the poem and the flight imagery at lines 58–64a have not lacked critical attention separately, I attempt a reading that brings together the vividly real, noisy seabirds and the pelagic bird-soul image. Far from appearing as mere background incidentals, the poet's treatment of the seabirds we first encounter resonates with contemporary ornithological knowledge, and suggests that they feature specifically as species that best convey the trials and endeavours of a sea-going speaker who observes, listens to and names seabirds. Speculating and conducting the journey to heaven, that is, involves a human-to-avian transformation, in which the pilgrim must inhabit and traverse the seabirds' territory. Moreover, the curious essence of seabirds as winged creatures that are always at home on the seas and journeying to a home elsewhere establishes them as what I term 'native foreigners', a paradox that highlights the seafarer's conflicting yearnings and, more widely, reflects the difficult dynamic between the earthly and celestial in the poem's perceptions of the soul's journey. As metaphoric relations dissolve into ambiguity even whilst they are established, this paradox suggests birds as ideal correlatives; birds' mysteries are aligned with uncertain adventures towards God beyond far horizons, towards a destination which is never reached in the poem.

Avian mysteries persist in Chapter Two. Naming birds to interpellate their worldliness and addressing their cryptic lives remain prominent in Anglo-Saxon ornithological dealings, but here I explore these interests in texts that, far from transcending materiality, are well known for repeatedly engaging us with the downright everyday. If the Old English riddles have often been read as texts that define, contain and wonder at phenomena, the recurring presence of birds in this collection may well confirm their centrality in these intellectual enquiries that seek to identify and know. Birds are conspicuous and prodigious transformers in the riddles, but I am particularly concerned here with birds not only as subjects of transformation but also as pedagogical agents – exacting and edifying creatures whose innate diversity and riddling existences engage them with the intellectual operations that the Exeter Riddles reflexively scrutinise. As nonhumans whose various natural mutations enthral us and defy our efforts to determine and classify, birds are embroiled in the hermeneutic channels and limitations of accessing knowledge because they demonstrate to us how wondering is a paradoxical act that perpetuates mystery even as we come to know. I focus specifically on three riddles outside the usual 'bird group' to explore a jay that actively and wittily defers identification, and an unidentifiable flock of birds that seem to mock the very act of naming. The chapter culminates with one particular diving water bird in a *scriptorium* riddle that transfigures a bird's feather into the technological implement that will inscribe further imaginative and linguistic transformations. In so doing, it reminds us of the fundamental involvement of bird kind in the physical, scribal production of letters generally, and, more pertinently, in the specific processes and creations of wondering and riddling in the Exeter Book.

Birds transformed by human agendas are at the heart of the next two chapters, which function in some ways as companions. *The Owl and the Nightingale* and *The Parliament of Fowls*, bird debate poems, are both significantly concerned with the ways in which birds are co-opted for literary uses; they are two of the finest bird poems in the medieval English canon, in fact, because their writers are not only highly knowledgeable about the broad cultural functions of birds, but also adeptly understand the instability and complexity of such fabrications. The sophisticated comedy of both poems involves a tension resulting from an undeniable ornithological realism pitched against familiar metaphorical representations that are wryly invoked and exploited. My reading of *The Owl and the Nightingale* understands it as a poem that self-consciously examines

Introduction

the effects of cultural authorities through the brilliant ploy of having the birds themselves make the attacks, holding to account the other's, or defending their own, species-ness. What seems to have happened in *The Owl and the Nightingale* is that humanised literary representations have gained so much sway through repeated interpellation that even the birds themselves, inconsistently, are convinced of their own cultural identities, adopting them as innate taxonomic identifiers. Both the owl and the nightingale are victims of this procedure, but it is the owl that forms the focus of Chapter Three, because the popular, multiple and conflicting versions of owl species in late medieval literary culture illustrate the effects I describe particularly well. Whilst this confusing hybridity of naturalistic and fictionalised owls is largely treated with levity in the poem, I am also concerned with the more serious implications that result from these cultural acts of speciation. As a popular bestiary creature, the owl is embroiled with some unsettling social realities, and in the poem the loathing directed at the bird as a result of successive literary inheritances alludes to some unpleasant and violent ends for owl kind.

In Chaucer's *Parliament of Fowls* we find birds again whose unpredictable, defiant behaviours undercut or resist wholesale cultural appropriation. Birds continue to elude and surprise through redirecting cultural transfigurations of the nonhuman. *The Parliament* is not the only text included here to make use of that conventional medieval form, the allegory, but it certainly does so the most overtly and thoroughly. Like my discussion of *The Owl and the Nightingale*, Chapter Four is sensitive to the ways in which birds are employed as filters for human interests in conspicuously artificial, formalised modes. Specifically, I pick up a theme that features elsewhere, the nonhuman voice, to examine in detail how Chaucer manages this particularity in an allegorical framework. One of the most famous passages in *The Parliament* involves a surprising moment when a goose, cuckoo and duck break away from speaking anthropomorphised English, and instead express their indignation in bird speak: '"Kek kek! kokkow! quek quek!"' (499). The moment can be easily dismissed as flippant and irrelevant, but the slippage between voices raises translation problems that have implications for medieval ideas about birds' voices and the functions of allegory itself as a mode that is often employed for nonhuman representation. I draw on the modern theory of 'biotranslation' from the field of biosemiotics to explore how Chaucer treats the possibility of translation between or across species. The well-known 'kek kek' line (499) in *The Parliament* assuredly represents a form of otherness that cannot be easily or accurately deciphered, but I argue that the movement between voices from line to line that are typically assigned articulate or inarticulate status in medieval theories of *vox* does not render the squawks incomprehensible, but as meaningful utterances in avian terms that bear the potential for translation, even if, ultimately, this must be poetically imagined. More broadly, then, the line opens up further possibilities for the operations of allegory in Chaucer's poem, by which linguistic translation from bird- to human-speak might recommend that we sometimes read allegorical 'translation' as a window to genuinely nonhuman interests that are artfully conveyed through Chaucer's crafted English.

Questions about vocal translations are subsumed into bodily translations in my final chapter, which examines avian-human metamorphosis in Gower's *Confessio Amantis*. We come full circle in this respect; the transformations of Tereus, Procne and Philomela in the 'Tale of Tereus' recall the enactment of migrating seabird flight in *The Seafarer*. Those pelagic travels are metaphorical, of course, in the sense that the seafarer does not actually become a bird, even if we assume that the disembodied flight of the seafarer's mind or heart is real enough. Gower's characters, however, literally change into birds in full-blown Ovidian metamorphoses. Although medieval translations and adaptations of Ovid's popular *Metamorphoses* did tend to allegorise for the purposes of Christian moralising, Gower does not. In his versions the tales illustrate particular morals to the hapless Amans, but the transformations do take place in their own right. The culminating, anticipated mutations at the tale's end are only the most obvious examples in a narrative preoccupied with violated and mutilated bodies that come apart and come together in pluralistic forms. Birds are not only central to thinking about these bodily boundaries and reconfigurations, but their tell-tale transformations embody and enable desire by dissolving the limitations of human existence into hybridity. Avian form is not incidental. Rather, human and avian histories converge intimately in the extended aetiologies that characterise Gower's re-telling of this ancient myth so that the characters, still cognitively human, are liberated or given fuller identity by avian mobility and voice.

Across my chapters birds engage a complex set of avian-human convergences that do perform typically, confirming and promoting the instructive and utilitarian roles of birds for mankind, but they also, in each case, grapple with birds as illuminating creatures of instability and uncertainty that are equally capable of reducing and dissolving human confidence, knowledge and identities. These moments, I suggest, deserve further attention for what they reveal about the birds that persist in the poetic imagination right across the Middle Ages. In what follows I offer readings of such birds in five medieval English poems familiar to modern readers, largely because, although all these texts feature birds prominently, there has been little or no attention to how detailed study of these birds can contribute richly to established or new interpretations of these poems. In all five cases, I seek the ways in which feathered physicality and transformation is embraced intimately and significantly as part of poetic strategy.

Plate 1 **Common tern** *Sterna hirundo*
© Brian Lawrence
þær him stearn oncwæð / isigfeþera 'there the tern answered them, icy-feathered' (*The Seafarer*, 23b–24a)

1

Native Foreigners: Migrating Seabirds and the Pelagic Soul in *The Seafarer*

> This indoors flying makes it seem absurd,
> Although it itches and nags and flutters and yearns,
> To postulate any other life than now.[1]
> (Louis MacNeice, 'Dark Age Glosses', 15–17)

> What came first, the seabird's cry or the soul
> Imagined in the dawn cold when it cried?[2]
> (Seamus Heaney, 'Small Fantasia for W.B.', 3–4)

Louis MacNeice's poem reminds us of how well endures one specific association of a very well-known sparrow with a central Anglo-Saxon 'image-complex': fire-lit hall and raging storm, transience and eternity.[3] The purported moment in Bede's *Historia ecclesiastica* when one king and his people reject their pagan beliefs for a promised Christian eternity pivots on a fictional augury in which a flying bird is entwined with the morphosis and fate of the human soul.[4] Bede's sparrow is allegorical: like man's journey from the unknown to human existence on earth, and then again to the

---

[1] Louis MacNeice, *Selected Poems* (London: Faber and Faber, 1998), p. 133.
[2] Seamus Heaney, 'Small Fantasia for W.B.', *Times Literary Supplement* (27 January 1989); subsequently published in Seamus Heaney, *Seeing Things* (London: Faber and Faber, 1991), p. 78. I owe thanks to Adam Nicholson who inadvertently suggested these lines as an epigraph.
[3] Kathryn Hume, 'The Concept of the Hall in Old English Poetry', *Anglo-Saxon England*, 3 (1974), 63–74 (p. 63).
[4] The other existing version of Edwin's conversion also attaches augury to the event. Unlike the sparrow in Bede, however, an ominous corvid threatens to overturn the conversion by 'croaking from an unpropitious quarter of the sky'; *The Earliest Life of Gregory the Great by an Anonymous Monk of Whitby*, ed. and trans. by Bertram Colgrave (Lawrence, KS: University of Kansas Press, 1968), pp. 96–7.

unknown, the bird flies in from the cold, through the banqueting hall and back out again into the tempestuous night, subject to the ineluctable transience of mortal life.[5] The *passer*, or *spearwa* in Old English, becomes responsible for a seminal moment in the history of the English people, assigned a significant rhetorical function in a pagan representation of life without Christ that simultaneously contemplates what that life might look like after conversion.[6] It resonates with and consolidates a scriptural legacy which designates birds a special status in thinking through this key theological anxiety and inquiry, a legacy which locates birds as ideal creatures to articulate the Christian pilgrim journey by aligning avian flight with the metaphorical peregrinations of the faithful who must 'soar to the unchangeable substance of God'.[7] The bird appears in Saint Augustine's lengthy exegesis of Psalm 83, for instance, where it is compared to the human heart or soul. Psalm 124.7 includes the *neodspearuwa* 'needful sparrow' that Ælfric alludes to elsewhere: *Ute sawl is ahred of grine swa swa spearwa* 'Our soul is freed from the snare just like the sparrow'. And in 101.5 the speaker compares himself directly: *ic spearuwan swa some / gelice gewearð, anlicum fugele* 'I became, in a way, like the sparrow – a solitary bird'.[8] Old English

---

[5] For the passage, see *Bede's Ecclesiastical History of the English People*, ed. and trans. by B. Colgrave and R. A. B. Mynors (Oxford: Clarendon Press, 1969), pp. 182–3. For the OE translation, see Thomas Miller, ed., *The Old English Version of Bede's Ecclesiastical History of the English People*, EETS OS, 95, 96 (London: Trübner, 1890–91), II.x (pp. 134–6). The relevant line reads: *cume an spearwa & hrædlice þæt hus þurhfleo* '[there] came a sparrow and [it] flew swiftly through the house'.

[6] *Spearwa* consistently glosses *passer* in OE translations. The term could carry the same general identification sense as *passer* likely did in Latin; Ælfric glosses *passer* as *spearewa oððe lytel fugel* 'sparrow or little bird': *Ælfrics Grammatik und Glossar*, ed. by Julius Zupitza (Berlin: Weidmannsche Buchhandlung, 1880), p. 307.

[7] *Saint Augustine, City of God: Books VIII–XVI*, trans. by G. G. Walsh and G. Monahan, The Fathers of the Church: A New Translation, 14 (Washington, D.C.: Catholic University Press of America, 1952), XI.ii (p. 188).

[8] Cf. Psalm 54.6 and Matthew 10.29–31. The psalms were certainly available to Anglo-Saxon monastics in Lat. psalters and, after Bede's time, in OE translations, such as the Paris Psalter. M. J. Toswell notes that although these translations postdate Bede, the vocabulary is noticeably close to the glosses in earlier Lat. psalters, and that the Metrical Psalter translates the version Bede is likely to have used, the Roman psalter; M. J. Toswell, 'Bede's Sparrow and the Psalter in Anglo-Saxon England', *American Notes and Queries*, 13:1 (2000), 7–12 (p. 9,

spearwa, it seems, was the bird of choice for representing the soul.[9]

Bede's sparrow usefully introduces us to key elements of the bird-human device at the heart of more than one poem in the Old English Exeter manuscript in which, as another Exeter Book poem states, a *fugles gecynd* 'bird's kind' is *fela gelices* 'much like [ours]'.[10] The poetic strategies of these texts specifically feature birds as metaphorical images for Christian ascension and transformation in profound contemplations envisaging or instructing the longed-for move from here to there. In the most extensive and fully realised version of this analogy, a fantastical bird inhabiting a utopian land twelve fathoms above earth is made an exegetical type for the *hæle hrawerig* 'body-weary man' (*Phoenix*, 554a). The allegory overtly couples the bird's eternal resurrection habits with both Christ and the thronging masses of saved souls who are continuously said to be *swa se fugel* 'as the bird' (558a, 585b, 597a). The phoenix is the *anhaga* 'lone-dweller' (87a), a bird-human union that the Exeter poets may have picked up from the psalms, particularly in cases where glossed psalters intentionally depict the sparrow as an

---

n. 1). References above to the psalms in OE are to the Paris Psalter (ASPR, 5); for Ælfric's allusion to the sparrow from Psalm 124 above, see 'Forty Soldiers' in *Ælfric's Lives of the Saints*, ed. by W. W. Skeat, EETS OS, 76, 82 (London: Trübner, 1881, 1885) p. 254. The *Ancrene Wisse* (early thirteenth century) also employs the solitary sparrow from these psalms as a paradigm for anchorite reclusiveness; see *Ancrene Wisse: A Corrected Edition of the Text in Cambridge, Corpus Christi College, MS 402 with Variants from Other Manuscripts*, ed. by Bella Millet, EETS OS, 325, 326, 2 vols (Oxford: Oxford University Press, 2005, 2006), vol. 1, III, especially chapter xvii.

[9] Donald K. Fry suggests that the specific choice of a sparrow in Bede signals the move from paganism to Christianity; Donald K. Fry, 'The Art of Bede: Edwin's Council', in *Saints, Scholars and Heroes: Studies in Medieval Culture in Honor of Charles W. Jones*, ed. by Margot H. King and Wesley M. Stevens, 2 vols (Collegeville, MN: St. John's Abbey and University, 1979), vol. 1, pp. 195–209 (203). For a study of the symbolic sparrow and its biblical sources in Bede's *Historia ecclesiastica*, see Janina Sara Ramirez, 'The Symbolic Life of Birds in Anglo-Saxon England' (unpublished doctoral thesis, University of York, 2006), pp. 167–95.

[10] The Exeter poems are in vol. 3 of ASPR. An interactive facsimile of the MS is available in *The Exeter DVD: The Exeter Anthology of Old English Poetry*, ed. by Bernard J. Muir and programmed by Nick Kennedy (Exeter: University of Exeter Press, 2006).

anhoga.[11] In this opening chapter, I address the bird-human *anhaga* in another Exeter poem that augments the 'much like' stratagem with what is, arguably, even greater sophistication.[12] Quite unlike the paradisiacal territories of *The Phoenix*, *The Seafarer* presents a *middangeard* 'middle-dwelling' (90b) situation closer to that we find in Bede. There is no elaborate depiction of otherworldly locations, nor the evangelical assuredness that comes with overt and complete allegory; nor, in fact, are birds even explicitly associated with human souls. As in the famous sparrow analogy, we encounter the same fluctuations between hall-life and the daunting outside world, the mind that weighs up the two in opposition, and birds that are associated with both these worlds.

The Seafarer poet, however, turns Bede's vision inside out. The speaker wilfully adopts the ascetic, torturous hardships of sea life to seek a mysterious *elpeodigra* 'foreign country' (38a) over the horizons, and 'indoors flying' ('Dark Age Glosses' [15]) becomes outdoors flying. Out here, in a real-world marine territory between cliffs and high sea, the seafarer encounters a very particular type of *anlic fugol* suited to the alienation and uncertainties that accompany his faith voyage; not a mythic species dwelling in fabled lands, nor even a solitary sparrow, but native European seabirds seen and heard off British shores. If MacNeice's poem recalls the biblical sparrow, then my second epigraph alludes to the currency of seabirds in another long-lived and even more pertinent bird-soul pairing: in Seamus Heaney's lines a seabird's distinctive call is the first in a series of imagined reifications of the spirit to be developed in the complete poem, hinting at an enduring and intimate

---

[11] As in Psalm 101 in the Lambeth Psalter. For the text, see U. Lindelöf, ed., *Der Lambeth-Psalter: eine altenglische Interlinearversion des Psalters in der Hs 427 der erzbischoefliche Lambeth Palace Library; I, Text und Glossar, II, Beschreibung und Geschichte der Handschrift; Verhältnis der Glosse zu anderen Psalterversionen; Bemerkungen über die Sprache des Denkmals*, Acta Societatis Scientiarum Fennicae, 35.i and 43.iii, 2 vols (Helsinki: Druckerei der Finnischen Litteraturgesellschaft, 1909–1914).

[12] On *The Phoenix*, see Ellard's excellent 'Going Interspecies, Going Interlingual', in which she explores this 'highly symbolic narrative that places bird–human interconnectivity at the heart of its ecosystems' (270). The first version of the present chapter appeared in 2010, and since then only Ellard has written at length on birds in OE poetry from an ecocritical perspective.

association.¹³ *Brimfuglas*, to give them their Old English name as it appears in *The Wanderer* (47a), are the most noticeable feature of ocean life in an extended passage of *The Seafarer* in which each bird is individually named.¹⁴ In a text that is conspicuously preoccupied with what is not material, and in which birds are ultimately pressed to metaphorical purposes, these real seabirds introduce a curious avian materiality. It is the literal/figurative nuance established in the seafarer's intentional interactions with named seabirds that form the focus of this chapter, because it prepares us for the synchrony between these early experiences and the much studied flight imagery at lines 58–64a when we encounter the *anfloga* 'lone-flier' (62b): externalised spiritual flight should specifically recall these observed and named seabirds, whose presence in the poem is informed by Anglo-Saxon ornithology. The poet does not reject or defuse the presence of real, experienced birds, but catches up as part of the ultimate metaphor their conspicuous being and relevance in specific real-world habitats.

Seabirds, so vividly brought to our attention in lines 19b–25a, become the ideal image for Christian pilgrimage because their winter ocean wanderings mirror what the seafarer must do. Birds seem to perform an action that, to borrow Johanna Kramer's words

---

13   The tradition of equating seabirds with human souls or sailors is ancient, but not easily traceable. Swans are not considered seabirds now, but presumably were to the Anglo-Saxons, as suggested by the kenning *swanrade* 'swan-road' (arctic swans do, after all, migrate over seas). In the anonymous *Life of Gregory*, Paulinus's soul journeys to heaven in the form of a swan (see Colgrave, *Life of Gregory*, pp. 100–1) and Exeter Book Riddle 5 describes a swan with spectral qualities (*ferende gæst* 'travelling spirit' [9b]). Mark Cocker notes the 'ghostly whiteness' that no doubt contributed to the 'common superstition that seabirds could become the embodied spirits of lost sailors'; Mark Cocker, *Birds and People* (London: Jonathan Cape, 2013), p. 218. Similarly, the 'crews of old whalers in the Arctic thought fulmars were the spirits of Greenland skippers'; Adam Nicholson, *The Seabird's Cry: The Lives and Loves of Puffins, Gannets and Other Ocean Voyagers* (London: William Collins, 2017), p. 28. These beliefs seems to rely on an oral transmission more than anything else, but some classical texts make these links between seamen and seabirds: e.g. Hermes as a skimming seabird (*Odyssey*, V.49–53), or the association of shipwrecked sailors and gulls in Greek epigrams, for which see P. M. C. Forbes Irving, *Metamorphosis in Greek Myths* (Oxford: Oxford University Press, 1990), p. 125.
14   Bosworth-Toller also gives *pyr-maw* 'sea-bird' as a putative alternative; s.v. (n.) *pur*.

on Anglo-Saxon theories of the Ascension, is 'liminal at its very core as an event that takes place between heaven and earth'.[15] This conflation of human and avian pelagic lone-dwellers articulates what we might refer to as the 'native foreigner': creatures which shift between land and sea, that have 'homes' in more than one land but are equally at home on the seas, and that annually return home but are equally characterised by their migrations. Seabirds appear to be native and foreign in this world, close and distant, in the way that human souls are between two homes temporarily: here in the *middengeard* but restlessly always on their way to the true, eternal *ham* 'home' (117) that exists over the watery horizons.[16] Moreover, this is an interspecies kinship and voyage that is troubled by instability as it verges between literal and figurative; the seafarer's attempts to make seabirds 'native' to his own existence and kind, that is, are often compromised because real birds alienate his attempts to construct metaphors. This dynamic, however, does not weaken the metaphor's effect, but powerfully reflects the paradoxical yearnings and fraught ontological status of the seafarer's own wanderings. Birds' strangeness is meaningfully depicted as at once native and yet entirely foreign to the human.

The seabirds in lines 19–25 are the most memorable elements of a physical space that is a hard and unavoidable aspect of the journey. In the final chapter of this book I explore fully reified, avian metamorphoses in Gower's *Confessio Amantis*. In *The Seafarer* these transformations are metaphoric flights, but imaginings which, nonetheless, depend upon the palpability of real avian encounters which inspire and are then incorporated into the speaker's salvific enterprise.

[15] Johanna Kramer, *Between Earth and Heaven: Liminality and the Ascension of Christ in Anglo-Saxon Literature* (Manchester: Manchester University Press, 2014), p. 6.

[16] Although the imagery in lines 58–64a is often identified with the soul, some scholars have recommended more refined distinctions between *hyge*, *modsefa* and *hreþer*. The bird-soul figure, therefore, might be more precisely described as the bird-aim (*hyge*) or the bird-mind (*modsefa*) at different points, but for the sake of consistency and clarity I will refer to the bird-soul throughout. Even if we choose not to see it actually as the soul flying out here, the poem as a whole still concerns the ultimate movement of the soul's earthly journey towards heaven, even if this specific flight is taken to be a future event.

Anglo-Saxon Ornithology

Anglo-Saxon encounters with real birds have been overlooked, no doubt because most references occur in texts in which it has long been presumed literary tropes govern how the natural world is presented. Recent work in various disciplines has determined to show more fully, however, that real birds were given more than symbolic relevance in many spheres of Anglo-Saxon culture. We might consider, for instance, how birds in Old English place-names suggest associative links between species and particular environments, or point to the rich assemblies of birds' names in the extant Old English glossaries (more of which below). Zooarchaeological studies, attempting to move 'beyond seeing animals as mere passive resources to be exploited' have explored how the broad range of domestic and wild bird species present on sites across Anglo-Saxon England can yield further ideas about the conspicuous and important roles birds played in the everyday lives of the people who inhabited these places.[17] This is particularly the case for domesticated species, but also for those used in falconry, whose remains are recovered from high status centres.[18]

We might expect the Anglo-Saxons to be familiar with domesticated species used for food or sport, but may be less persuaded by this sort of interest in wild birds. The evidence, however, strongly suggests that Anglo-Saxon experiences of birds were not generic or limited, and that they observed and responded to species from a wide range of habitats.[19] In the 'remarkably long' list of landmarks in Anglo-Saxon place-names and charters, wild birds are clearly associated as conspicuous, observed elements of location. Markers

---

[17] Kristopher Poole and Eric Lacey, 'Avian Aurality in Anglo-Saxon England', *World Archaeology*, 46:3 (2014), 400–15 (pp. 410–11).

[18] For Anglo-Saxon raptor remains see Keith Dobney and Deborah Jaques, 'Avian Signatures for Identity and Status in Anglo-Saxon England', *Acta zoological cracoviensia*, 45 (2002), 7–21.

[19] See the extensive list of archaeological Anglo-Saxon records in D. W. Yalden and U. Albarella, *The History of British Birds* (Oxford: Oxford University Press, 2009), pp. 130–4. For taxonomic and linguistic discussion, see Eric Lacey, 'Birds and Words: Aurality, Semantics and Species in Anglo-Saxon England', in *Sensory Perception in the Medieval West*, ed. by Simon C. Thomson and Michael D. J. Bintley (Turnhout: Brepols, 2016), pp. 75–98.

such as *on masen mere* 'to the tit-mouse's pond', *turtlingcford*, possibly 'ford where the turtle dove is seen', or *wrænnan leah* 'the wren's wood' indicate how 'intimately aware' people were of birds as part of their everyday experiences with their surroundings.[20] With specific reference to sea or coastal birds, a place such as Foulness Island in Essex (*fughel-ness* 'bird-headland') likely refers to large flocks of wading and wildfowl species on the marshland. These associations are supported, too, by archaeological finds; excavations at the Anglo-Saxon coastal site of Bishopstone in Sussex, for instance, have turned up the remains of numerous sea or wader birds, marking them as characteristic inhabitants in and around human settlements in coastal regions.[21] Moreover, the naming of particular seabird species in *The Seafarer* and the focus on their calls suggest that these birds did make an impact as avifauna of particular habitats, enough, at least, so that the poet could rely upon their presence to recreate a particular environment and feeling. For the Anglo-Saxons, as Andrew Whitehouse has argued of birdsong in modern times, it is possible that birds' 'sound-making' was an important component of 'place-making'.[22]

Identifying or visualising seabirds has a special relevance in *The*

---

[20] Della Hooke, 'Beasts, Birds and Other Creatures in Pre-Conquest Charters and Place-Names in England', in *Representing Beasts in Early Medieval England and Scandinavia*, ed. by Michael D. J. Bintley and Thomas J. T. Williams (Woodbridge: Boydell Press, 2015), pp. 253–82 (271 and 276). The section on bird-related place-names is by some way the longest in this essay. See also, Carole Hough, 'Place-Name Evidence for Old English Bird-Names', *Journal of the English Place-Name Society*, 30 (1998), 60–9.

[21] The saltmarshes of south Essex have been subject to periods of reclamation over the centuries, but the habitat certainly existed in the early Middle Ages and would have been attractive feeding territory to resident and migrating coastal birds as much then as now. See also OE *pipere* under 'Redshank' in the glossary. For the Bishopstone excavation, see Poole and Lacey, 'Avian Aurality', 406. The connection between coastal regions and seabirds or wetland birds may also be reflected in a series of eighth-century *sceattas* portraying birds whose 'long legs and beaks indicate waders, appropriately, considering the coastal attribution of the series'; Anna Gannon, *The Iconography of Early Anglo-Saxon Coinage: Sixth to Eighth Centuries* (Oxford: Oxford University Press, 2003), pp. 113–14. See also Marion M. Archibald and Michael Dhenin, 'A Sceat of Offa of Mercia' <http://www.britnumsoc.org/publications/Digital%20BNJ/pdfs/2004_BNJ_74_4.pdf> [accessed 15 March 2016].

[22] Whitehouse, 'Listening to Birds in the Anthropocene', 58.

Seafarer beyond evocation, which enables the poem's particular visions of pilgrim-journeying. Bede's sparrow is a fitting image of Christian transformation largely because of its biblical pedigree. The migrating seabird, though, provides *The Seafarer* poet with a potent image for the migrating soul for reasons that attend more to the bird itself. As echoed by Bartholomaeus's description of *larus*, seabird species occupy a revealing space between land, sky and sea, along liminal, coastal territories which are prominent in *The Seafarer* – the uneasy boundary between the renounced *eorðwelan* 'earth-wealth' (67a) for which the speaker laments, and the paradoxically desired hardships sought on the *atol yþa gewealc* 'terrible tossing of waves' (6a).[23] Seabirds breed right on these terrestrial margins, many on high sea cliffs that tower over the waves, but travel for vast distances to find food, often for huge spans of time, particularly in winter when they become truly sea-bound creatures, travelling hundreds, even thousands of miles.[24] They inhabit a watery realm – *mæwes eþel* 'the gull's home' (*The Husband's Message*, 26b) – that might well seem otherworldly or alien, and certainly was treated symbolically in this way in patristic texts that are likely influences upon the poems' sea-pilgrimage motif, most notably in Augustine's familiar analogies.[25] The religious journeys of both human bodies and souls, that is, are so well depicted not only by birds generally, whose most noticeable ability is flight, but by birds who master this skill over nonhuman habitats – mysterious and dangerous seas that stretch beyond the human eye.

---

[23] The seafarer makes four distinct breaks from the seascape to address land-living: see lines 12–17, 27–30, 39–46 and 55–7.

[24] Seabirds exemplify the solitude that the psalms traditionally attribute to the sparrow. The whooper and Bewick's swans migrate from the Arctic circle to winter in Britain. The gannet, like most true seabirds, disperses and flies great distances out into the Atlantic in winter. Gulls in winter are generally marked by the same pattern, but they do inhabit coasts all year round, too. See distribution maps for, e.g., herring gull and kittiwake (*BWP*, vol. 1, pp. 743 and 760). The curlew is not technically a seabird, but is associated with winter estuarine territories, is migratory and 'commonly solitary' (*BWP*, vol. 1, p. 660). White-tailed eagles (sea eagles) are generally linked with 'sea coasts', and are 'dispersive, or migratory' and 'typically solitary' (*BWP*, vol. 1, p. 306).

[25] See, e.g., *Expositions on the Psalms*, CVII.vii. Cf. another Exeter poem, Cynewulf's *Christ II* (850–63).

The Anglo-Saxons were certainly aware of birds' ability to migrate, in the ornithological sense. Aristotle's observations on birds were available to churchmen through the likes of Pliny, who mentions 'this migration of birds of passage over seas and lands', and Isidore's remarks on birds like the swallow and stork which are 'migratory and return at certain seasons', whilst others 'stay in the same location'.[26] Old English poetic descriptions of journeying ships that speed *famigheals, fugole gelicost* 'foamy-necked, most like a bird' on the *swanrade* 'swanroad' (*Andreas*, 497 and 196b), in fact, recall in inversion Pliny's comparison of swans' and geese's flight patterns with 'the beaked prows of ships'.[27] As we will see in Chapter Two, the mysteries of flight attend the Exeter Book bird riddles, too: in one, a swan is defined by its unreachable flights far *ofer folc* 'over the people' (7.6a), and in another a barnacle goose is described according to the myth that its unfathomable disappearance is explained by its origin as a mollusc. But the Anglo-Saxons, keenly aware of their own migrations *ofer ganotes bæð* 'over the gannet's bath' or *swanrade* 'with the swan road' (*Beowulf*, 1861b and 200a) and wary of invasions from Nordic foreigners across the North Sea, surely understood and responded to birds' migrations in the broadest sense, too, as creatures which paradoxically 'stay in the same location' and are always on the move, soon to be gone and out of sight.[28] Birds are equated with frightening but compelling territories outside human knowledge, like the exotic realms to which Isidore links birds' unknowable wanderings in his introductory passages to birds, and which lead to their most characteristic

---

[26] *HN*, X.xxxiii; *Etym.*, XII.vii.1. Cf. Pliny's reference to the swallow: *HN*, X.xxxiv. Cf. also Aldhelm's enigmas on the swallow (47) and the nightingale (22) which both reference the migratory habits of these species.

[27] *HN*, X.xxxii. I provide my own translation here of Pliny's comparison to emphasise a more direct reading of (adj.) *rostrato* than does Rackham. Lat. (n.) *rostrum* 'beak' refers to both a bird and the galley of a ship.

[28] For discussion of Anglo-Saxon perceptions of their own continental migrations, see Nicholas Howe, *Migration and Myth-Making in Anglo-Saxon England* (New Haven, CT: Yale University Press, 1989). Howe describes their initial migrations from the continent as the 'founding and defining event of their culture' (p. ix).

quality, that which gives them their Latin name (*avis*).²⁹ Isidore's portrayal of birds resonates with the opening to another poem from the Exeter collection:

> Monge sindon geond middangeard
> unrimu cynn, þe we æþelu ne magon
> ryhte areccan ne rim witan;
> þæs wide sind geond world innan
> fugal ond deora foldhrerendra
> wornas widsceope ...
>
> (*The Panther*, 1–7)³⁰

[Many are the countless species across the earth; their nature we cannot rightly reckon, nor know their number, for the masses of birds and earth-treading beasts are widely scattered throughout the world.]

Seabirds that cannot be fully known, at home on the pathless and equally foreign oceans that the seafarer perversely seeks out, best embody this marvel of avian behaviour.

Avian Encounters – Naming and Listening

The short section in *The Seafarer* listing six coastal species has frequently attracted scholars who show an interest in the birds for birds' sake, particularly from those wanting to examine birds in Old English texts or English literature generally. The list of species has been seen by some as 'the first bit of true-sounding, wild-inspired

---

²⁹ *Etym.*, XII.vii.3. Cf. Pliny's comments on storks, which focus on the mysterious aspect of their migration: 'Where exactly storks come from or where they go to has not hitherto been ascertained' (*HN*, X.xxxi). The sense of foreignness associated with some birds is evident, too, in examples like MLat. (*falco*) *peregrinus* which meant 'pilgrim', but also, as in classical Lat., 'foreign'. Cf. also OE *wealhhafoc* 'foreign-hawk', recorded in numerous glossaries. For a possible connection between these two terms, see Philip A. Shaw, 'Telling a Hawk from an *Herodio*: On the Origins and Development of the Old English Word *Wealhhafoc* and Its Relatives', *MÆ*, 82:1 (2013), 1–22 (pp. 8–9).

³⁰ Cf. the opening to *The Phoenix*: *Hæbbe ic gefrugnen þætte is feor heonan / east-dælum on æplast londa /... Nis se foldan sceat / ofer middangeard mongum gefere* 'I have heard that there is far hence in eastern parts a noblest land ... that corner of the earth is not easy of access to many throughout this world' (1–4).

field ornithological record since the Romans'.[31] Margaret E. Goldsmith devotes much effort to seeing the poem as a faithful, ornithological depiction. For her, the 'singling out of several birds implies a close interest in their habits and calls' and she proposes that 'the birds of his poem must be familiar sights round the seashore if he is to draw his audience of landsmen with him in imagination'.[32] Although Goldsmith does not relate her conclusions to the larger themes and structures of the poem, in her opening she does place her identifications broadly in the context of literal and allegorical approaches: 'ornithological unlikelihoods' (should they exist) make the idea of allegorical intent ... less far-fetched'.[33]

Most attention, then, has come from those wishing to compile pre-modern nomenclatures. Little work has been done to examine ways in which the presence of birds in the poem challenges us to reframe our knowledge of Anglo-Saxon perceptions of species relations and distinctions, to recognise that these were, in fact, nuanced, competing, experiential, and that this understanding requires us to reconceive how we interpret the figurative roles of birds in the poem. One response that does represent recent ecocritical interests correctly identifies the seabird passage as significant. Matt Low has recognised in these lines evidence of a 'concrete place'; for him the repetition of *þær* 'there' (23b) is the key word implying an evident literalism, giving emphasis as it does to location.[34] Oddly, Low does nothing more than assign the birds 'prevalent' status, and his analysis ends typically, by remarking how the physicality of place

---

[31] James Fisher, *The Shell Book of Birds* (London: Ebury Press & Michael Joseph, 1966), p. 44. Fisher is so convinced of the veracity of the birds' presentation in the poem that he even ventures a location (Bass Rock, East Scotland) and an approximate date in the year (20–27 April).

[32] Margaret E. Goldsmith, 'The *Seafarer* and the Birds', RES, 5:19 (1954), 225–35 (pp. 225 and 226). See also Eric Lacey, 'Birds and Bird-lore in the Literature of Anglo-Saxon England' (unpublished doctoral thesis, University College London, 2013), pp. 83–99. Lacey's thesis is a recent, substantial study of bird taxonomy and augury in Anglo-Saxon England, but I was unable to view the text until very near completing my own manuscript for publication, and have, therefore, not been able to address the research therein.

[33] Goldsmith, '*Seafarer* and the Birds', 226.

[34] Matt Low, '"Heard gripe hruson" (The hard grip of the earth): Ecopoetry and the Anglo-Saxon Elegy', *Mosaic*, 42:3 (2009), 1–18 (p. 10).

reflects the speaker's torment in 'traversing these hostile environments'.[35] A closer, bird-centred reading of the relevant lines, however, suggests how the poet establishes a complex interrelation between human and bird which is particularly dependent on the acts of listening and naming.

Rather like Bede's sparrow, the seabirds' signification is not clear cut, a characteristic that the poet exploits, and for which ambiguity their physicality is largely responsible.[36] They are overtly linked to the hall-life by the seafarer, and yet remain resolutely a part of the terrifying sea-storm environment, as intrinsic to the *iscealdne wæg* 'ice-cold way' (14b) as the *hrimgicelum* 'icicles' (17a) and *hægl scurum* 'hail showers' (17b) that precede them:

> Hwilum ylfete song
> dyde ic me to gomene, ganetes hleoþor
> ond huilpan sweg fore hleahtor wera,
> mæw singende fore medodrince.
> Stormas þær stanclifu beotan, þær him stearn oncwæð
> isigfeþera; ful oft þæt earn bigeal,
> urigfeþra; ne ænig hleomæga
> feasceaftig ferð frefran meahte.[37]
>
> (*The Seafarer*, 19b–26)

---

[35] Ibid., 11. More recently, Helen Price has given the birds a little more attention, but is more concerned with the wider ecosystem of land and water in the elegies; Helen Price, 'Human and Nonhuman in Anglo-Saxon and British Postwar Poetry: Reshaping Literary Ecology' (unpublished doctoral thesis, University of Leeds, 2013), pp. 289–92.

[36] The equivocal sparrow can signify both a pitiable mortality and the 'meaninglessness' of the 'pagan faith', as Bruce Mitchell and Fred C. Robinson interpret it, but also the enlightened and eternal soul following conversion; Bruce Mitchell and Fred C. Robinson, *A Guide to Old English*, 5th edn (Oxford: Blackwell, 1992), p. 269.

[37] The *earn* (white-tailed eagle) can be confidently identified, and the *swan* and *mæw* labelled at genus and family level, respectively. Which swan and which gull we are dealing with is less certain. Whooper swan has been suggested more than once (Goldsmith, 'Seafarer and the Seabirds', 226–7), which fits well with the scene and theme of migration, but the mute swan with its familiar 'musical' flight is more associated with *song* (see Exeter Riddle 7 and *Etym.*, XII.vii.18–19). OE *swan* derives from an Indo-European onomatopoeic cognate broadly meaning 'sound'; see W. B. Lockwood, *The Oxford Book of British Bird Names* (Oxford: Oxford University Press, 1984), s.v. Swan. Moreover, OE does have two terms for the genus: *swan*, and that which appears in *The Seafarer*, *yflete*. In the glossaries, these terms correspond to different Lat. names (*olor* and

[Sometimes I took the swan's song for my game, the gannet's sound and curlew's cry for men's laughter, the gull's singing for the mead-drink. There storms beat stone cliffs, there the tern answered them, icy-feathered; very often the eagle yelled, dewy-feathered; no protecting kinsman can comfort the desolate soul.]

There is a comparable effect in the much briefer reference to seabirds in *The Wanderer*:

> Đonne onwæcneð eft wineleas guma,
> gesihð him biforan fealwe wegas,
> baþian brimfuglas, brædan feþra,
> hreosan hrim ond snaw, hagle gemenged.
>
> (*The Wanderer*, 45a-8b)

cygnus, respectively), indicating that Anglo-Saxons may have differentiated, although this is inconsistent. If we are to go on which species was most likely to be seen over the *swanrade*, the arctic migrating whooper (or Bewick's) seems more likely, whose modern name refers to its distinctive trumpeting call. For further discussion on the possible distinctions, see Peter Kitson, 'Swans and Geese in Old English Riddles', *Anglo-Saxon Studies in Archaeology and History*, 7 (1994), 79–84. *Ganet* seems straightforward, but is problematic in that the term glosses more than one lemma in the glossaries. The undeniable portrait of a labelled juvenile gannet in the Sherborne Missal (British Library, MS Add. 74326; c. 1400), however, makes it clear that this term was applied to this species by at least the late medieval period. Lockwood also gives an attestation from 1274 (*British Bird Names*, s.v. *Gannet*). The prevalence of this white species, the largest British seabird, nesting en masse on coastal cliffs (Bass Rock has the world's largest colony), could hardly have been missed by Anglo-Saxon observers, though, and there is no reason why the word might not have been assigned to this species even if it was also used as a more general term for sea-fowl. The *huilpe* and *stearn* have never been positively identified. For a full discussion on possible species, see Goldsmith, 'Seafarer and the Birds', 228–9 and 230–4, respectively, and Lacey, 'Birds and Bird-lore', pp. 93–5. Following most editors, I translate *huilpe* as 'curlew' on the basis of cognates in modern Germanic languages (e.g., Mn Dutch *wulp*; see Lockwood, *British Bird Names*, s.v. *Whaup*), the distinctive 'bubbling' or 'whaup' call of this species (*BWP*, vol. 1, p. 660), and its common presence in British coastal regions. Poole and Lacey recommend the whimbrel instead ('Avian Aurality', 408), but these species are very similar and it is impossible to say which might be intended. The whimbrel also causes the same problems as *stearn* (usually translated as 'tern') because it is a brief, summer passage migrant. *Stearn* does appear in the glossaries, but all we can say with any likelihood is that it names some sort of gull or gull-like species. The kittiwake (as suggested by Goldsmith) or fulmar might be other possibilities.

[Then the friendless man wakes again, sees before him dark waves, seabirds bathing, spreading feathers, rime and snow falling mingled with hail.]

We do not have particular species in this passage, but we do have specific behaviours described – the *baþian brimfuglas brædan feþra* which place us beyond the realm of mere symbolism. In both cases, nature is not simply an indicator of mood or a depiction of the hostile forces opposing the human and human society.[38] The developed details in *The Seafarer* shift the scene more fully, though, from conventional tableau to interconnected and affective ecosystem, in which the human speaker will attempt to engage in a complicated manoeuvre that involves simultaneous association and distancing. The elements of 'concrete place' that Low recognises in *The Seafarer* include rocky sea cliffs; the seafarer is not just afloat on featureless, generic waters, but more precisely situated in a littoral environment, to which the storm and the tern are linked by alliteration. That characteristic of seabirds as creatures of terrestrial margins is heightened by this reference – the speaker has land in sight even whilst on the ocean (birds, indeed, can even be a navigational sign of land). It is the names and calls of the seabirds that are most 'prevalent', however, not only as evocative elements of the wild, but as the aspects with which the seafarer shows most interest, overtly drawing parallels between human and nonhuman realms.

The act of naming species is a central part of the effect in this passage, not only because it involves precision, or because we are dealing with birds other than the literary-invested raven and eagle, but because naming practices in themselves were central scholastic activities – in grammars and in Isidore's extensive etymological lists, and also in reading or writing the different types of glosses that accompanied important Latin texts. Birds appear in a good number of extant glossaries, and the vernacular terms often show close observation of species' appearances, calls and habits; to name

---

[38] Few critics now argue for a shared authorship, but the role of birds in these poems is remarkably similar. Perhaps this commonality implies a wider identification of seabirds with the themes of journeying and solitude which is treated with particular specificity by these poets.

birds meant to know birds to some degree, to recognise that this or that Latin avian term equated to an English name rooted in some form of actual or potential experience.[39] It is reasonable to speculate, then, that the intellectual monastic environment in which *The Seafarer* was likely written and copied made available or familiar other examples of bird-naming.[40] Naming seabirds is meaningful beyond establishing a generic backdrop because it engages with an attention to linguistic detail that does not, to judge from evidence like the glossaries, ignore experiences with the physical, natural world.

This is particularly the case when we consider the role that bird sounds appear to have played in the procedures of Anglo-Saxon naming. The authors of the Bishopstone study propose that birdsong and calls were, in fact, 'key aspects of people's daily lives': for them, literary evidence supports a wide range of species discovered in the excavations to reveal an archaeacoustic reconstruction.[41] They cite other archaeological evidence to demonstrate how perceptive Anglo-Saxons were to avian aurality – a series of coins, for instance, depicting the five senses, in which hearing is represented by a bird perched on a person's shoulder.[42] Vernacular bird names

---

[39] Birds are numerous in glosses and glossaries. See *Ælfrics Grammatik*, pp. 307–8; Second Antwerp glossary: Wright-Wülcker, pp. 131–3 (here erroneously attributed to Ælfric), and David W. Porter, ed., *The Antwerp–London Glossaries: The Latin and Latin–Old English Vocabularies from Antwerp, Museum Plantin-Moretus 16.2 – London, British Library Add. 3224*, vol. 1 (Toronto: Pontifical Institute of Medieval Studies, 2011); Brussels glossary: Wright-Wülcker, pp. 284–7; Second Corpus glossary: Wright-Wülcker, pp. 1–54, and J. H. Hessels, ed., *An Eighth-Century Latin–Anglo-Saxon Glossary, Preserved in the Library of Corpus Christi College, Cambridge* (Cambridge: Cambridge University Press, 1890); Harley 3376 glossary: Wright-Wülker, pp. 192–247, and R. T. Oliphant, ed., *Harley Latin-Old English, edited from British Museum MS Harley 3376* (The Hague: Mouton, 1966); Épinal-Erfurt Glossary: J. D. Pheifer, ed., *Old English Glosses in the Épinal-Erfurt Glossary* (Oxford: Clarendon Press, 1974); and the Cleopatra glosses, particularly Second Cleopatra glossary: Wright-Wülcker, pp. 258–61, and J. Quinn, 'The Minor Latin-Old English Glossaries in MS. Cotton Cleopatra A. III' (unpublished doctoral thesis, Stanford University, 1951). For discussion of OE bird names, see the glossary in this volume.

[40] All the birds listed in the poem, except *huilpe*, are attested in at least one of the extant glossaries: e.g., in the Second Antwerp glossary we find *ylfete* (6), *earn* (10), *stearn* (11), *mæw* (30), and in the Second Cleopatra glossary, *ganot* (1).

[41] Poole and Lacey, 'Avian Aurality', 400 (abstract).

[42] Ibid., 403.

in Old English glossaries, in fact, reveal a preponderance of species named according to appearance, habitat or behaviour, but many more relate to song or call. Numerous bird names are onomatopoeic: *finc* 'finch', *hroc* 'rook', *crawe* 'crow', *cio* 'chough'. There are many more, too, that associate a particular species with distinctive sound: *swan* 'swan', *nihtegale* 'nightingale', *raredumle* 'reed-boomer' (bittern), *hæferblæte* 'goat-bleater' (snipe).[43] Onomatopoeic names were native to Germanic languages, but a key source like Isidore may also have encouraged the practice.[44] A lexicographical focus on bird sounds is evident in *The Seafarer*'s seabird passage; two of the birds listed have what are likely to be onomatopoeic names, the *huilpe* and *mæw*.[45] Moreover, the speaker foregrounds the birds' calls; all six utter sound, emphasised through the poet's range of sonic nouns. There are some similarities with the Exeter bird riddles, which are also rich in aural effects and further emphasise the impact of sounds: the swan (Riddle 7), like its *Seafarer* counterpart, *singað* (9a), and there is a shared vocabulary of nouns and verbs for song or call between the elegy and the riddles. The jay (Riddle 24), a bird noted for its remarkable ability to imitate the voices of all sorts of other creatures (including the *mæwes song* [6b]), can *giellan* 'cry out' (3b) another's *hleoþor* 'sound' and *reord* 'voice' (5). *Hleoþor* appears in the seabird passage itself, and the other two appear in the later *anfloga* passage (53b, 62b).

---

[43] Names relating to habitat, behaviour or appearance include: *þisteltwige* 'thistle-twig' (goldfinch), *duce* 'duck', *glida* 'glider' (kite), *hegesugge* 'hedge-sucker' (hedge-sparrow), and *rudduc*, 'ruddy one' (robin). Monosyllabic, onomatopoeic names tend to have a Proto-Germanic/Proto-Indo-European origin, but the compound terms seem to be of Anglo-Saxon (and Old Saxon) invention. For detailed references, see my own discussions in the glossary, and the studies listed there.
[44] *Etym.*, XII.vii.9.
[45] Bosworth and Toller define *huilpa* as 'the name of a bird so called from its note'; Bosworth-Toller, s.v. (n.) *huilpa*.

Avian Encounters – Strange Relations

The birds' calls establish a distinct ubiety, but they are also central to another striking aspect of *The Seafarer*. The speaker attempts to engage with these animate elements of his surroundings in a manner that reflects the sort of environmentally-sensitive action Jeffrey Jerome Cohen has encouraged us to recognise and to perform. In a poem that requires its speaker to consistently 'curve into anthropocentric sel[f]' in tending to the state of his soul, when it comes to the birds he will also 'extend apprehension outward into the ecomateriality', an action that becomes central to his internal scrutiny. The seafarer becomes 'palpably embroiled' through his own volition.[46] The seafarer's experiences draw purposeful, explicit connections between species' calls and aspects of land- and hall-life.

This association with the seabirds has attracted mixed responses. At one end of the spectrum, some have gone so far as to suggest 'something akin to pleasure' in this sequence, close to a 'masochistic smugness', as Nicholas Jacobs puts it.[47] He even suggests congruence with a passage from *Guthlac A* (739–45) which depicts the natural world favourably in a spring depiction. Because instances like *Guthlac* show us that 'a distrust of the natural world' is not a 'universal feature', it is possible that in *The Seafarer*, as in some speculated Irish sources, the 'pleasures of nature afford a fair exchange for those of civilisation'.[48] Jacobs's response, however, is rare, and even he is speculative. Most, aligning the scene with conventional nature tropes in Old English poetry, see the seafarer's identification with birds working anthropocentrically and conversely. That is, the association is designed to remind us that the seafarer *lacks* company

---

[46] Jeffrey Jerome Cohen, ed., *Inhuman Nature* (Washington, DC: Oliphaunt, 2014), p. ii. In *The Wanderer*, something similar occurs: afflicted with *sorg ond slæp* 'sorrow and sleep' (39a), the speaker hallucinates that preening seabirds are his beloved lost kinsmen; he *onwæcneð* 'awakens' (45a) into an unintended embroilment, where birds and men are momentarily one and the same to him.

[47] Nicholas Jacobs, '*The Seafarer* and the Birds: A Possible Irish Parallel', *Celtica*, 23 (1999), 125–31 (p. 128). Cf. C. A. Ireland, 'Some Analogues of the O.E. *Seafarer* from Hiberno-Latin Sources', *Neuphilologische Mitteilungen*, 92 (1991), 1–14 (pp. 7–8).

[48] Jacobs, '*Seafarer* and the Birds', 127.

(or company that counts, anyhow) and, therefore, the birds are only relevant as indicators of human absence. Any likeness is spurious in this analysis because *gomene*, *hleahtor* and *medodrince* are intended with gloomy irony.[49] Jennifer Neville cites the end of the seabird passage (25b–6) when the seafarer expresses deep grief as clear evidence that the scene is of no inspiration to the speaker, pitching it against the very moment from *Guthlac* with which Jacobs finds an element of similarity.[50]

This prevailing interpretation is not one that I deny or dismiss. Contrasts between human and nonhuman elements in the poem are present and significant, and the general expression of suffering makes 'new-found exultation' seem excessive, even if it 'welcomes discomfort' for the 'striking of moral postures'.[51] The seafarer's paradoxical choice at the heart of the poem, as Frederick S. Holton demonstrates, produces a rich sea imagery, capable of symbolising a range of contradicting meanings.[52] This same paradox recommends more nuanced ways of reading the seafarer's mood and relation to the birds, which are a particularly striking aspect of this seascape. Whether travel occurs for pilgrimage or other reasons, whether it is allegorical or actual, the persistent emphasis on choosing *hean streamas*, / *sealtyþa gelac* 'the high seas, tumult of the salty waves' (34–5) in contrast to land-dwellers *wingal* 'flushed with wine' (29a) can imply sincerity in the seafarer's business as much as irony – *dyde* is not so much making do, but repeated (*Whilum*, *ful oft*), proactive, and willing adaptation. Taking ascetic pleasure in the birds' presence and their substitutive acts suits well the concept of *peregrinatio*; they can be simultaneously desired and deplored. Recognising moments like these reveals connections that are not linear or simple (birds' presence equals grievous human absence), but subtle and

---

[49] Conversely, on the absence of irony in these lines, see B. J. Timmer, 'Irony in Old English Poetry', *ES*, 24 (1942), 171–5.
[50] Jennifer Neville, *Representations of the Natural World in Old English Poetry*, CSASE, 27 (Cambridge: Cambridge University Press, 1999), p. 36. For P. R. Orton, the birds are 'pathetically inadequate substitutes'; P. R. Orton, 'Form and Structure of *The Seafarer*', *Studia Neophilologica*, 63 (1991), 37–55 (p. 40).
[51] Jacobs, '*Seafarer* and the Birds', 128.
[52] Frederick S. Holton, 'Old English Sea Imagery and the Interpretation of *The Seafarer*', *Yearbook of English Studies*, 12 (1982), 208–17.

interrelated. The connections between species are inconsistent, but this dynamic is part of a cohesive use of the bird figure across the text, and in attending to it we can appreciate another way in which the long debated literal and allegorical aspects of the text might co-exist.[53] Indeed, *The Seafarer*'s birds, stubbornly literal as well as powerfully figurative, are perhaps one of the key elements of the text that do point the way towards this co-existence. In the later part of the poem these complex bird-human relations, permeated by competing affinities and differences, do not so much point towards what the seafarer has left behind as look forwards to anticipate in more literal terms the closeness of bird and man that occurs when the seafarer imagines his *modsefa* 'spirit' (59a) enacting a migration across oceans (60–4a). The profound bird-soul will also require us to hold in one view likeness and difference.

These tensions between species, however, are prepared for in the speaker's dealings with real seabirds. The final lines of the seabird passage are characteristic: *ne ænig hleomæga / feasceaftig ferð frefran meahte* 'no protecting kinsman can comfort the desolate soul' (25b–6). Immediately following the list of species, its syntactical position implies that we read the line as a comment in response to the preceding correspondences, an indication as to how the seafarer relates to the birds, or why they are important. On the face of it, these lines provide evidence of the seabirds' negative impact, as Neville argues. For those who favour the idea that nature is only a hostile opposite, words such as 'miserable' or 'wretched' for *feasceaftig* are most appropriate. Others choose to translate it as 'desolate', and Bosworth-Toller offers 'poor, destitute', both of which allow more easily for the contented suffering of a voluntary exile

---

[53] For allegorical interpretations, see, e.g., G. V. Smithers, 'The Meaning of *The Seafarer* and *The Wanderer*', *MÆ*, 26:3 (1957), 137–53, and 'The Meaning of *The Seafarer* and *The Wanderer* (continued)', *MÆ*, 28:1 (1959), 1–22. The most famous example of a literal interpretation is Dorothy Whitelock, 'The Interpretation of *The Seafarer*', in *Early Cultures of Northwest Europe*, ed. by Cyril Fox and Bruce Dickins (Cambridge: Cambridge University Press, 1950), pp. 261–72. Richard North remarks that '*The Seafarer* is more about nautical fact than figure', that 'the seafaring is real enough'; Richard North, 'Heaven Ahoy! Sensory Perception in *The Seafarer*', in *Sensory Perception in the Medieval West*, ed. by Simon C. Thomson and Michael D. J. Bintley (Turnhout: Brepols, 2016), pp. 7–26 (25 and 26).

who renounces worldly values.⁵⁴ All of them, however, allow us to interpret lines 25b–26 as a forlorn exclamation from the seafarer that there is no one to help, not simply because he is at sea and his kinsmen on land or dead, but because they cannot help with a journey which must be confronted alone. For some, these lines immediately following the list of birds clarify why the speaker is unhappy – because birds are all he has for company, not humans. There is another way of reading this, though, which inverts the previous reading; that is, the seafarer turns to birds for game and laughter and song because no human is able to comfort him.⁵⁵ It is precisely because *ne ænig hleomæga / feasceaftig ferð frefran meahte* that the birds are necessary and desirable as companions. *Meahte* 'can', lends the sentence a gnomic quality; in this life there is no comfort to be had from other men. Unlike typical instances, then, the birds are brought purposefully into the human frame, not defined against it.

Specifically, it is the birds' cries that summon nostalgic thoughts of human companionship for the seafarer. Returning to the emphasis on sounds in this passage reveals this meeting of contradictory attitudes in the intricate patterning of bird-human likeness and difference. The aural identification with birds is embedded in the poet's composition of the passage, and resonates with those preoccupations and responses to birds' sounds that we discussed above. The structure of the Old English line produces contrast, but also suggests parity between the bird and human.⁵⁶ This is particularly

---

54 See, e.g., Richard Marsden, ed., *The Cambridge Old English Reader* (Cambridge: Cambridge University Press, 2004), and Ida Gordon, ed., *The Seafarer*, rev. edn (Exeter: University of Exeter Press, 1996). See also, Bosworth-Toller, s.v. (adj.) *feasceaftig*.

55 North reads the passage along these lines: he comments that the 'question is not how much the Seafarer bemoans all this feathered wildlife ... but how soon he comes to regard it as superior': 'the eagle and his part are welcome to take their [kinsmen's] place'; North, 'Heaven ahoy!', pp. 14–15.

56 For this reason, Roy F. Leslie has suggested alternative punctuation in the passage: 'If we place a stop after *song* at the end of line 19, *ylfete song* becomes an additional object of *gehyrde* (18) in the first sentence, and we have a one-to-one correspondence in the second: the cry of the gannet for pleasure, the curlew's call for the laughter of men, and the gull singing for the mead-drinking'; Roy F. Leslie, 'The Editing of Old English Poetic Texts: Questions of Style', in *Old English Poetry: Essays on Style*, ed. by Daniel G. Calder (Berkeley, CA: University of California Press, 1979), pp. 111–25 (118).

evident in lines 21–2 which use the caesura most symmetrically to create the effect, supported by the placing of *fore* 'in place of' at the beginning of the B lines, indicating that the birds stand for the human, not in opposition:[57]

> ond huilpan sweg   fore hleahtor wera,
> mæw singende   fore medodrince.
>
> (21–2)

[and curlew's cry for man's laughter, the singing gull for the mead-drink.]

Human merriment and bird voices are bound up together in dense alliterative patterns; there is a triplet of words denoting sound (*song, sweg, singende*) and a cluster of words circling around the consonants of men's *hleahtor*. Aspects such as this can indicate straightforward substitution, in which raucous or jarring bird calls are made to stand ironically for more pleasant, articulate human sounds. From a conventional perspective, the seafarer is presumably miserable because a curlew or gannet's calls do not actually sound like human merriment. Laughter, perhaps the most distinctively human sound here, may well seem opposed to the shrieks of seabirds because it is associated with 'the bright world of the Germanic hall'.[58] For Hugh Magennis, the reference to men's laughter is part of the 'ironic image' of the whole passage. But he also recognises in his study of laughter in the poem that this human sound (like Holton's sea imagery) suffers from contradictions, that it is 'double-sided', an image of relief and dismay.[59] Birds, too, directly paralleled with 'double-sided' laughter at this moment, are blurry sites of meaning. The ironic contrast of human laughter with the curlew's cries simultaneously suggests

---

[57] Jacobs examines the grammatical evidence for the possibility of *fore* meaning 'in preference to' (127), although he comes to the conclusion that the precise meaning of the word is 'not wholly conclusive'; for him, the ambiguity, in line with my own argument, establishes 'some complexity of tone' (128). In any case, either translation supports that the birds can be seen as a replacement for human companionship, and understands that this is not necessarily negative. Jacobs, '*Seafarer* and the Birds', 127–8.

[58] Hugh Magennis, 'Images of Laughter in Old English Poetry with Particular Reference to the "hleator wera" of *The Seafarer*', *ES*, 73:3 (1992), 193–204 (p. 204).

[59] Magennis, 'Images of Laughter', 204.

kinship through the alliteration, which not only links *huilpan* and *hleahtor* (echoed, too, in *hleomæga*), but binds *hleahtor* to the gannet's *hleopor* in an even closer linguistic resonance.⁶⁰ Poole and Lacey comment that the collocation of curlew cry and human laughter intentionally recalls the formulaic phrase *hearpan sweg* 'the harp's sound', a detail which they take to infer the bird's musicality, rather than just an evocation of hall-life.⁶¹

This shuttling effect between difference and similarity is also conveyed in the vocabulary used to denote voices and sounds in the seabird passage. As demonstrated in the Exeter bird riddles, the stock of Old English words conveying sounds could variously and broadly mean 'voice', 'cry', 'speech', 'song', and be applied to both human or nonhuman agents.⁶² In these poems, there is a playful confusion between voices that are simultaneously conflated and distinguished so that, as Robert Stanton puts it, 'observable sounds of birds ... become one with the representation in a human system of signification'.⁶³ Something of this ambiguity seems intentional in *The Seafarer* as well. The swan's *song* and gull's *singende* may imply an element of personification, particularly for the Anglo-Saxon mind which associates song as a typical part of hall pleasures, but the terms can exist neutrally as expressions of the birds' natural voices, too, which also can be said to sing. The same goes for *sweg* (which can mean 'confused sound, din', or the opposite, 'articulate

---

60   Neville, in fact, translates *hleopor* as 'laughter'; Neville, *Representations*, p. 36.
61   Poole and Lacey, 'Avian Aurality', p. 408. The authors suggest whimbrel as the owner of *sweg*. For *hearpan sweg*, see, e.g., *Beowulf*, 3023b.
62   *Sang* 'song', e.g., a term applied to human or angelic vocal production as well as that of birds or animals. See Bosworth-Toller, s.v. (n.) *sang*, sense 1(a) and (b). *Sanges* occurs in Exeter Riddle 57, the solution to which is most often assumed to be some species of bird. Poole and Lacey, following Audrey Meaney, go so far as to suggest that Anglo-Saxons distinguished even more specifically: for them *sang* 'refers to bird calls in neutral tones', whereas *winsum* [*sang*] 'singles out calls that were seen as particularly beautiful'; Poole and Lacey, 'Avian Aurality', pp. 402–3. For Meaney's comments, see, Audrey Meaney, 'Exeter Book Riddle 57 (55) – A Double Solution?', *Anglo-Saxon England*, 39 (1996), 187–200 (189). Meaney's assumption, however, is based on one recorded use of *winsum sang* in Ælfred's *Metrical Psalter*.
63   Robert Stanton, 'Mimicry, Subjectivity and the Embodied Voice in Anglo-Saxon Bird Riddles', in *Voice and Voicelessness in Medieval Europe*, ed. by Irit Ruth Kleiman (New York, NY: Palgrave Macmillan, 2015), pp. 29–46 (33).

sound', such as that of birdsong) and *bigeal* (from *bigiellan*, 'to celebrate with song', 'to scream').[64] As Stanton remarks about the bird riddles, this vocabulary involves a 'tension between natural, instinctive utterance and conventionally assigned meaning'.[65] Institutional distinctions between articulate human speech and inarticulate nonhuman sound that pervade scholastic theories, and which might be said to highlight opposition in the seabird passage, are not consistent in poetic treatments, or, indeed, in the vernacular language itself.[66] Old English sound-words, as in Modern English, are broad in their scope and application, encompassing, distinguishing and combining any number of human, nonhuman and inanimate subjects which might produce sounds of various and contiguous types. In a particular context, of course, a writer can intend a particular meaning of *sang*, but a poetic text such as *The Seafarer*, which explicitly correlates bird and human sounds, appears to rely upon the potential ambiguity for its overall effect, so that sound types are blurred into a cross-species category. Onomatopoeic names (*mæw*, *huilpe*), bound up in grammars concerned with defining voices, and taxonomies which translate birds' calls into human-replicated and human-assigned terms, demonstrate this particularly well; to speak the name (as the seafarer does) is to also enact the call the bird makes, melding human and avian vocalisations. When the birds make sound, perhaps the seafarer thinks of how they recall, even seem to imitate, human utterances.[67] They encourage a strange, unstable correlation which can raise equal sorrow or solace.

[64] Bosworth-Toller, s.v. (n.) *sweg*, senses 1 and 2(a), and (v.) *bi-gellan*.
[65] Stanton, 'Mimicry, Subjectivity, and the Embodied Voice', p. 39.
[66] For further discussion of this topic in an Anglo-Saxon context, see ibid. An Anglo-Saxon reference to the conventional model of articulate and inarticulate voice types can be found in Aldhelm's *De pedum regulis*.
[67] Gulls, e.g., although not the species directly related to men's *hleahtor*, are well known for their distinctive laugh-type calls. The herring gull has a proverbial laugh-type cackle, transcribed as 'kyow' or 'gagagag' (*BWP*, vol. 1, p. 745). *Mæw* was the native term for gull, in common use up until the seventeenth century, and is presumed to imitate the yelping made by many species. It is unclear which type of gull is represented by Anglo-Saxon *maew*, but if not the herring gull, perhaps the common gull (*BWP*, vol. 1, p. 737) or the kittiwake with its 'laughing "ha-ha-ha"' (ibid., p. 761). The last two species are similar in appearance and may not have been distinguished. Goldsmith identifies kittiwake with *stearn*; Goldsmith, 'Seafarer and the Birds', 234.

The artful linking of bird and human in *The Seafarer* reveals an unstable pattern of correspondence and discord. The birds and their calls oscillate between human and nonhuman worlds for the speaker, at one and the same time loosed from their natural environments to partake figuratively in the human realm, whilst remaining distinctly nonhuman. The assimilation suggests a kinship between species, even a form of comfort perhaps (in *The Wanderer*, this comfort is explicit, albeit momentary [52a]), but also exposes the ultimate foreignness of human and nonhuman species, despite the connections the speaker makes. Indeed, the poet presses these differences between species further, even to the extent that the natural world puts up an apparent resistance to the speaker's attempts to engage, as though to give reflexive attention to the inconsistencies inherent in the metaphor procedures.

Unsurprisingly, these resistances are located in the interplay of voices.[68] Although the seafarer does not speak out to the birds, there is an implied discourse in the repeated utterances. In the sense that the birds are company now, their vocalisations replacing the sounds of revelry back on land, the seafarer engages with their utterances, but what is more apparent is the dialogue existing between birds, and birds with their environment. The vocative is raised when the storms beat cliffs, a noisy action promoted to the status of utterance through parallel syntax: *þær stanclifu beotan, þær him stearn oncwæð*. The tern 'answers' to the storm's swell against rock (another vocal term that can be applied to animate and inanimate subjects in Old English).[69] The eagle, too, may well be joining the conversation: *ful oft þæt earn bigeal*. It is unclear to which subject *þæt* applies – the *stearn*, the storm or the cliffs – but the pattern of syntax ending the

---

[68] In *The Wanderer*, it is avian actions, as well as voices, that are responsible. When the *wineleas guma* 'friendless man' comes round from his stupor, it is the disappointing sight of birds *baþian* 'bathing' and *brædan feþra* 'preening feathers' that brings on his *sorg*. The initial act of remembering comrades, momentarily correlated with the seabirds in the speaker's dazed state, has a positive effect (as suggested by *georne* 'eagerly' [52b] and *gliwstafum* 'joyfully' [52a)]), but this is shortlived.

[69] Bosworth-Toller, s.v. (v.) *on-cweðan*, senses 1 and 2. The *him* in 23b is sometimes translated as 'himself', but the effect remains the same – the tern does not answer the seafarer.

line (noun-verb) and adjacent *isigfeþera / urigfeþra* combine to give a sense of interrelation.⁷⁰ The whole passage, therefore, falls into two parts. The first of these has the seafarer correlate human and nonhuman worlds by his own volition, but the second frames him out. The interactions continue without him; the *stearn* answers to storm, waves and cliffs, itself perhaps, but not him.

There may be a similar effect in *The Wanderer* at the moment when, immediately following the speaker's encounter with seabirds, he envisages *fleotendra ferð* 'the souls of the floating ones' (54a), entities that ambiguously incorporate the seabirds and the *maga gemynd* 'memory of kinsmen' (51a). He *greteð* 'greets' (52a) the *secga geseldan* 'companions of men' (53a) or *ferð*, a verb that includes the senses of 'to speak to', or 'call upon'.⁷¹ *Sorg bið geniwad* 'sorrow is renewed' (50b), it seems, because these mysterious beings *swimmað oft onweg* 'always swim away' (53b), *no þær fela bringeð / cuðra cwidegiedda* 'do not bring there many familiar voices' (54b-55a). *Cwidegiedd* is a term with very few recorded uses, and variously translatable as 'speech', 'song', 'utterances', 'exclamations' and 'sayings'. As with other sound-words in *The Seafarer*, it is telling because it allows for a range of meanings which can attach it to both avian and human subjects represented by *fleotendra ferð*.⁷² This same word, however, can lead the birds back to their own physical realm, quite unattached to human meaning. Whilst the *ferð* can be said to make so little sense to the wanderer because he hallucinates or because they are spirits, if we read them as birds, the wanderer's

---

⁷⁰ For discussion of *þæt*, and the possibility that *bigeal* is a sound specifically aimed *at* a referent, see Gordon, *Seafarer*, p. 36, n. 24. Some critics view the *isigfeþera/urigfeþra* collocation with suspicion; see ibid.

⁷¹ Bosworth-Toller, s.v. (v.) *gretan*, sense 2. Some editors translate according to this definition.

⁷² Marijane Osborn notes that the word 'combines human and avian elements'; Marijane Osborn, 'The Vanishing Seabirds in *The Wanderer*', *Folklore*, 85 (1974), 122–7 (p. 124). There is a cluster of ambiguous nouns and verbs in this passage that hints at an intentional avian-human ambiguity (e.g., *geondhweorfeð*, *fleotendra* and *swimmað*) similar to that I argue for above with the seafarer's encounters with seabirds. For Osborn, 'the birds function very much as an objective correlative, first to an emotion, then to an idea' (122). Bosworth-Toller *Supplement* provides one reference relating to birds for the suffix of the word; s.v. (n.) *gid*, sense 2 (4).

words or gestures with which he *greteð gliwstafum* 'greets joyfully' (52a) are more pitiable because they are met, not with human (or humanised) responses, but unfamiliar avian sounds, or, alternatively, birds that do not make any sound at all. Like the overt parallels that the seafarer draws between human and avian sounds that move uneasily towards destabilisation, a cry out to seabirds mistaken for comrades is cut short because it is impossible for the birds to give him the sort of communication he desires.

In both cases, parallels disperse, but the birds remain. If the seafarer associates with these creatures in the first half of the sequence, what happens in the second is that the birds signal their own foreign agencies, which have nothing to do with human meanings. The vocalisations that suggest their potential for metaphor turn back towards the living creature. Birds can be part of that 'backdrop against which society struggles to defend itself', but the modulation between human and nonhuman is not a simple binary.[73] These birds are, in Rosi Braidotti's words, 'a field of forces, a quantity of speed and intensity, and a cluster of capabilities' that 'can do a great deal', even within the figuration process.[74] More precisely, these birds do answer – they 'talk back' perversely, through resisting. The seafarer's attempts to connect, whether positively or negatively, are frustrated because these vividly real birds make it impossible for nonhuman creatures to function smoothly or wholly as metaphor.

The Lone-Flier's Migrating Act

For most critics of this elegy, it is not the real seabirds but the numinous, mysterious bird-soul that attracts attention. *The Seafarer*'s enigmatic *anfloga* has been much studied for what it tells us about Anglo-Saxon perceptions of minds and souls, or to discover

---

[73] Neville, *Representations*, p. 56.
[74] Rosi Braidotti, 'Animals, Anomalies, and Inorganic Others', *Publications of the Modern Language Association of America*, 124:2 (2009), 526–32 (p. 528).

the pagan and Christian sources informing it.[75] The ultimate effect of the bird-soul, however, comes as the result of complex relations between species in the initial avian encounters. It is not simply a passing echo, but critical to the ultimate relevance of seabirds in this Christian poem about real and speculative transcendence. The pivotal moment when the speaker properly considers himself and his own seaward journey not only projects us towards spiritual (and bodily) journeys, but returns us to the intricate coming-togethers of bird and human in those scenes with sprayed feathers and lonely calls. Considering these two moments in the poem more closely also reveals how conflicting literal and allegorical strands that beset the poem can meaningfully co-exist. The profound pilgrimage towards heaven to which all Christians should aspire necessitates an intricate metaphor which can be concurrently literal and figurative, native and foreign to the human, because it mimics the negotiations between land and sea, body and soul, earthly and heavenly in the seafarer's pursuit of spiritual transformation, but also reveals an important strangeness (a foreignness) between nonhuman and human.

The bird-soul figure appears at a thematically key, and structurally central, moment. The passage is significantly placed at the poem's centre, at a turn in its structure (marked by the *Forþon* conjunction [64]) when the speaker's vision moves outwards from the seascape to consider more universally the *contemptus mundi* theme. Again, something like this occurs in *The Wanderer* (likewise marked by *Forþon* [58]), suggesting transition between real and metaphorical birds. The speaker, having woken to the seabirds, *Þonne* 'Then'

---

[75] The best known of these studies is Peter Clemoes, '*Mens absentia cogitans* in *The Seafarer* and *The Wanderer*', in *Medieval Literature and Civilization: Studies in Memory of G. N. Garmonsway*, ed. by D. A. Pearsall and R. A. Waldron (London: Athlone Press, 1969), pp. 62–77. See also Vivian Salmon, '"The Wanderer" and "The Seafarer", and the Old English Conception of the Soul', *Modern Language Review*, 55:1 (1960), 1–10; F. N. M. Diekstra, '*The Seafarer* 58–66a: The Flight of the Exiled Soul to its Fatherland', *Neophilologus*, 55 (1971), 433–46; and Neil Hultin, 'The External Soul in *The Seafarer* and *The Wanderer*', *Folklore*, 88:1 (1977), 39–45. For general discussion, see Alexandra Sanmark, 'Living On: Ancestors and the Soul', in *Signals of Belief in Early England: Anglo-Saxon Paganism Revisited*, ed. by M. Carver, A. Sanmark and S. Semple (Oxford: Oxbow, 2010), pp. 162–84 (165–8).

(49a) thinks on he who *sendan sceal swiþe geneahhe / ofer waþema gebind werigne sefan* 'very often must send over the binding of the waves a weary spirit' (56–7), and, shortly after, his *modsefa* 'spirit' (59a).

The fullest development of the bird-soul image, though, comes in *The Seafarer*. It is separated by some thirty-eight lines from the seabird description, but the two are linked by the introduction of another (seventh) named species (*geac* 'cuckoo' [53]):

> Forþon nu min hyge hweorfeð   ofer hreþerlocan,
> min modsefa   mid mereflode
> ofer hwæles eþel   hweorfeð wide,
> eorþan sceatas,   cymeð eft to me
> gifre ond grædig,   gielleð anfloga,
> hweteð on hwælweg   hreþer unwearnum
> ofer holma gelagu.
> (*The Seafarer*, 58–64a)

[Therefore, now my desire roams beyond the breast-locker, my spirit with the sea-flood, over the whale's home travels widely, (over) earth's expanses, comes again to me, eager and greedy; the lone-flier yells, urges the breast to the whale-path without hesitation, over reaches of oceans.]

Recognising a fuller correlation between the seabirds and the flying soul is one way of approaching the complications critics of this poem have always faced in explaining the passage in which the spirit appears. Although it is agreed that the speaker's disembodied perceptions or soul are depicted in some sort of bird-like travel over the oceans, there is disagreement about exactly how this action is performed: whether the soul-travelling should be taken literally or metaphorically, and precisely what are the identities and relations of the *hyge, modsefa, anfloga* and *hreþer*. To what extent, in fact, should we perceive the bird as a feature of any of these, or the *anfloga* be associated with the other entities?[76] For my purposes,

---

[76] North has most recently argued for the importance of differentiating between these cognitive entities, and I accept his recommendation that *hyge* indicates an 'aim' or 'purpose', which guides the reconnaissance flight of the *modsefa* 'mood-sense', and its return to urge the body and soul to follow suit; North, 'Heaven ahoy!', pp. 15–21.

the prior dealings with seabirds recommend that the ambiguity surrounding these issues (like that concerning the compatibility of the poem's literal and allegorical elements) does not require a neat reconciliation. Rather, the palpability of birds seen and experienced on the seas informs the effect that many argue for in the poem's presentation of the 'lone-flier', a physicality that suggests 'more literal movement than mere thought'.[77]

The flight of the soul itself in *The Seafarer* has been seen as entirely metaphoric, and as a literal journey by the disembodied soul or mind. The question of whether the *hyge* and *modsefa*'s flights are real or not echoes the nexus of real/figurative relations we encountered earlier on. Real birds, on the one hand, may suggest to us the realism of a pilgrimage journey or anticipate souls or minds genuinely taking flight beyond the confines of the body, a literal, nautical enactment of the birds' peregrinations. On the other, birds fly in a real sense that can only be achieved imaginatively by humans as a prospective thought experiment. Even if there is actual sallying forth beyond the body, this literal sense is still only a precursory cognitive venture which is *figuratively* like a bird's flight. However, the metaphoric assimilation of man and bird is not reductive. The physical connotations and strong sense of avian voices or actions earlier in the poem are intrinsic to a bird-human metaphor that is imbued with those same experiential understandings and interactions. One approach, in fact, can even lead into the other; a literal *modsefa* sallies out and returns to incite the seafarer to undertake a perilous sea-journey, which is both real and a metaphor for spiritual, ascetic sufferance, the 'fulfilment of an ideal' that will be reified upon death and, more so, upon judgement when, to borrow from *The Wanderer, ealre þisse worulde wela weste stondeð* 'all this world's wealth stands wasting' (74).[78]

Close scrutiny of the *anfloga* passage reveals that it is not only characterised by the sorts of nuances which both assimilate and distance birds and humans in the seabird scene, but that the language

[77] Hultin, 'The External Soul', p. 40. Clemoes argues for a metaphoric flight of the mind in both poems, whilst claiming also that *sendan* (*Wanderer*, 56a) seems too vivid to convey imagined happenings; Clemoes, '*Mens absentia*', p. 74.
[78] Diekstra, 'Flight of the Exiled Soul', 433.

is also particularly suggestive of the actions of migrating. This is made most apparent by the addition of another bird only a few lines before which serves to re-adumbrate the connection between birds and souls in the coming metaphor. As is emphasised in most analyses of the cuckoo's purpose, the bird urges *sefan* ... / *on flodwegas feor gewitan* 'the mind ... to travel far upon the ocean paths' (51–2). The cuckoo's *geomran reorde* 'mournful cry' (53b) may be a reminder of earthly temptations in the welcoming season of spring, and in this regard has often been traced to analogous instances in Welsh sources to account for this reasoning of the bird's presence.[79] As much as any of the birds, the cuckoo brings contradictions. It is *sumeres weard* 'summer's guardian' (54a), a land-returner come to breed, and thus associated with those attractive vernal qualities the seafarer is keen to avoid (48–9). It is also, though, a prompt to seek out the open seas well beyond land, and its encouragement is linked clearly to the human spirit's journeying desire through the verb attending each subject: the seafarer's will or mind *monað* 'urges' (36a) his *ferð to feran* 'spirit to set out' just as the cuckoo *monað* (53a). As the bathing *brimfuglas* in *The Wanderer* incite an imaginative association, and thus will *sendan* out the soul upon the waves, so does the cuckoo.

With this persistent reference to journeying, surely another relevance to the cuckoo is that it specifies again the importance to the poem's theme of birds that fly great distances, that return *ham* each year but other times mysteriously travel *ofer hwæles eþel hweorfeð wide,* / *eorþan sceatas,* recalling the 'wildernesses' and 'pathless ways'

---

[79] See, e.g. Ernst Sieper, *Die altenglische elegie* (Strasbourg: Trübner, 1915), pp. 70–2, and Nicholas Jacobs, 'Celtic Saga and the Contexts of Old English Elegiac Poetry', *Études celtiques*, 26 (1989), 95–142 (pp. 122–3). See also, though, 'De cantibus avium', which mentions how *cuculus cantans scottos iter ire perurget* 'the singing cuckoo drives off the Irish to go on the journey' (13). [S]*cottos* 'Irish' is amended to *socios* 'companion' by Pieter Burmann (see Buecheler and Riese, *Anthologia latina,* p. 197), but all three MSS in which this poem is extant clearly show *scottos* and I do not see sufficient grounds for this change. Whilst 'De cantibus avium' is not known as a source for the Exeter poems, the cuckoo parallel and the general astonishment expressed at the diversity of the nonhuman world may suggest a shared scholarly frame of reference.

with which Isidore associates birds.[80] The cuckoo, then, recalls the former seabirds, and all are present in a multiplex figure that combines bird and Christian pilgrim as migrating species: the *anfloga*, a *hapex legomenon* that in this context seems to adapt the more usual *anhaga* term attached to birds elsewhere (as in the psalters). The *anfloga* has been the subject of much study, and readers tend to argue for either the cuckoo or the seafarer's soul as its identity.[81] With the earlier interactions and correlations between species in mind, however, this enigmatic being seems best read as a hybrid. To be sure, the *anfloga*'s vocalisation (*gielleð*) convincingly echoes the cuckoo's *reord*, and on this basis Gordon argues that it cannot be the soul because the 'emphasis on the cries, which could have little or no metaphorical significance, would make such an image absurd'. She also dismisses the possibility of a seabird because 'there has been no previous mention of a sea-bird to connect with the *anfloga*'.[82] Gordon is right that seabirds are not mentioned immediately prior to the *anfloga*, but the earlier references to seabirds are the dominant avian presence in the poem, and thus seem well intended to inform our interpretation of the *anfloga*. Specifically, the lone-flier's call may remind us of the central feature of the earlier birds' effect on the speaker – it is their voices which are prominent. In contradiction to Gordon's remark, it makes excellent sense for the *anfloga* to call out, bird-like. One of the earlier seabirds, the *earn*, in fact, shares a preterite form of the same verb (*bigiellan*) used to express the *anfloga*'s cry. The utterance made by the figure should not faze us, nor encourage us to see its identity singularly as the cuckoo, but to recognise how numerous avian referents are conflated with the human in an image of solitary flying. The seafarer is not separate from the cuckoo or seabirds at this point, but intimately linked

---

[80] Anglo-Saxon knowledge of the cuckoo's migratory habits would have been available in *Etym.*, XII.vii.67, and in *HN*, X.ix.
[81] For the cuckoo, see Sieper, *Die altenglische elegie*, pp. 70–7; Whitelock, 'Interpretation of *The Seafarer*', pp. 265–6; P. R. Orton, '*The Seafarer* 58–64a', *Neophilologus*, 66:3 (1982), 450–9; Marsden, *Old English Reader*, p. 227. For the soul, see Salmon, 'Old English Conception of the Soul'; Diekstra, 'Flight of the Exiled Soul'; and Hultin, 'The External Soul'.
[82] Gordon, *The Seafarer*, p. 41, n. 62b.

through the soul's mimicking distinctive vocalisations as it enacts far-wandering avian flight.[83]

This migratory *lust* 'desire' (36a) of heaven-seeking minds, spirits and birds, evident in the poem's journeying vocabulary throughout, is concentrated in the *anfloga* passage through continuous references to urgency, movement and distance, right before we reach the structural *volte* in the poem. *Hweorfeð* occurs twice in three lines (58a, 60b), meaning 'move', 'roam' or 'wander', but the senses of 'turn' or 'change' also work in line 58 in which the *hyge* initiates or itself performs a metamorphosis of sorts, out beyond the body and into mobile form. *Ofer* also comes twice in the same number of lines (and again at line 64), conveying a vivid upwards or extending action – 'above', 'over', 'beyond', 'across'. It joins *wide*, *eorþan sceatas* and the double whale kenning to imply an expanse which the *modsefa* is keen for the breast to traverse *nu, unwearnum*. In moving as a migrating bird across these spaces, the seafarer is *mid mereflode*, not merely *ofer*, as akin to the environment as he is to the bird. So, too, like the periodic returning action of the cuckoo and the seabirds, the *hyge* and *anfloga cymeð eft to me*, urging the speaker on the life-long return journey *ham*.

Seafaring does not stop when we reach the poem's homiletic concluding passage. The most significant travelling begins when one recognises and eschews the temporality and decay of the world, is

---

[83] There is no need to specify a particular seabird species; it is the characteristic of the general seabird that is pertinent. Identification elsewhere of a white bird with the soul (Exeter Riddle 7, Paulinus's swan-soul in *Gregory the Great*) may encourage us to identify with more typical seabird species, most of which in the early passage are, of course, white (*ylfete, ganet, mæw, stearn*). The *earn* does broadly come under the 'seabird' category, however, because of its breeding and hunting habitat (it is commonly named the sea-eagle in modern terminology), and the adult, at least, has a white tail and is characteristically pale in colour overall, unlike the very dark juvenile. On the evidence of the flier's *gifre ond grædig* desire, Richard North recommends specifically, in contrast to my focus on whiteness, that 'Most likely it [*anfloga*] is meant to come in the black shape of a predator'; North, 'Heaven ahoy!', p. 14. In the final section of his chapter, North aims to 'study the poet's materialization of *hyge* and *mōdsefa* into a bird of prey', but does not specifically mention raptors again until the very end when referring to a possible Norse analogue for the *anfloga* (pp. 21–2), which deals with ravens. See also, John C. Pope, 'Second Thoughts on the Interpretation of *The Seafarer*', *ASE*, 3 (1974), 75–86 (p. 84).

enjoined by these revelations and then follows the *modsefa*'s lead to mimic seabirds' pelagic wanderings, the soul in its temporary dwelling heading onwards until it is finally released and can make its own, disembodied final flight.[84] Literally and metaphorically, this resignation and wilful commitment is prompted by the flight of real birds. At the very moment when the seafarer thinks of setting over the sea he moves with conviction into his *contemptus mundi* theme. The conjunctive *Forþon* 'For this reason, therefore, for' (64b) leads us from the lone-flier image prompting the seafarer's own irresistibly urged journey *ofer holma gelagu* directly into a rejection of the pleasures available in *þis deade lif / læne on londe* 'this dead life / loaned on land' (65b–66a).[85] A fear of worldly and bodily demise as *Yldo him on fareð* 'Age comes upon him' (91a) is overcome by faith in God, towards whom the seafarer will journey successively in mind, body and soul by enacting the ocean-wandering bird's flight. Birds, too, offer structural unity between lines 1–64a and 64b–124.

The Native Foreignness of Seabirds

In the second epigraph to this chapter Heaney implies a ready association between seabirds and souls, but the lines also echo the central paradox that has characterised the seafarer's dealings with birds by calling into question the exact relationship that exists between bird and soul. To what extent are seabirds satisfactory metaphors for the yearning Christian soul? How closely can the human soul be associated with the flights and habits of these sea-wanderers?

---

[84] These stages of succeeding flights might be complicated by a further example: when the body is finally reunited with the soul on Judgement Day. For a 'doomsday' interpretation, see Smithers, 'Meaning of *Seafarer* and *Wanderer*' ([1957] and [1959]). On the relationship of body and soul in Anglo-Saxon thought, see the two versions of the *Soul and Body* poem and Exter Riddle 43. The typical master/servant relationship is implied in *The Seafarer* if we imagine that it is the masterful soul itself that ventures out and returns to urge the body.

[85] There has been a great deal of critical discussion about the precise meaning of *Forþon* in this poem and *The Wanderer*; see, e.g. Nicholas Jacobs, 'Syntactical Connection and Logical Disconnection: The Case of *The Seafarer*', *MÆ*, 58 (1989), 105–13. However we translate the term, though, it always implies a bridging movement.

Heaney's question resonates with these conundrums because it addresses habits of metaphor; bird and soul are so intimately and repeatedly unified that it becomes hard to distinguish the two ('What came first?'). As with *The Seafarer*'s *anfloga*, on the one hand Heaney's subjects are ambiguously conflated: is it the bird or the soul that we hear 'when *it* cried'? On the other, though, the lines signal incompatibility between literal and figurative, between a palpable 'seabird's cry' and the 'soul / Imagined', and the questionable correlation of 'Inside or outside' (1). In *The Seafarer*, the affinities between bird and human speaker finally cohere in the metaphoric *anfloga* vision, but something of that earlier resistance to bird-human embroilment lingers. Of *The Seafarer*'s bird-soul, too, we might ask 'What came first?'.

I have argued that it is right to see both avian and human referents in this calling creature, but it is also true that the passage is marked by obscurity. There is no firm evidence that heaven precisely is where the seafarer is headed, nor imagery of what it looks like. It is always implied, always stays the *incertum* that is over the horizon (to refer back to Bede) where it must be speculated. As North memorably puts it, the poem only involves an 'intuition of heaven'.[86] The future is uncertain, and *Forþon nis þæs modwlonc mon ... / þæt he a his sæfore sorge næbbe, / to hwon hine Dryhten gedon wille* 'So there is no man so proud-spirited ... / that he never has worries about his seafaring as to what his Lord will do' (39–43). The same mystery pervades the *anfloga* which encourages the body to head for this unspecified destination; it is both an avian species separate to the *hyge* and *modsefa*, and a third term to describe whatever human element has soared out from the breast.

Birds do not achieve complete or overt assimilation with the human, but this, paradoxically, is part of the migration metaphor's powerful effect in articulating the theological predicament faced by the seafarer. Throughout the poem, his bleak contemplation oscillates between dichotomies: between hot and cold, land and sea (and their respective lifestyles), earth and heaven, between distress over exile from comfortable land-living (the 'dead life') and a resolve

---

[86] North, 'Heaven ahoy!', p. 8.

to face miserable sea-dwelling, between body and psychological components (mind, aim, heart, soul, spirit), and between human and nonhuman worlds. The seabirds, and the cuckoo, inhabit extremes; they are land-dwellers that wander far to other homes in mysterious lands over the reaches of the great oceans, characterised by flight which enables them to transcend from one realm to another. The seafarer himself associates the birds with conflicting locales: with land, kinsmen and merrymaking, and with the alienating sea, as creatures that do not respond to his human efforts. We are intended to recall the seabirds in the bird-soul because it is seabirds that function as the ideal image for the transformative experiences the seafarer seeks in the struggles between difficult opposites, the movement between which incites both despair and joy about the tempting pleasures that must be left behind in this world for the arduous, miserable journey towards *ecan eadignesse* 'eternal blessedness' (120). In this, seabirds not only model the seafarer's necessary actions, but may also recall Christ, the ultimate type, whom Kramer sees 'inhabiting a both/and condition ... permanently betwixt and between' in Anglo-Saxon Christian doctrine. The seabird, too, 'dwells in two places at once'; *mid mereflode*, it is ever at home and moving towards home at once.[87] Just so, the forlorn Christian soul has two homes and must find it within himself to reject one in favour of miserable trials that lead to the hoped-for joys of the original home, but making, for now, the foreign and inhospitable sea a home alongside the birds.

Observations of migratory avian flights also seem to have been bound up with wider Anglo-Saxon ideas of foreignness. In *Beowulf*, for instance, sea travel is prominent – nautical actions performed *ofer* that are neatly associated with pelagic birds in the familiar sea kennings. As Robert L. Schichler has argued, the potential political implications of this are further suggested by references outside poetry that link ocean-going bird flight with the tensions that come with foreign affairs, threats and travel. Schichler proposes that effective foreign alliances appear to be identified in numerous texts with the gannet's bath:

---

[87] Kramer, *Between Earth and Heaven*, p. 7.

Cuð wæs þæt wide   geond feola þeoda,
þæt afaren Eadmundes   ofer ganetes beð
cynegas hyne wide   wurðodon swiðe,
burgon to þam cyninge,   swa him wæs gecynde.
(*Anglo-Saxon Chronicle*, Worcester Manuscript
[D], year 975)[88]

[It was widely known throughout many nations over the gannet's bath that kings widely honoured him (Edmund's son) greatly, submitted to that king, as was natural to him.]

Seabirds might also be equated with more suspicious perceptions of foreignness, as when Beowulf travels *fugle gelicost* 'most bird-like' (218b) *ofer lagu-stræte* 'over the sea-way' (239a) and arrives on the Danish coast to be met as a hostile stranger. To be sure, in *The Seafarer* birds are linked with the ferocity and danger of the sea surge. As Neville has shown, the presiding image of foreigners is pejorative; foreigners 'are heathens, animals, monsters, devils, and objects of hatred'.[89] The very term that defines the seafarer as foreigner, *elþeodig*, occurs in *Elene* repeatedly to designate the Hun tribes as hostile (57b, 82b, 139a). In *The Seafarer*, however, as in *The Wanderer*, it is clear that foreignness takes on a more positive valence in the pilgrimage context – alienation or exile from one's nativeness is a desirable, if paradoxical, state. Anglo-Saxon attitudes to foreignness could be contradictory, and this fine discrimination between belonging and not belonging is evident in *The Seafarer*'s contemplations of an estranged *ham*.

---

[88] E. Classen and F. E. Harmer, eds, *An Anglo-Saxon Chronicle from the British Museum, Cotton MS., Tiberius B. IV* (Manchester: Manchester University Press, 1926), p. 50. Cf. Peterborough manuscript (E), and also Winchester manuscript (A) in which Oslac is banished over the gannet's bath in 975; see Michael Swanton, ed. and trans., *The Anglo-Saxon Chronicles*, rev. edn (London: Phoenix Press, 2000). For discussion of the positive associations of the gannet's bath, see Robert L. Schichler, 'From "Whale-Road" to "Gannet's Bath": Images of Foreign Relations and Exchange in *Beowulf*', *Reading Medieval Studies*, 28 (1999), 59–86 (pp. 72–5).

[89] Jennifer Neville, '"None Shall Pass": Mental Barriers to Travel in Old English Poetry', in *Freedom of Movement in the Middle Ages: People, Ideas, Goods*, The Harlaxton Symposium, 2003, ed. by P. Horden (Donington: Shaun Tyas/Paul Watkins, 2007), pp. 203–14 (206).

The poet of *The Seafarer* transforms an inherited bird-soul image into a specific vision of the solitary foreigner necessarily set upon the waves. The ocean-going actions of the seafarer, frequently mentioned, are the ways of the seabirds: both *hean streamas, sealtyþa gelac / ... cunnige* 'experience the high streams, the tossing of salt waves' (34b–5), their overlapping paths inhabiting and navigating a shared environment. This species likeness, however, continuously reveals a tension. Just as migrating bird and man are native foreigners in themselves, the metaphoric relations bringing them together on this premise are characterised by a native/foreign dynamic as figurations are simultaneously constructed and dismantled, firstly in the tensions that hamper those interactions the seafarer instigates, and finally in the oblique *anfloga* image which suggests but does not confirm metaphoric correlation. The potency of species affinity lies right on the threshold of like and unlike, because birds are both knowable and unknowable, like the divine and *hyht in heofonum* 'joy in the heavens' (122a) in this present journey towards *ham*, but which are yet to be reached. The seafarer rejects *þis deade lif / læne on londe*, but the dead life only continues in another sense on the raging seas. Whilst it is the exile-path towards an envisaged true home, it is also associated with the harsh vagaries of postlapsarian life; the seafarer, like Adam in the Old English *Genesis B*, must choose to *on flod faran* 'to travel on the sea' (832a) as a consequence of sin. The seafarer's (and the wanderer's) journey is conducted in *this* life and, as such, his narrative devises and enacts a stratagem for reaching a pilgrim goal that, for now, lies beyond oceanic horizons. In order to *hycgan hwær we ham agen, / ond þonne geþencan hu we þider cumen* 'to ponder where we may have a home and then think how we may arrive there' (117–18), the seafarer embraces birds' otherness as a necessary component of an image that, like the sea itself, casts the speaker between opposites. Their evasive connections to the seafarer place the nonhuman beyond the human, *ofer* our mortal ken, in line with the mysteries of God himself.

To return to the bird with which we began, Bede's sparrow reminds us of the same predicament. We are dealing here with that which *prorsus ignoramus* 'we absolutely do not know', but through and towards which a faith in the Lord may enlighten and lead us.[90] The wandering birds present an enviable ability to mimic in constructing a solution to the soul's progress and fate (to the *hu*), but their enigmatic, unfathomable characters which we cannot know also dislocate the human from the nonhuman in being a reminder of the ultimate mysteries of God in heaven and our return, distance journey to him. The duality of birds in *The Seafarer*, at the centre of a poem which deals with complex sets of interlocking dualisms, embraces representations in the Augustinian mode, whereby literal and symbolic signifiers co-exist. The seabird, in this sense, is a sign (*signum*) *est quod et se ipsum sensui et praeter se aliquid animo ostendit* 'which is itself sensed (or apprehended in itself) and which indicates to the mind something beyond the sign itself'.[91] E. G. Stanley seems to make a similar point with direct reference to Old English poetry in his well-known observation that 'the Anglo-Saxons treated allegory in a manner which revealed a relation of fact to figure so close that the figure was an inseparable aspect of the fact'.[92] Stanley's point, though (as when he states that 'the thought gives the flower'), is that the figurative precedes and governs the sense of realism in these representations.[93] *The Seafarer*'s birds suggest alternative and more complex procedures at work; factual and figurative birds are, indeed, inseparable in *The Seafarer*, and remind us that a heaven-bound spiritual transformation begins with a necessary, physically experienced journey here on earth towards unknown horizons.

---

[90] *Bede's Ecclesiastical History*, pp. 182–3.

[91] *De dialectica*, 5. Latin and translation cited in Mark E. Amsler, *Etymology and Grammatical Discourse in Late Antiquity and the Early Middle Ages* (Amsterdam: John Benjamins, 1989), p. 49. In relation to Augustinian allegory, Juan Camilo Conde Silvestre and Juan Carlos Conde Silvestre suggest that 'at the level of reception, the interpretation of the images in lines 4–64 of *The Seafarer* is built on the hermeneutic addition of another signified and its referent to the ones literally attributed to the textual signifiers', thus 'account[ing] for the validity of both the literal and the allegorical interpretations'; Juan Camilo Conde Silvestre and Juan Carlos Conde Silvestre, 'The Semiotics of Allegory in Early Medieval Hermeneutics and the Interpretation of *The Seafarer*', *Atlantis*, 16:1 (1994), 71–90 (p. 88).

[92] E. G. Stanley, 'Old English Poetic Diction and the Interpretation of *The Wanderer*, *The Seafarer* and *The Penitent's Prayer*', *Anglia*, 73 (1955), 413–66 (p. 452).

[93] Ibid., p. 434.

Plate 2 **Barnacle goose** *Branta leucopsis*
© Brian Lawrence

þa ic of fæðmum cwom / brimes ond beames on blacum hrægle; / sume wæron white hyrste mine 'when I came out of the embrace of water and wood in a black garment, some of my wear was white'
(Exeter Book Riddle 10, 6b–8)

2

Avian Pedagogies: Wondering With Birds in the Exeter Book Riddles

BIRDS IN THE EXETER BOOK RIDDLES are an important subject of wonder, the various and unique transformations of particular species described in a scheme of nearly one hundred riddles that marvel at nonhuman phenomena, both animate and inanimate. Anglo-Saxon riddles as a whole had serious, didactic purposes and, despite their unique characteristics, the Old English riddles' clear connections to the Anglo-Latin examples make it likely that they also served some form of pedagogic role in a monastic environment.[1] Certainly their formulaic injunctions, instructing that

---

[1] The Anglo-Saxon Lat. riddles clearly demonstrate their 'heavily didactic element'; Andy Orchard, *The Poetic Art of Aldhelm*, CSASE, 8 (Cambridge: Cambridge University Press, 1994), p. 158. As an indication of the Anglo-Latin riddles' popularity, two codices from Canterbury (Cambridge, University Library, MS Gg.5.35, and London, British Library, MS Royal 12.C.xxiii) include the collections from Symphosius, Aldhelm, Tatwine and Eusebius, alongside a range of other educational texts common to European schools, such as Prudentius's *Psychomachia* and Lactantius's *De ave phoenice*. For a full list of manuscripts including Anglo-Saxon riddles, see Fr. Glorie, ed., *Variae collectiones aenigmatum Merovingicae aetatis*, Corpus Christianorum, Series Latina, vol. 133, pp. 152–62. For discussion of riddles generally in Anglo-Saxon learning, see Patrizia Lendinara, 'The World of Anglo-Saxon Learning', in *The Cambridge Companion to Old English Literature*, ed. by Malcolm Godden and Michael Lapidge (1991; repr. Cambridge: Cambridge University Press, 1994), pp. 264–81 (276–7). Uncertainties over dating or locating the Exeter Book's origin, along with the vernacular riddles' curious blend of literary and oral influences, make it difficult to clarify their exact purpose, but the largely religious content of the codex (particularly the likes of the three exegetical Christ poems that open the compilation) suggest a likely pedagogic purpose as a whole. Most recently, Mercedes Salvador-Bello has identified the Exeter Book as 'the literary product of a team of compilers from a reform-orientated scriptorium'; Mercedes Salvador-Bello, *Isidorian Perceptions of Order: The Exeter Book Riddles and Medieval Latin Enigmata*, Medieval European Studies Series, 17 (Morgantown, WV:

we *frige* 'ask' or *saga* 'say' *hwæt* 'what' or *hu* 'how' something is or comes to be, fit with the intellectual lines of inquiry evident in the Latin riddles. Superficially, then, birds feature on one level in the 'catalogue of diversity' to be pondered, guessed and classified by naming a solution.² As scholars of the Exeter Riddles have long known, however, their unique form of vernacular riddling presents audiences with sophisticated, often divergent forms of learning and hermeneutics in their own right, and in this chapter I explore how birds' peculiarities become part of the collection's self-reflexive pedagogic aims and strategies.

As in Chapter One, we are never far from the mysterious qualities of birds' foreignness, and this compelling avian aspect will ultimately concern us more with how the Riddles' strategies reveal ignorance as much as enlightenment. I see avian quiddities as particularly apt in this dialogic game, because the lives and behaviours of these proximate strangers exemplify well the distinctive interplay of the known and unknown in riddling discourses; in being both nameable and anonymous they suit riddles' tendencies to obfuscate and disambiguate concurrently. Birds are a significant element in the miscellany, that is, because they enact a series of diverse transformations that redouble their participation in the Riddles' preoccupations with wondering. As subjects of wonder, they naturally perform a bewildering range of perpetual sleights and shifts that transgress species and territory boundaries, making their diversity excellent riddle material. Within riddling frameworks, however, this unpredictable diversity achieves a heightened focus because it meets with further transformations imposed by metaphor and paradox. Under these linguistic operations, birds also become pedagogical agents in a 'dramatized form of education', to borrow Robert Stanton's phrase, by resisting categorisations and exposing epistemological limitations, particularly when

West Virginia University Press, 2015), p. 499. On the OE riddles' possible monastic provenance and scholarly context, see Craig Williamson, ed., *The Old English Riddles of the Exeter Book* (Chapel Hill, NC: University of North Carolina Press, 1977), pp. 5–12.

2   Russell Poole, *Old English Wisdom Poetry*, Annotated Bibliographies of Old and Middle English, 5 (Cambridge: D. S. Brewer, 1998), p. 13.

it comes to naming.³ In short, they teach us something about the processes of learning and knowing. This is nowhere more obvious than in the bird's most typifying component, the feather, when it is transformed in the *scriptorium* into an essential implement. In this respect, birds share something with various other nonhuman subjects in the Riddles, but in a literary context becoming a quill has a special purpose beyond that of other artefacts, particularly in a body of writings that so often seems aware of its own artful existence. In this most material of senses, birds are responsible for constructing and obscuring knowledge, for creating the Riddles' linguistic play that promises and refuses a cognitive transformation towards clarity and understanding.

How To Wonder

Wondering is a central preoccupation in the Exeter Book, and very often an act directed at the natural world.⁴ In the Old English *Physiologus* we encounter wonder in three of the world's *unrimu cynn* 'countless species' (2a): the panther's *wrætlice gecynd* 'strange kind' (9a), a *miclan hwale* 'great whale' (3b), and an unnamed *fugle / wundorlicne* 'wonderful bird' (1b–2a), usually identified as the partridge on the text's moral application, and which is reminiscent of another Exeter feathered creature – the *wundrum fæger* 'wonderfully handsome' phoenix (*Phoenix*, 85b). The Riddles are no exception: *wundor* abounds, in numerous grammatical forms.⁵

---

3   Stanton, 'Mimicry, Subjectivity and the Embodied Voice', p. 30
4   Brian MacFadden has suggested that *wundor* is what characterises numerous texts in the Exeter Book manuscript; Brian McFadden, 'Sweet Odours and Interpretative Authority in the Exeter Book *Physiologus* and *Phoenix*', *Papers on Language and Literature*, 42:2 (2006), 181–210. Outside this manuscript, as well, examples of the word imply the important and varied act of wondering. See, e.g., *Solomon and Saturn*: *Ac hæwt is þæt wundor ðe geond ðas worold færeð* 'But what is that wonder that travels throughout this world?' (280). For further examples in other literature, see the extensive entry for *wundor* in Bosworth-Toller, and s.v. (adj.) *wrætlic, wraetlice* and *seld-*.
5   Twenty-three of the Riddles include a form of the word. The list is longer if we include synonyms (*wrætlice, sellic*). After Williamson, *Old English Riddles*, p. 464: adj. *wundorlic* 'wondrous/wonderful'(88.19), *wunderlicu* (18.1, 20.1, 24.1, 25.1),

The subjects are frequently described or describe themselves using the word, or through other terms which equate to the same or very similar meaning: *wrætlic* (21.2) or *sellic* (29.3), for instance, both of which are variously glossed as 'wondrous', 'strange' or 'curious'.[6] On the basis of examples like the *Physiologus* and *The Phoenix*, we may be inclined to think of Anglo-Saxon *wundor* in a traditional exegetical context, in which marvelling at animals reveals their analogous functions in scripture. Wonder here is like the creature itself, disposable once the job of interpretation is done. The conspicuous presence of *wundor* in the Riddles may encourage us to seek correlations or trace a uniform conceptualisation across the Exeter texts, to place the Riddles alongside discourses that seek to replace *admiratio* with 'the *scientia*, or knowledge, to which it led' or to 'reduce the scope of the unexpected or sudden', or that use wonder to appropriate.[7] Along these lines, Brian McFadden has argued in two articles concerning the Exeter texts (one on the Riddles) that many of these poems are concerned with textual interpretation as 'ability to control' in response to political and cultural anxieties, offering poems that allay any 'astonished uncertainties', and 'contain threatening aspects of the natural world'.[8] For him, the way to deal with the riddles is to solve them correctly so that the 'wonder of the being is stripped away', and thus tamed into submission

---

wundorlicu (29.7), *wundorlice* (29.1, 87.1), *wundorlicran* (Riddle 31.5); n. *wundor* 'wonder/miracle' (47.2, 67.5, 69.1, 90.1 [the last riddle in this list is in Latin, but in some Anglo-Saxon texts *wundor* is given for *mirum*]), *wundres* (60.10), *wundra* (21.8, 84.35); adv. *wundrum* 'wondrously/wonderfully' (35.1, 36.2, 50.1, 68.2, 84.1, 22 and 41). A final two riddles use compound words: *wundorworuld* 'wonder-world' (39.17) and *wundorcræfte* 'wonder-skill' (40.85). This list only includes those riddles with direct use of one of the forms of *wundor*. Verb forms of the word do not appear in the riddles, but synonyms do: *wafian* 'to wonder, be amazed' (84.42).

[6] My numbering of the Riddles follows that of ASPR.
[7] Caroline Walker Bynum, *Metamorphosis and Identity* (New York, NY: Zone Books, 2005), p. 43. Bynum's discussion on wonder focuses on twelfth- and thirteenth-century perceptions, but can usefully be applied to consider how Anglo-Saxon wondering correlates or differs. Russell Poole's comment on the 'unexpected or sudden' summarises Morton W. Bloomfield's discussion of wisdom poetry generally; Poole, *Old English Wisdom Poetry*, p. 7.
[8] Respectively, Brian McFadden, 'Sweet Odours', 81, and 'Raiding, Reform, and Reaction: Wondrous Creatures in the Exeter Book Riddles', *Texas Studies in Literature and Language*, 50:4 (2008), 329–51 (p. 333).

through human understanding.⁹ Similarly, Jennifer Neville, writing on wisdom poetry, argues that 'as Old English poets write about human beings who are circled, confined and defined by the hostile forces of the natural world, they enclose the natural world in their representations of it and confine it to the roles that they desire for it'.¹⁰

As the previous chapter revealed, though, engaging the mysterious or unknown can have different outcomes. It can treat foreign subjects in a manner which does not dismiss their material, actual relevance, or dissolve them into simple analogy. Nor is wonder always located in an elsewhere, dealing with the exotic or mythic, as the Old English riddles make very clear. As Caroline Walker Bynum is aware in her discussion of medieval wonder discourses, 'You can only marvel at something that is, at least in some sense, there'.¹¹ For all that we can argue that wonder in Old English riddles might be aimed at tackling something beyond the apparent subject of wonder itself – scriptural elucidation, fear, domination – the lack of answers in the codex certainly makes this very difficult to achieve satisfactorily. Moreover, as scholars have repeatedly noted, the Riddles' subjects have a knack of reasserting their materiality; what has been described as 'the daily realisms of Old English life', or a 'sharp sense of wonder for the ordinary slice of life' that might lead us to feel that the Anglo-Saxons were 'careful observers of the world about them'.¹² The extent to which the Riddles' birds evidence genuine ornithological experience or mere book-learning continues to be the subject of critical debate, encouraged by the eclectic mix of forms, registers and influences in which the domestic worlds of Anglo-Saxon lived experiences butt up alongside and overlap with

---

9   McFadden, 'Raiding, Reform and Reaction', 335.
10 Neville, *Representations*, p. 178.
11 Bynum, *Metamorphosis*, p. 73.
12 Charles W. Kennedy, *The Earliest English Poetry* (Oxford: Oxford University Press, 1943), p. 134; Patrick Murphy, *Unriddling the Exeter Riddles* (University Park, PA: Pennsylvania State University Press, 2011), p. 9; and Williamson, *Old English Riddles*, p. 12, respectively. This typifying feature has been associated with the genre of wisdom poetry more generally: 'The characterisation of Anglo-Saxon wisdom as truthful, simple, fresh to the point of childlikeness and directly responsive to personal observation of Nature ... is not dead even now'; Poole, *Wisdom Poetry*, p. 23.

more elevated subject matter.¹³ On the one hand, to take Riddle 9 as an example, the writers and audiences of the riddles 'need not have included assiduous bird-watchers ... [because] the cuckoo's natural history was a famous *story*', but, on the other, 'since the cuckoo ... has always been a regular summer visitor to England, its nest-parasitism would have been observed in Anglo-Saxon times'.¹⁴ Or the swan (Riddle 7) simultaneously 'does not resemble ... any bird to be seen in today's waterways' and clearly represents personal observation.¹⁵ Most of the species included in the Exeter bird group riddles do have literary antecedents, and may well require us to turn to books, but it is also noticeable that the collection does away with mythic or exotic species in a way that its Latin predecessors do not. All the species are to be found wild on British shores: the swan (OE *swan*), the nightingale (OE *nihtegale*), the cuckoo (OE *geac*), the barnacle goose (MLat. *bernaca*), the jay (OE *higera*).¹⁶ At the least, the formulaic opening to a number of the Riddles must give

---

13   The same has been argued for the Old English Riddles' closest literary model, Aldhelm's *Enigmata*. Cf. Celica Milovanović-Barham, who remarks on the impression in some of these enigmas that 'material [is taken] directly from nature' and described 'with considerable precision and accuracy'; Celica Milovanović-Barham, 'Aldhelm's *Enigmata* and Byzantine Riddles', *ASE*, 22 (1993), 51–64 (p. 51). See also M. L. Cameron, 'Aldhelm as Naturalist: a Re-Examination of Some of His *Enigmata*', *Peritia*, 4 (1985), 117–33.

14   Jennifer Neville, 'Fostering the Cuckoo: *Exeter Book* Riddle 9', *RES*, New Series, 58 (2007), 431–46 (p. 434) [italics original], and Dieter Bitterli, *Say What I Am Called: The Old English Riddles of the Exeter Book and the Anglo-Latin Tradition* (Toronto, Buffalo and London: University of Toronto Press, 2009), p. 37.

15   John D. Niles, *Old English Enigmatic Poems and the Play of the Texts* (Turnhout: Brepols Publishers, 2006), p. 111. For studies that treat the swan in real, observable terms, see Richard Wells, 'The Old English Riddles and Their Ornithological Content', *Lore and Language*, 2 (1978), 57–66, and Kitson, 'Swans and Geese', p. 79.

16   Aldhelm's *Enigmata* includes biblical, textbook birds like the night-raven (Enigma 34), eagle (Enigma 57) and dove (Enigma 64), or birds that are highly unlikely to have been seen in Anglo-Saxon England, like the ostrich (Enigma 41). The Exeter Book 'bird group' is defined for the purposes of this study as including Riddles 7–10 and 24, but I will later include Riddle 57 which, although it has never convincingly been solved as one species or another, is widely regarded to have a bird as its solution. Riddle 74 has been solved as a bird riddle by two scholars, but neither with wider acceptance: for whooper swan (OE *ylfetu*), see Kitson, 'Swans and Geese', pp. 79–81; for sea-eagle, see K. S. Kiernan, 'The Mysteries of the Sea-Eagle in Exeter Riddle 74', *Philological Quarterly*, 54 (1975), 518–22.

the impression that an object or a creature has been or *can* be seen: *Ic wiht geseah wundorlice* 'I saw a wondrous creature' (29.1).

In my reading, these two strands come together to demonstrate how wondering at birds' *wrætlice* 'strange' behaviours is one way in which we can come to understand more fully what it means to wonder in the Exeter Riddles. Birds are the stuff of learning, deeply involved with pedagogic interests in these texts, but they are also stubbornly real in that they get away, tantalisingly, from attempts to pin them down. These two aspects are not at odds, and, contrary to previous interpretations, enrich our wondering not through closing down, controlling or stripping away, but through opening up and perpetuating mystery, turning us again to the 'traditional authority of close observation'.[17] The call for us to name, as the riddles do both explicitly and implicitly, is a dialogic, perpetuating engagement that incorporates the nonhuman into intricate patterns with human endeavours in a move that reflects *The Seafarer*'s treatment of the seabird image. Strategies for wondering through naming gesture back to the physical being, so that even as we move forwards towards a desirable solution, the mysteries inherent in material, subjective presence remain a fundamental aspect of the wondering process. In this, the bird riddles present an excellent example of the nonlinear, paradoxical form of wondering that Patricia Dailey proposes for the Old English riddles. For her, the texts do not do away with their literal objects; they 'reinvest the object itself with a found strangeness and mystery, its truer way of cohabiting the world'.[18] In what follows, I suggest that the bird riddles 'reinvest' their avian subjects' intrinsic, often unknowable, worth when their unpredictable swerves and diversions place them outside linguistic and epistemological schemes.

---

[17] Elaine Tuttle Hansen, *The Solomon Complex: Reading Wisdom in Old English Poetry* (Toronto and London: University of Toronto Press, 1988), p. 135.

[18] Patricia Dailey, 'Riddles, Wonder and Responsiveness in Anglo-Saxon Literature', in *The Cambridge History of Early Medieval English Literature*, ed. by Clare A. Lees (Cambridge: Cambridge University Press, 2013), pp. 451–72 (p. 470).

Avian Transformers

> Innate repertoire supplemented by highly developed and widely used capacity of both sexes for accurate mimicry of various sounds, e.g. ... Buzzard *Buteo buteo*, Kestrel *Falco tinnunculus*, Grey Partridge *Perdix perdix*, Crane *Grus grus*, Magpie *Pica pica*, Carrion Crow *Corvus corone*, and Starling *Sturnus vulgaris* ... motorbike horn, human voice, whistled songs, barking dog, and (probably) lawnmower.[19]
>
> (Jay, *Garrulus glandarius*)

The modern ornithological description above of a jay's remarkable mimic abilities not only echoes Riddle 24 itself (to which I will soon turn), but might also remind us of a characteristic of the Exeter Riddles as a whole. Birds appear alongside and are woven into a rich fabric of Anglo-Saxon existence that points towards a prosaic, real-world element. They are as much a part of ordinary life, that is, as onions, rakes, dough, bellows, the ox and plough, the motion of tangible beings and objects. We are dealing with species in the broadest sense here, speculating on the appearance (Lat. *species* 'form') of an individual kind or sort, an act that begins with looking (Lat. *specere* 'to look'), then sifts and weighs up similarity and difference to progress towards speaking a name.[20] If one of the effects of the Exeter Riddles is, in the words of a grammarian echoed by Aldhelm, to reveal the *occultum similitudinem rerum* 'hidden similarity of things', birds not only feature within this marvel, but exemplify these intricate interrelations through their distinctive transformative abilities.[21] Some objects become wondrous to us when they are subjected to imposed transformations (an ox-hide turned to vellum; an onion metaphorically conceived as a phallus), but birds already enthral us with their various and conspicuous modulations that help us to recognise how boundaries come together and come apart in the textual 'ecosphere' that the Riddles construct – a shifting, interrelated vision of species on *þes middangeard missenlicum / wisum gewlitegad* 'this earth adorned in diverse ways' (31.1–2a).

---

[19] BWP, vol. 8, pp. 19–20.
[20] See J. A. Simpson and E. S. C. Weiner, eds, *The Oxford English Dictionary*, 20 vols, 2nd edn (Oxford: Oxford University Press, 1989), s.v. (n.) *species*.
[21] Donatus, *Ars grammatica*, ed. by Heinrich Keil (Leipzig: Teubner, 1864), p. 402.

Birds, consummate transformers, can reveal to us the interwoven lives of worldly phenomena because they transcend classifications in remarkable ways.

The Exeter birds are always in motion, pursuing through various mutations Isidore's 'pathless ways'.[22] The swan (Riddle 7) is paradoxically silent and loud, and travels afar. The cuckoo (Riddle 9), also a far-traveller, grows to be a huge bird that far outsizes the nest of its host and its usurped earlier identity, so moving from cuckoo to host-species to cuckoo again. The barnacle goose (Riddle 10) undergoes a remarkable metamorphosis, emerging and deriving from another creature entirely, and, like two other birds, does a disappearing act for half the year.[23] The nightingale (Riddle 8) and jay (Riddle 24) change their voices as they please, also appropriating new identities. Implicit in these processes, too, is another avian mutation, the seasonal moult. The denuded bird, of course, naturally so or plucked, is evident in those riddles that mention the quill, particularly Riddle 51.

The swan and the barnacle goose demonstrate birds' strange ability to inhabit a range of territories.[24] Although birds are largely recognised as aerial creatures, they actually master all three key ecological realms. In Riddle 57, birds confusingly *tredað bearonæssas, hwilum burgsalo* 'tread the woody headlands, sometimes the town-dwellings' (5) even whilst being creatures of *lyft* 'air' (1a), but the poets of the swan and barnacle goose riddles exploit this transgressive quality more precisely to maximise obfuscation – what

---

[22] For another study that suggests intentional links between the bird riddles, see Audrey L. Meaney, 'Birds on the Stream of Consciousness: Riddles 7–10 of the Exeter Book', *Archaeological Review from Cambridge*, 18 (2002), 119–52.

[23] Riddle 10 is the earliest record we have of the barnacle goose myth, which seems to have come about to explain its absence from British shores during the breeding season. See Edward Heron-Allen, *Barnacles in Nature and Myth* (Oxford: Oxford University press, 1928).

[24] The variety of terrains birds inhabit is recorded in the seventh-century *Liber de ordine creaturarum*. It is not only noted that birds live in a variety of habitats (salt sea, fresh water, open country, wood and fen), but that each type of bird is generated from a particular expression of water. Birds which fly at extreme heights, for instance, are born from cloud precipitation. See *Liber de ordine creaturarum: un anónimo irlandés del siglo VII*, ed. by Manuel C. Díaz y Díaz (Santiago de Compostela: University Press of Santiago de Compostela, 1972). See also the ninth-century OE *Martyrology* which follows *De Ordine* on this subject.

creature is this that inhabits land, sea and air? The swan is visualised from the ground upwards as though to mirror the ascent to air, and the poet repeatedly mentions its three habitats. At first it *hrusan trede* 'tread[s] earth' (1b) or *wado drefe* 'stir[s] up waters' (2b), the bird's first two elements, sharing its sometime *wic* 'dwelling' (2a) with *hæleþa byht* 'men's homes' (3b). *Hwilum* 'Sometimes' (3a), however, the swan takes to the *hea lyft* 'high air' (4b) and *wolcna strengu* 'cloud's power' (5b), distanced from mankind: the windy air *byreð* 'carries' it away *ofer folc* 'over the people' (6a). All these transitions are clearly indicated for us by the series of conjunctions or adverbs (*þonne, oþþe, hwilum*). Finally, in the last line, all three are brought together: when the swan is not on the *flode ond foldan* 'river or earth', it is a *ferende gæst* 'travelling spirit' (9) of the skies.

The barnacle goose, too, performs a similar ascent from earth to sky. The genesis of the bird moves from the *firgenstreamum* 'mountain streams' (2b) to the *sunde* 'sea' (3b), its rise emphasised by way of contrast to the double reference to initial immersion: the bird is *underflowen* 'underflowed' (2b) and *besuncen* 'sunk' (3b). At the same time, the creature's *lice* 'body' (5b) is *getenge* 'resting upon' (4b) a *liþendum wuda* 'floating piece of wood' (5a) (the remnant of another living being caught in the motion of perpetual change), bound to its earthliness by its beak *on nearwe* 'in confinement' (1a). Like the swan it transcends to its principal realm part way through the riddle, and finally has *feorh cwico* 'animate life' (6b) when it *ahof* 'lift[s] up' (9b) to the air. Unlike the barnacle goose, the cuckoo's migration was common knowledge, but there are close similarities between the descriptions of these two birds immediately adjacent to each other in the manuscript. The cuckoo is likewise marked by transformative stages (*Þa* [3b], *oþþæt* [7a], *siþþan* [9b], *oþþæt* [10a]), and its *widdor ... siþas* 'wider journeys' (10b–11a) beyond the nest and foster mother anticipate the goose's flight up and away from the *fæðmum* 'embracing arms' (6b) of *brimes ond beames* 'wave and wood' (7a). As the cuckoo obtains its animate spirit part way through the riddle, so the goose achieves *feorh cwico* 'living spirit' (6a) when it departs from the mollusc cocoon.

The nightingale and the jay enact transformations of a different type. Both are vocal virtuosos, but the focus with each is their marvellous skill in shifting voice, even to the point where they seem like different species altogether. Where the barnacle goose riddle is striking for the terms that highlight movement and haptic becoming, Riddle 8 is characterised by a vocabulary that emphasises voice.[25] More precisely though, it presents a series of vocal transformations which border on excess.[26] These are clustered for effect in the opening lines:

>   Ic þurh muþ sprece   mongum reordum,
>   wrencum singe,   wrixle geneahhe
>   heafodwoþe   hlude cirme,
>   healde mine wisan   hleoþre ne miþe,
>   eald æfensceop,   eorlum bringe
>   blisse in burgum,   þonne ic bugendre
>   stefne styrme;   stille on wicum
>   sittað nigende.   Saga hwæt ic hatte,
>   þe swa scirenige   sceawendwisan
>   hlude onhyrge,   hæleþum bodige
>   wilcumena fela   woþe minre.
>
>   (Riddle 8)

[I speak through the mouth with many voices, sing with modulations, frequently vary my head-voice, call loudly, keep up my ways, do not hold back from speech. Old evening-singer, I bring to noblemen bliss in the towns; when I cry with bending voice, still in the homes they sit quietly. Say what I am called, who, like an actress, the entertainer's song loudly mimics, proclaims to men many greetings with my voice.]

The motif of frequent variation continues: the *bugendre / stefne* 'bending voice' sings *wilcumena fela* 'many greetings'. This sense of dextrous manipulation is enhanced by the principal meaning of *wrenc* ('trick, artifice, wile, stratagem'), and the /wr/ consonantal pairing associated with the sleight or shift is picked up again

---

[25] A number of scholars attending to this riddle have noticed this distinctive feature. See Stanton, 'Mimicry, Subjectivity, and the Embodied Voice', p. 36; Bitterli, *Say What I Am Called*, pp. 47–8 and 54; and Robert DiNapoli, 'In the Kingdom of the Blind, the One-Eyed Man is a Seller of Garlic: Depth-Perception and the Poet's Perspective in the Exeter Book Riddles', *ES*, 81 (2000), 422–55 (p. 57).

[26] Cf. *BWP*, vol. 5, pp. 634–6: the nightingale's voice is 'remarkable for its richness, variety and vigour' (p. 634).

in *wrixle*.²⁷ As with the seabirds in Chapter One, the terminology applied to this vocalist is rich in terms that ambiguously combine human and avian sounds, and are employed similarly to suggest convergence, not distinction. The bird's voices, particularly, might function as clues to the speaker's identity because *reorde* is a word attached to bird sounds in other instances in the Exeter manuscript: the jay mimics the *glidan reorde* 'kite's voice', and, as we have already seen, the cuckoo in *The Seafarer* is also assigned this term (53b). So, too, do the flocking birds in *The Phoenix* sing with *reordum* (338b). The word has a wide range of meanings relating to voice, and can equally describe specifically human articulations or language as well.²⁸ The use of this word, then, is clearly intentional, because it leads us into the figurative representation of the nightingale as a performer of numerous types – the *æfensceop* 'evening-poet'; the reverent ecclesiast (suggested by the quiet or bowing [*nigende*] action of *stille* listeners); the *scirenige* 'actress', singing the *sceawendwisan* 'entertainer's song'.

Other words for voice in the riddle also bring together avian-human references. *Hleoþre*, for instance, which I translate as 'speech' above, but which, like *reorde*, could also be used to describe a bird's note. There is the gannet's *hleoþor* in *The Seafarer*, the *guðfugles heloþor* 'warbird's cry' in Riddle 24 (5a), and in an echo of the content of Riddle 8, we *geheraþ hleoðrum brægdan oðre fugelas* 'hear other birds modulate their songs' in the *Metres of Boethius* (13.47b–48a).²⁹ So, too, could *stefn* 'voice' and *cirm* 'cry' convey both avian and human sounds.³⁰ Some recall human vocalisations much more fully (*sprecan* almost exclusively refers to human speech in Old English texts). *Heafodwoþ* 'head-voice' – recalling Pliny's intricate description of the nightingale using musical terminology – seems to present the bird's voice as contrived, rational song, although

---

²⁷ Both words descend from Proto-Indo-European **wreik* 'to turn'.
²⁸ Bosworth-Toller, s.v. (n.) *reord* and (v.) *reordian*.
²⁹ Bosworth-Toller, s.v. (n.) *hleoþor*, sense 2.
³⁰ *Stefn* appears in Riddle 24, and *cirm* describes the noises of the elusive birds in Riddle 57.

wope, appearing again in the final line, can also mean more broadly 'sound, cry, noise'.³¹

This proliferation of voices does two important things: it makes it abundantly clear that aurality is central to this speaker's identification, and secondly, we are led to believe that working towards the correct answer has something to do with thinking of the subject in figurative terms as a human performer. This is no throwaway metaphor, though, designed just to mask the speaker's identity. Nor is it dispensable once we have an answer, which might have the effect of reducing the birds' natural vocalisations to nonhuman noise which can only metaphorically be described as 'musical'. As Robert Stanton has recently argued, this riddle 'produces difficult questions about the nature and function of voice' because 'the nightingale betrays a keen awareness of the power of a modulated voice to participate in human performance practices'.³² This blurring of vocal boundaries has even wider implications, however, when considered in the light of the other bird riddles. These creatures are some of the most transgressive wonders to appear in the whole riddle collection because they seem to establish their own parameters, exploiting their own diversities to obscure identification. It is not so much that the nightingale has a remarkable voice as the fact that this voice is plural, always altering its guise. These vocal re-makings are distinctive examples of the various transformations I notice in the bird riddles above. Moreover, some birds seem to exploit these abilities intentionally to deceive others. The cuckoo, for instance, plays 'dead' (young birds were thought to be born twice, once as a dead egg and then again when they hatch), and then plays at being another bird altogether, a convincing enough act to fool the surrogate mother into caring for the impostor *swa arlice swa hire agen bearn* 'just as properly as her own children' (9.6).³³ All these birds fool our senses in one way or another.

---

31 Bosworth-Toller, s.v. (n.) *wope*, senses 1 and 2. For Pliny's well-known elaboration on the nightingale's vocal skills, see *NH*, X.xliii.
32 Stanton, 'Mimicry, Subjectivity, and the Embodied Voice', p. 39.
33 For other riddles that depict the 'born unborn' egg paradox, see Symphosius's Enigma 14, Eusebius's Enigma 38, and Bern Riddle 8. For all texts see Glorie, *Variae collectiones aenigmatum*, 133 and 133a. See also *Etym.*, XII.vii.79.

The Multiple Identities of the Jay

The riddle that best conveys this duplicitous quality of birds comes some way into the collection. Riddle 24, most usually solved as the jay, picks up where Riddle 8 leaves off and develops the theme of vocal manipulation to extraordinary new levels.[34] Like the nightingale, the jay employs a rich (and noticeably similar) vocabulary of sound, varies her voice and is a bird that *onhyrge* 'mimic[s]'. Birds, attended by that qualifying determiner 'some' (Lat. *aliae*) in Isidore, exemplify well the 'sometimes' motif that runs through the riddles, but the jay tops the lot: *hwilum* is anaphorically repeated seven times. We are dealing with a bird here that is not only a true mimic, but also changes its voice almost every half line:

> Ic eom wunderlicu wiht,   wræsne mine stefne,
> hwilum beorce swa hund,   hwilum blæte swa gat,
> hwilum græde swa gos,   hwilum gielle swa hafoc,
> hwilum ic onhyrge   þone haswan earn,
> guðfugles hleoþor,   hwilum glidan reorde
> muþe gemæne,   hwilum mæwes song,
> þær ic glado sitte.   . X. mec nemnað,
> swylce . ᚠ. ond . ᚱ.   . ᚩ. fullesteð,
> . ᚾ. ond . I .   Nu ic haten eom
> swa þa siex stafas   sweotule becnaþ.
>   (Riddle 24)

[I am a wondrous creature. I vary my voice: sometimes bark like a dog, sometimes bleat like a goat, sometimes honk like a goose,

---

[34] Others have argued for woodpecker, based on what seems to be a confusion over Lat. *pica* (jay, magpie) and *picus* (woodpecker) in the Anglo-Saxon glossaries. Isidore clearly distinguishes between *pica* and *picus*; *Etym.*, XII.vii.47. For a full discussion on this topic see Williamson, *Old English Riddles*, pp. 207–8. As both magpie and jay seem to have been known as mimics to the Anglo-Saxons through Pliny (*NH*, 10.xlii; the reference to a kind of *pica* that feeds on acorns may well be a jay) and Isidore (*Etym.*, XII.vii.46; magpie only), I follow most here in solving *higoræ* as 'jay'. In early MLat., both birds were called *pica*, as in classical Latin. Distinction between the species, however, may be apparent from the fact that the Second Antwerp glossary gives *higere* for Lat. lemma *gaia*, and the Brussels glossary adds *gagia* to *picus* ~ *higera* (both are etymons to ME *jay* via OF *gai*). Further, a separate term, *agu* (cf. Old Saxon *agestra*), is used to gloss *pica* in the Second Antwerp glossary (Wright-Wülcker, p. 132) which implies some level of differentiation.

sometimes yell like a hawk, sometimes I mimic the ashy eagle – cry of the warbird – sometimes the kite's voice I speak with my mouth, sometimes the gull's song, where I sit gladly. G they name me, also Æ and R. O helps, H and I. Now I am called as these six letters clearly indicate.]

This riddle seems to present itself in the guise of an animal-sound list from the popular Latin pedagogical tradition (*voces animantium*), but its place amongst the Exeter Riddles complicates things considerably. If this little poem teaches us the Old English animal noises, we are also acutely aware that it is not the actual animals named that make these noises – some other being is articulating sounds that are supposedly proper to other creatures.[35] In this way, Riddle 24 self-reflexively manipulates voices and identities to produce a speaker that is simultaneously singular and plural. Here is a *wunderlicu wiht* that truly combines and switches species to evade its own self-conscious, self-changing classification: a jay is a dog, or a goat, or a goose!

What Riddle 24 does so well is to show how birds in these riddles enrich hermeneutic procedures by all at once establishing and dissolving boundaries. In this sense, birds are already riddles in themselves because their contradictions and mutations encourage us to see them in new terms without the help of poetic transposition – the silent sounder, the unborn born, bird that is another bird. Metaphoric layering to various degrees, the rhetoric of consonance, is central to riddling; part of the art of presenting and solving these

---

[35] These wordlists are in the tradition of Suetonius and Isidore. Besides Ælfric's *Grammar* (*Grammatik*, pp. 128–9), see Aldhelm's *De pedum regulis*, which includes all the species that appear in Riddle 24, except the gull; Aldhelm, *De metris et enigmatic ac pedum regulis*, in *Monumenta Germaniae Historica*, ed. by Rudolf Ehwald, Auctores Antiquissimi, 15, (Berlin: Weidmann, 1919), pp. 179–80. For discussion, see Patrizia Lendinara, 'Contextualized Lexicography', in *Latin Learning and English Lore: Studies in Anglo-Saxon Literature for Michael Lapidge*, ed. by Katherine O'Brien O'Keeffe and Andy Orchard, 2 vols (Toronto: University of Toronto Press, 2005), vol. 2, pp. 108–31 (116–18), and Jonathan Hsy, 'Between Species: Animal-Human Bilingualism and Medieval Texts,' in *Boolldly Bot Meekly: Essays on the Theory and Practice of Translation in the Middle Ages in Honour of Roger Ellis, The Medieval Translator*, 14, ed. by Catherine Batt and René Tixier (Turnhout: Brepols, forthcoming). I am grateful to Jonathan Hsy for allowing me to view the proof of this essay.

conundrums is to negotiate a path between the layers, to ascertain to what extent, if at all, we are dealing with metaphor.[36] When we hear that a *Moððe word fræt* 'moth ate words' (47.1a), is this intended literally? As it turns out, yes; insects that bore through books do at least give the distinct impression that they are consuming the pages and, therefore, words too. But we are also required to read this figuratively; bookworms do not digest words intellectually and are none-the-*gleawra* 'wiser' for the habit (6a). If we are to take the metaphor a step further and transfer insect characteristics to humans, we could also say that some inattentive monastic 'bookworms' are left equally ignorant. Birds intensify this process because their transformations have a habit of literalising what we might at first consider to be metaphorical. The meshing of metaphorical and literal aspects occurs in *The Seafarer*, but there conflicting aspects contribute to a cohesive metaphorical scheme. In the Riddles, when literal qualities pull away from metaphorical assimilation they often undo or impede the steps we make towards an answer. In the paradox of the cuckoo in Riddle 9, do we take the subject to be actually dead, or dead in some figurative sense? In this instance the sense is literal, on both sides of the orphan/cuckoo metaphor; the impact of the human foster story in part comes from the young child left for dead by its parents, and in terms of birds' oviparity (the young chick inside the egg was yet to be endowed with spirit). How far should the ambiguity of *byht* and *wic* in Riddle 7 perplex us?[37] Swans do not build human dwellings, but they do naturally inhabit land, like man, as much as they do water and the air. Deciphering the metaphor in this example may then extend to imagining how far the creature being described actually takes to the air (which, of course, it truly does).

---

[36] The dynamic of literal and metaphorical elements in the riddles has been addressed throughout much of the poems' critical history. Doane, for example, attempts to 'account for ... and to discount certain features in just the right amount' so that we can tread a careful line between the two; A. N. Doane, 'Three Old English Implement Riddles: Reconsiderations of Numbers 4, 49 and 73', *Modern Philology*, 84 (1987), 243–57 (p. 243).

[37] Bosworth-Toller, s.v. (n.) *wic*, senses 1–3 ('dwelling, place, abode, habitation'; 'place where a thing remains'; 'collection of houses').

The jay in Riddle 24 redoubles and collapses metaphors to articulate a perpetual movement between likeness and difference that correlates riddling strategies with species classifications; in the same way that literal and metaphorical modes are blurred, so are the markers of species. A mimicking bird is the perfect subject to convey the slippery nuances involved in species identifying because it can convincingly incorporate the trademark voices of other creatures (even inanimate 'species', as the epigraph above shows) into its vocal range in a way that at least seems to transfer likeness towards something that is uncannily the same, even indistinguishable. As Isidore's magpie proclaims, 'if you did not see me, you would deny that I am a bird'.[38] Outright, the jay presents itself as *swa* 'like' other creatures, and the fact that it imitates birds *and* mammals can hardly be accidental – the correlations between species oscillate more closely between near-kind and not so near. The question of metaphor is foregrounded here: the jay's voice is only *like* a goat's, but at the same time this is not a human-imposed conceit. The jay does genuinely imitate the animal in the way only some birds can, a detail that is brought closer to our attention by the use of onomatopoeic vocalisations (*beorce, blæte, græde, gielle*) which convey the animal utterance with some degree of accuracy, as though to replicate the jay convincingly sounding these other voices.

There is another valence to contend with, involving onomatopoeia. These words are, of course, contrived human signifiers, albeit ones that aim for authenticity. Despite the fact, then, that the human subject is not included in the jay's repertoire, human vocalisations do appear in other forms. The poem's runes are the most obvious way. These additional semiotics do not divert our focus away from avian matters, though. Rather, they bind us even more tightly into the jay's trickery by extending the number of translation hurdles. A dog or hawk or gull's voice is filtered through another bird's voice that translates to us through a human narrator, that

---

[38] Isidore is citing Martial here; *Etym.*, XII.vii.46. The similarity of Isidore's magpie to Riddle 24 may suggest it as a source. Cf. Isidore's description of the parrot: 'it pronounces articulate words so that if you did not see the bird you would think a human was speaking' (*Etym.*, XII.vii.24).

must then be processed through a further series of codes – runes must be matched to their corresponding letters in the Roman alphabet, which then need rearranging to present us with the solution. A tactic that might seem to undermine the elusive character of this particular subject (because it gives us a strong helping hand with the answer) actually does the opposite, then, because it gestures towards open-endedness, not finality, when it moves outwards into human modes of signifying.

The jay has yet another trick, however, that turns our careful proceedings back on themselves so that human language is presented not as a simple superimposition that anthropomorphises the bird, but as part of the jay's own voice all along. Dieter Bitterli has noted before now that the runes 'extend the catalogue of the jay's mimicry to the realm of human language'.[39] But the appropriation occurs even without these symbols. It is easy enough, particularly given the characteristic prosopopoeia of Anglo-Saxon riddles, to assume anthropomorphism. Once we remember that we are dealing with no ordinary bird here, though, but one that is renowned for mimicking even the human voice, the boundaries change again – the human speaker reciting the poem can very plausibly be one of the many voices adopted by the jay itself, thus craftily integrating the human voice that at first sight seems to be absent from the catalogue. The jay is not personified, but is actually speaking the poem. If we take this to be the case, then Isidore's etymological association of the poet and the mimicking corvid is fully realised; the riddler or performer and the jay consume each other's voices.[40]

The jay, with its most human-like capabilities, is the most pointedly transformative of all birds in the collection because its own hide-and-seek game imitates riddling strategies. Both require us to revise continually what we think we know, or what we think we have safely defined. In this sense, birds teach us something about the complexity of taxonomic endeavour. In the case of the jay, we are presented with a creature whose identifying feature is that it

---

[39] Bitterli, *Say What I Am Called*, p. 97.
[40] 'The magpie (*pica*), as if the word were "poetic" (*poetica*), because they pronounce words with a distinct articulation, like a human'; *Etym.*, XII.vii.46.

Avian Pedagogies

shares the identifying (vocal) feature of numerous other creatures. When this bird tells us, like the nightingale, that it *muþe gemæne* 'speak[s] with my mouth', what appears to be a crucial clue, and is, turns out to be what is also least trustworthy. In its use of typical onomatopoeic utterances and its listing of conventional species, Riddle 24 is akin to the *voces animantium* list, a familiar medieval teaching tool which, amongst other purposes, functioned as a form of taxonomic index:

> ealswa be nytenum: *canis latrat* hunt byreð, *lupus ululat* wulf ðytt, *equus hinnit* hors hnaegð, *bos mugit* oxa hlewð, *ouis balat* scep bleat, *sus grunnit* swin runað.[41]
>
> [It is the same for animals: the dog barks, the wolf howls, the horse neighs, the ox lows, the sheep bleats, the pig grunts.]

Riddle 24 recalls these texts, but we are dealing with a very different beast because the animal sounds are embedded within the vocal capabilities of another animal, thus scrambling the conventional procedure of assigning specific defining sounds to specific creatures. As playful as we might find Riddle 24, there is, perhaps, a more disconcerting underlying note. Fear or discomfort are not feelings we might immediately associate with our responses to the riddles, but if vocalisations were a way in which Anglo-Saxon scholars classified some nonhuman subjects, the jay is especially contrapuntal, even threatening, to notions of species containment. McFadden has suggested that the 'correct' procedure for solving these riddles requires that 'rather than taking the traits of the object as inherent to that object, the solver sees them metaphorically [and harmlessly] shared with simple objects and thus evades the verbal trap'. The jay, as just one example, shows us how difficult this approach can be – precisely what is inherent or simply metaphorical is too difficult to tell, and, in effect at least, may not even be different. It is not possible to 'reduce the subject to simplicity'.[42]

---

[41] *Ælfrics Grammatik*, pp. 128–9.
[42] McFadden, 'Raiding, Reform, and Reaction', 335. McFadden argues that the Riddles are the product of 'actual or potential threat posed by Viking incursions and the blurring of boundaries between civil or ecclesiastical affairs'; ibid., 329.

All avian transformations in the riddles, vocal or otherwise, perform this sort of exercise. They loosen category definitions, so that speciation does not so much involve identifying precise characteristics that close off this or that kind of being from other kinds, as it requires us to permit categories that open up to cross- or inter-species affinities. The jay's multiple identity straddles the delicate boundaries between the literal and metaphorical so dextrously that we cannot be sure which avian-avian, or avian-animal, or avian-human vocal relations to trust. On the whole, though, wondering at the world in this way does not demand that we fear these interrelations, because, as Michael Lapidge and James L. Rosier claim for Aldhelm's enigmas, 'the human learning process involves classification and the intelligible ordering of experience; but it also involves the ability to transcend conceptual categories'.[43] Indeed, the lack of answers in the Exeter manuscript can even encourage willingness to admit uncertainties, to recognise but not circumscribe the web of sprawling, inclusive contiguities between animate and inanimate individuals. Metaphorical relations can help us to understand more fully the complex ordering of things in less expected ways, to see how what may appear ostensibly just similar can enact a flattening out of metaphor, or dissolve into more integral or tangible correspondences than we might have first suspected.

Birds with No Names

Superficially, at least, these complex negotiations are intended to lead to the ultimate act of classification – naming itself. This, however, proves very difficult if a creature's defining characteristics cannot be accurately surveyed, or, indeed, that creature is capable of manipulating its own characteristics. In medieval thinking, of course, these two stages are inextricably interlinked in many cases because onomastic principles are guided by etymology, according to which the name of a given thing is determined by its intrinsic

---

[43] *Aldhelm: The Poetic Works*, trans. by Michael Lapidge and James L. Rosier (1985; repr. Cambridge: D. S. Brewer, 2009), p. 61.

nature. Isidore of Seville's hugely popular *Etymologiae* elaborates at great length on this theory:

> Etymology (*etymologia*) is the origin of words, when the force of a verb or a noun is inferred through interpretation. ... The knowledge of a word's etymology often has an indispensable usefulness for interpreting the word, for when you have seen whence a word has originated, you understand its force more quickly. Indeed, one's insight into anything is clearer when its etymology is known.[44]

In the Exeter Riddles' most immediate model, the *Enigmata*, the etymological principle governs Aldhelm's descriptions.[45] The task of illuminating *rerum enigmata clandistina* 'the hidden mysteries of things' is engaged in Isidorian discovery.[46] Crucially, there are titular solutions, which make clear that we are not in the business of guessing here; we begin with a word and work backwards to understand its 'force' by delighting in the process of the first person subject revealing its own meaning through defining its properties.[47] The swallow, to take an avian example, demonstrates nicely that 'the characteristics of a thing or creature should not be divorced from its name and etymology' by revealing itself through an esoteric play on its own name that requires readers to know that its

---

[44] *Etym.*, I.xxx.1–2. *Etymologia* derives from Greek **etymos* 'true, real, actual'.

[45] See Nicholas Howe, 'Aldhelm's *Enigmata* and Isidorian Etymology', *ASE*, 14 (1985), 37–59.

[46] *The Enigmata*, preface (lines 7–8), in *Aldhelm: The Poetic Works*. Unless otherwise stated, all references to the *Enigmata* in Latin are to *Through a Gloss Darkly: Aldhelm's Riddles in the British Library MS Royal 12.C.xxiii*, ed. and trans. by Nancy Porter Stork (Toronto: Pontifical Institute of Medieval Studies, 1990). Translations are from *Aldhelm: The Poetic Works*. I use Lapidge and Rosier's 'Enigma' throughout in reference to Aldhelm's poems rather than Stork's 'Riddle'. Numbering of the Enigmas is taken from Stork.

[47] Titular solutions are also provided for the riddles by Eusebius, Tatwine and Boniface, and are a feature of the influential century of enigmas from the late classical author Symphosius. See, however, Orchard, who argues that the usual contrast with the OE riddles' distinct lack of answers is less exact; in many manuscripts answers are added in the margins by a later hand (and, therefore, not part of the original exercise), or involve highly difficult encryptions; Andy Orchard, 'Enigma Variations: The Anglo-Saxon Riddle-Tradition', in *Latin Learning and English Lore*, 2 vols (Toronto: University of Toronto Press, 2005), vol. 1, pp. 284–304.

Greek name derives from a particular flower, the drops of which the bird uses to cure the sore eyes of its young.[48]

In the *Enigmata*, Isidorian principles are clear enough and, such was Aldhelm's conviction in Isidorian theory, 'it could hardly have been otherwise'.[49] Scholars have sought similar preoccupations in the Old English riddles.[50] As a set, the Exeter Riddles promote their interest in naming loudly and frequently: we are invited to perform the very act of naming through the formulaic injunction *saga hwæt ic hatte* 'say what I am called', or, more specific to the etymological principle, *hu ic hatte* 'how I am called' or *frige hwæt ic hatte* 'find out what I am called'.[51] The typical patterns of the Riddles ('I am a strange creature ... name me'; 'I saw a strange creature ... name it') implicitly recommend an inverted Aldhelmian approach. Starting from the opposite side of the etymological coin, we proceed towards the correct solution by careful elimination. But the Exeter Riddles, of course, do something very different; despite all this insistence on naming, there are no answers, and thus no names. Even the six riddles which offer runic clues do not provide immediate answers because they must still be deciphered. Whether any prefaces or answers were ever provided in the manuscript or an earlier copy, or were intended to be at a later date (as in the case of some marginal additions in the Anglo-Latin riddles) is unknown. What we do know, as Neville points out, is that the scribes responsible for copying and assembling the Riddles 'did not intend solutions to be given, because they are not there'.[52] This famous characteristic

[48] Howe, 'Aldhelm's *Enigmata*',p. 38. The bird's Greek name (*chelidon*) derives from the greater celandine plant (Greek *chelidonia*). For the plant, see *Etym.*, XVII.ix.36. For the myth that swallows cure sore eyes with droplets from the flower's juices, popularised in later bestiary materials, see *NH*, X.xxxiv–v.
[49] Howe, 'Aldhelm's *Enigmata*', 58.
[50] See Salvador-Bello, *Isidorian Perceptions*.
[51] These formulas are found in Riddles 1, 3, 8, 10, 12, 19, 23, 62, 66, 73, 80, 83 and 86 (*saga hwæt* or *hu*); 14, 16, 26 and 27 (*frige hwæt*). Cf. *Dic mihi quae est illa res* 'Tell me what that thing is' in one Lat. prose riddle (79); Martha Bayless and Michael Lapidge, eds, *Collectanea Pseudo-Bedae*, Scriptores Latini Hiberniae, 14 (Dublin: School of Celtic Studies, Dublin Institute for Advanced Studies, 1998), p. 130.
[52] Jennifer Neville, 'Precarious Insights into Wooden Artefacts', in *Trees and Timber in the Anglo-Saxon World*, ed. by Michael D. J. Bintley and Michael G. Shapland (Oxford: Oxford University Press, 2013), pp. 122–43 (124).

draws us back into some familiar avian conundrums. Like birds, who are equally foreign and familiar, or who slyly reveal themselves through a sequence of concealments, the Riddles flaunt and deny the possibility of naming. As we will see, in the case of one bird riddle that comes right at the end of the first set in the manuscript, birds' abilities to preserve, or tease respondents with, their anonymities, open up a gap between words and things to expose complications in the naming game, thus obscuring Isidore's 'insight' by which 'anything is [made] clearer'.

In his study of the etymological principle as part of the wider Anglo-Latin influence on the Old English riddles, Bitterli focuses on birds to make his point. In his reading of Riddle 7, 'swan' is revealed through rhetorical patterns across the verbs *swigan* 'to silence' (1a), *swogan* 'to resound' (7a) and *swinsian* 'to sing' (7b): 'At least for OE *swinsian* 'make melody' and *swan* ~ *swon* (and its Germanic cognates) this etymological connection is indeed linguistically plausible and even very likely'. In Bitterli's analysis, then, the bird riddles 'typically centre on the identifying characteristic that, according to medieval birdlore, distinguishes the animal from other species'.[53] As we have seen, though, if birds have a defining characteristic, it is that they rarely stay the same – their predictability is their unpredictability. Identifying traits are always in question in riddles, and this is certainly the case with birds. Many of the birds in the Riddles call attention to sounds that they produce, including some whose songs produce their names directly, reminding us that birds have a special status above other animals groups, in that many literally sound out their own classifications.[54] Onomatopoeic avian names abound in Old English as well as Latin, which raises a question about just how well the intrinsic vocal element of a species that assigns it a particular name manages to

---

[53] Bitterli, *Say What I Am Called*, p. 37
[54] Of those that have vocally onomatopoeic names, the cuckoo's voice is not mentioned in the Riddle, but its Lat. name is onomatopoeic (*cuculus*) and Eric Lacey designates OE *geac* onomatopoeic status, too, as he does *higera* 'jay'; Lacey, 'Birds and Words', pp. 83–4. The birds in Riddle 57 have never been satisfactorily identified, but if the final half-line is anything to go by the species may have an onomatopoeic name.

translate into a human language system. When Isidore tells us, for instance, that the 'peacock (*pavo*) has its name from the sound of its call' or the 'raven (*corvus*), or *corax*, takes its name from the sound of its throat, because it croaks (*coracinare*) with its voice', we are aware that whilst the sound can be approximately articulated in human speech, the etymology itself here only refers us back to the birds' calls, not to any meaningful human-devised term that explains their songs.[55] Birds' voices generally present a more complicated case for etymology. The very principle Bitterli seeks to demonstrate in the Riddles specifically through birds is made unstable by the subjects themselves, most directly in the case of the jay: what we believe properly defines other animals is also, confusingly, what simultaneously distinguishes and dissolves the jay's identity across and into other creatures. Safe values and characteristics that supposedly lead us to a name are at risk. They show us, as Andrew Welsh has remarked of riddling characteristics, that 'In the process ... of reading the unknown in terms of the known ... the unknown never completely fits into the known'.[56] In another riddle involving birds – a domestic cock and hen (OE *hana* and *hæn*) – we are told in the final sentence that the decoded answer is finally *undyrne* 'unsecret' (42.15b). Arguably, birds' evasive transformations significantly complicate our ability to expose their wonder. They remain *dyrne*.

In the previous chapter, I suggested that the bird names in *The Seafarer* might be considered in the context of wider Anglo-Saxon interests in vernacular bird names. The Riddles, present in the same manuscript and overtly calling attention to naming, may highlight this potential scholastic context even further. Specifically, they may recall the inconsistences or difficulties attending the issue of naming birds in the Riddles that are reflected elsewhere in Anglo-Saxon school texts in which naming practices are central

---

[55] *Etym.*, XII.vi. 48 and 43, respectively. Medieval understandings of voice (*vox*), based on the Lat. models of authors like Priscian and Donatus, did indeed relegate birds' calls to the status of inarticulate. This is a theme I tackle fully in Chapter Four.

[56] Andrew Welsh, *Roots of Lyric: Primitive Poetry and Modern Poetics* (Princeton, NJ: Princeton University Press, 1987), p. 32.

preoccupations in medieval conceptions of grammar and logic. In the monumental efforts of scholars and scribes in monastic centres to integrate Christian-Latin knowledge and texts into English learning, birds featured alongside a host of other topics relevant to the Anglo-Saxon world. Translation projects were not only explicitly concerned with the benefits, strategies and difficulties of translating into English, but also showed great interest in making a diverse range of phenomena available in the vernacular. Many of the extant class glossaries, for instance, provide categories that mirror the everyday range of items and creatures appearing in the Exeter Riddles: agricultural implements, wild creatures, insects, birds, plants and trees, armoury, meteorology, nautical objects. Old English bird names in the extant glossaries do not, on the whole, show verbatim translation from the Latin, but a striking observation of calls and songs (as indicated by the number of onomatopoeic names), or appearances and behaviours which move us outside the intellectual sphere into contact with the physical natural world. There was a didactic value to knowing vernacular birds' names, whether to illuminate unusual terms that turned up in curriculum texts, or for use in classroom Latin-learning exercises, like colloquies.

This apparent interest in clarifying bird names and relating book-learnt ornithological knowledge to genuine or potential experiences in an English monastic setting is demonstrated nicely in some of the Canterbury school glosses of the well-known list of impure animals from Leviticus 11.[57] In the oldest extant version (St Gall, Stiftsbibliothek Cod. Sang. MS 913), a glossator tells us that the purple gallinule does not exist in Britain (*porphirio non fit in brittania*), and that ibises are long-beaked, African birds (*auis in Africa habens longum rostrum*). Even better known is the debate over the bird listed as *larus*: a heron to one individual, but apparently re-identified as a gull by Hadrian.[58] Attaching the right name to the

---

[57] These appear in the Leiden Glossary (originally compiled in St Gallen from English materials), of which a number of continental copies were made, and which have been shown to originate in the school of Hadrian and Theodore in late seventh-century Canterbury.

[58] The text reads: *laru(m) hragra adrianus d(ici)t meum e(ss)e*. 'Heron' is given directly as OE *hragra* here, but OE *mæw* (gull) is Latinised. Bernhard Bischoff and

right bird was, in some cases at least, not to be overlooked.

Scrupulous attention to bird names in these glosses also reveals the flip side to this exercise, though – naming birds, particularly when translating between languages, can be troublesome. As the St Gall Leviticus glossary reveals, matching name and thing could be tricky; the *onocratulus* is like a small duck, yet not the same, and is not found in England (*onocratulum: quasi anata; non eadem est tamen, nec nos habemus*).[59] Isidore's reflections on the huge diversity of birds represented by a 'single word' hint at similar difficulties; the impossibility of discovering 'how many kinds of birds there are' is concomitant with linguistic concerns about the general task of naming itself. Isidore's remarks, for instance, resonate with those of Ælfric in a grammatical and lexical context. Ælfric calls attention at the very end of his *Grammar* to the decisions involved in generally assigning names in English when he admits that *We ne magan swa þeah ealle naman awritan ne furþon geþencan* 'We cannot, however, name, write or further know everything'.[60] Some creatures, it is suggested, are unknown, do not have English names (perhaps accounting for the gaps in the Second Cleopatra glossary), or maybe not satisfactory names. The sentiments of both these writers may reflect scholarly perceptions more widely: 'De Cantibus avium', a tenth-century Latin poem in the *voces animantium* style conveys what seems to have been a conventional expression about the challenges that birds represented:

> Quis volucrum species numeret, quis nomina discat?
> Mille avium cantus, vocum discrimina mille.
> Nec nostrum (fateor) tantas discernere voces.[61]
>   ('De cantibus avium', 1–3)

Michael Lapidge, eds, *Biblical Commentaries from the Canterbury School of Theodore and Hadrian*, CSASE, 10 (Cambridge: Cambridge University Press, 1994), pp. 288 and 535.

[59] Ibid., p. 288. For complications concerning *onocratulus*, see the glossary in this volume, s.v. *Bittern* and *Pelican*.
[60] *Ælfrics Grammatik*, p. 322.
[61] Buecheler and Riese, *Anthologia latina*, pp. 218–19. The obstacles of specifying birds' calls are evident in the prose *voces animantium* lists. Humorous examples occur in Aldhelm's *De pedum regulis*, in which the master conversing with his student states that *ciconiae gratulant vel glottorant vel critalant* 'storks cry or rattle or make a stork noise'. The repetitive nonsense Lat. verbs in examples like

[Whoever counts the types of birds, who learns their names? There are a thousand songs of birds, a thousand different voices. Nor do I, myself, claim to distinguish such voices.]

Whilst birds were just one of many categories to be translated from Latin into English, this tradition of thought in early medieval texts that emphasises avian diversity relates birds intimately to serious lexical quandaries. In the process of identifying or assigning names, inadequate or unstable linguistic categories correlate and slip with precarious taxonomic boundaries to expose an unavoidable, sometimes impossible, balancing act which attests to the delicacy of such operations. Birds not only form part of the general difficulties of translating, but establish further, specifically avian hurdles because their sheer multiplicity, abundance and transformations are overwhelming.

If, as seems highly likely, the authors of the Exeter Riddles worked in a monastic setting, the overlap of literary discourses read and produced in these environments that deal with birds' names could recommend a shared set of interests and endeavours. The class glossaries, in their principal function, also aim to provide names for everyday items and implicitly raise some of the onomastic problems addressed elsewhere more directly (and creatively in the Riddles' case). As Nicholas Howe remarks, 'glossaries must posit a perfect correspondence between two Latin words or, even more questionably, between a Latin and an Old English word'.[62] Glossaries of varying types were important didactic tools in numerous circumstances, existing and functioning in the same literary circles as the popular Anglo-Saxon riddles, which also served as pedagogic resources. In the case of the popular collections of Anglo-Latin *enigmata*, it is certain that a number of them were both created by churchmen who composed grammar works, and, in their various

---

this indicate the specificity of particular calls, some of which apparently defy translation. See Aldhelm, *De metris*, p. 180.

[62] Howe, 'Aldhelm's *Enigmata*', 58. It is acknowledged that glossaries were an important source for Aldhelm's *Enigmata*. Howe makes the comment that 'some of his riddle solutions may be rephrased as glossary items'; ibid. See also, J. Marenbon, 'Les sources du vocabulaire d'Aldhelm', *Bulletin du Cange*, 41 (1979), 75–90 (pp. 79–83).

copies, circulated alongside these grammar or metrical treatises. The exact purposes of the Exeter Riddles are less clear, but their numerous connections with the Anglo-Latin tradition imply that they may well have functioned in a similar relationship with the same sorts of scholarly texts. Their authors were likely to be familiar, that is, with glossaries (and glossing activities) that accompanied important texts such as the *Etymologiae* and Ælfric's *Grammar*, in which the challenges of naming are addressed.[63]

Of the few Old English Riddles that still elude entirely satisfactory solutions, one, as if by way of demonstration, seems to be describing a group of birds. On that aspect of Riddle 57, at least, most are agreed.

> Ðeos lyft byreð   lytle wihte
> ofer beorghleoþa.   Þa sind blace swiþe,
> swearte salopade.   Sanges rope
> heapum feorað,   hlude cirmað,
> tredað bearonæssas,   hwilum burgsalo
> niþþa bearna.   Nemnað hy sylfe.
>
> (Riddle 57)

[The air bears little creatures over the hillsides. They are very black, swarthy, dark-coated. Bountiful of song, they journey in groups, cry loudly, tread the woody headlands, sometimes the town-dwellings of the sons of men. They name themselves.]

These creatures *hlude cirmað* (like the nightingale in Riddle 8 [3b]), the *lyft byreð* the birds in the same way it does the swan (4b–5a) and barnacle goose (9b), and both the swan and the birds of Riddle 57 *tredað* 'tread' when alighted, inhabiting opposing human and nonhuman

---

[63] All the birds identified in the Riddles (excluding barnacle goose) appear in the glossaries, including the hens from Riddle 42, and swallow (OE *swealwe*) and crow (OE *crawe*) – two of the most favoured solutions to Riddle 57. All the Riddle birds can be found, e.g., in the Second Cleopatra glossary (Wright-Wülcker, pp. 258–61). Glossaries and glosses were important features of manuscripts containing key source texts. In British Library, MS Royal 12.C.xxiii, the well-glossed copy of Aldhelm's *Enigmata* has seventy-five OE glosses, including a bird-related one that Nancy Porter Stork suggests may be a borrowed OE term from Latin (*nycticorax*); *Through a Gloss Darkly*, pp. 48–9. British Library, MS Cotton Cleopatra A.iii (in which birds are listed in all three glossaries) also includes a glossed text of the *Etymologiae*.

Avian Pedagogies

territories.⁶⁴ As in Riddle 8, too, paronomasia occurs on the same letters (*sw*) in *swiþe, / swearte*, which may also function onomatopoeically to convey the sound of flight or voice. Unlike these birds in earlier Riddles, however, there is little consensus about a solution for Riddle 57, only that for most readers the 'subject is quite firmly assigned to the category *bird*'.⁶⁵ Whatever its immediate sources or contexts may have been, Riddle 57 manifests the sorts of anxieties over naming birds and their characteristics evident in those texts discussed above – these are birds that apparently name themselves, but (still) cannot be named.⁶⁶ The history of this pithy riddle involves a longer list of possible avian suggestions than any other bird riddle, each scholar attending closely to the few details of bird and habitat, with most attempting to clinch identification according to the creature's most obviously bird-like trait, its voice, which, in line with many Old English bird names, should lead us to an onomatopoeic title. The refusal of this riddle to give up a convincing avian name has encouraged some to consider other airborne possibilities, including gnats, hailstones, bees, musical notes, demons and thunderclouds.⁶⁷ In recent times, scholars have reconsidered old solutions. Audrey L. Meaney has argued for swifts, Andrew Welsh has suggested swal-

⁶⁴ *Lyft* in relation to birds, seems to be supported by Anglo-Saxon scientific thought on the workings of flight. Meaney draws a parallel with Ælfric: in his *De temporibus*, he remarks that *On ðam [lyfte] feloð fugelas swa swa fixas swymmað on wætere. Ne mihte heora nan fleon, nære seo lyft ðe hi berð* 'Birds fly in the air, just as fish swim in water. Nor might any of them fly, if the air did not bear them.'; Ælfric, *De Temporibus anni*, ed. by H. Henel, EETS OS, 213 (Oxford: Oxford University Press, 1942), p. 72. Cf. Ælfric's *Hexameron; Exameron Anglice or The Old English Hexameron*, ed. by Samuel J. Crawford, Bibliothek der angelsächsischen Prosa, 10 (Hamburg: H. Grand, 1921), lines 137–8, and OE *Maxims II*, lines 38b–39a.

⁶⁵ Nigel F. Barley, 'Structural Aspects of the Anglo-Saxon Riddle', *Semiotica*, 10 (1974), 143–75 (p. 169) [italics original]. Cf. Audrey L. Meaney, who notes that the riddle gives a 'precise and accurate ... description of a piece of bird behaviour'; Meaney, 'Exeter Book Riddle 57', 200.

⁶⁶ The translation of line 7b to read 'They name themselves' is now widely acknowledged, rather than 'Name them yourselves'. As Elena Afros explains, 'the form *nemnað* can stand for present indicative first, second and third person plural as well as for imperative plural'; Elena Afros, 'Linguistic Ambiguities in Some Exeter Book Riddles', *Notes and Queries*, 52:4 (2005), 431–7 (p. 433).

⁶⁷ For a list of solutions to the Riddle up to 1981, see Donald K. Fry, 'Exeter Book Riddle Solutions', *Old English Newsletter*, 15:1 (1981), 22–33 (p. 24). Avian solutions include swifts, house martins, swallows, jackdaws, crows and blackbirds.

lows, and John D. Niles, focusing on the final line, like many others before, proposes another onomatopoeic candidate. For Niles there is 'little doubt' that the answer must be crows (OE *crawan*), in response to which Patrick Murphy has conferred that this is the 'most likely self-naming black bird we are ever likely to snare'.[68]

What Riddle 57 ultimately points us towards, intentionally or otherwise, is birds' defining ability to escape or devalue human nomenclatures. Whatever the solution that was originally intended, Patrick Murphy and Donna Beth Ellard are surely right to point to 'avian anonymity', at least as much as anything specific or definitive in the riddle. But where Murphy believes their anonymity points us away from birds as the correct answer (he argues for letters of the alphabet – OE *bocstafas*), I prefer to see this 'unremarkable' quality as precisely that which makes them remarkable; *lytle wihte* that 'no one can discover' or *naman awritan ne furþon geþencan*.[69] Despite the seeming vagueness, the internal correlations with other bird riddles point us towards those same wondrous transformations, characterised by paradox: they shift between human habitations and more foreign parts, they fly and tread, they produce song and also cry loudly, and if we take the final half line to refer to distinctive voices, as with the nightingale and the jay, this defining characteristic is also the most suspicious element, for these voices reveal and disguise themselves simultaneously.

---

[68] Murphy, *Unriddling the Exeter Riddles*, p. 83. For swifts, see Meaney, 'Exeter Book Riddle 57'. Welsh argues swallows on the premise that this bird '"swallows," as every living creature does', and also names itself in 'the airborne image of a vortex or whirlpool'; Andrew Welsh, 'Swallows Name Themselves: Exeter Book Riddle 55', *American Notes and Queries*, 3:2 (1990), 90–3 (p. 91). See, however, Lockwood, who proposes that OE *swealwe* derives from Proto-Germanic **swalwō*, 'the literal meaning of which was cleft stick, the name having been motivated by the forked tail'; Lockwood, *British Bird Names*, s.v. swallow. Perhaps, then, swallows name their characteristic shape in flight. For crows, see Niles, *Old English Enigmatic Poems*, p. 129, first suggested in Ferdinand Holthausen, 'Ein altenglisches Rätsel', *Germanisch-Romanische Monatsschrift*, 15 (1927), 453–4.

[69] Murphy, *Unriddling the Exeter Riddles*, p. 82, and *Ælfrics Grammatik*, p. 322. Ellard recognises an 'aerial vibratory assemblage of constant change', and refers us to Ælfric's grammatical category of 'mixed speech' as an aid towards solving the riddle: the birds 'name themselves … in the *"gemenged stemn"* [mixed speech] of their own species'; Ellard, 'Going Interspecies', 278 and 277.

Moreover, the switchback evasions of the dark birds in Riddle 57 place them firmly in line with an important effect of the Exeter Riddles' strategies: they expose the limits of epistemological aims, even within texts that urge us to exceed limitations and certify uncertainties, and thus contribute to the formulation of wonder. Some riddlers seem to draw attention to this aspect, as if to mock the *poncol mon* 'thoughtful man' (2.12b) or *þam þe bec witan* 'those that know books' (42.7a) who may end up not [one] *wihte þy gleawra* 'wit-the-wiser' (47.6a). Book-learning is apparently of little help in Riddle 57 – if Isidore is anything to go by, even the great authorities admit the impossibility of the task when it comes to birds – and the ambiguity of its final hemistich reminds us of a central feature of the Old English collection, that we are instructed to conduct a naming act by subjects (often in the first person) who persistently remind us of the obstacles involved in doing precisely this. The wording of line 6b in Riddle 57 highlights this particularly when we read *nemnað* as imperative; the idea is not to delight in tracing and explicating etymological roots, but rather, to do the naming yourself – in effect, to place oneself in the model of Adam. This is a performance that exists in Anglo-Latin riddles, too, but the absence of any titular or marginal solutions in the Old English riddles forces participation in a very genuine sense. Any anthropocentric confidence of the sort encouraged by Genesis in this manoeuvre, however, is deflated by the lack of answers against which to check one's efforts. What the Riddles do is set up a perpetual self-reflective circularity; when some speakers request a respondent to *frige* 'ask' of their name, the answer must inevitably be (in a manuscript culture at least): 'Guess!' There is a sense here in which the solution to at least some of the Exeter Riddles is locked in the physicality of the respective subject and, without any governing authority to nod success or not to any particular guess, the only option available is for one to turn back to the thing itself.

In her discussion of wonder surrounding the reinvested object concept, Dailey observes that by 'forcing us to think through the means of how we come to know the creature described in language', these texts highlight 'a link in epistemological knowing and a limit inscribed in naming': 'Responding to a riddle and naming an object might mimic a certain process of coming to know things in the surrounding world either directly or through literary precedents, yet naming the object of the riddle does not divulge the mystery it evokes'.[70] The bird riddles expose and contribute to precisely these sorts of limitations. In Riddle 57, the grammatical ambiguity of line 6b demands, on the one hand, that we partake in the typical naming game, and on the other states that the birds, in fact, name themselves, neither requiring our intervention, nor, in fact, allowing us this privilege. The birds of Riddle 57 are like those self-naming onomatopoeic birds we discover in Isidore, the calls of which are made names when rendered in Latin letters, but whose intrinsic sense only folds back into the avian selves to 'leueþ noo signe neiþir tokene of here passage'.[71] Naming birds, as we have seen, does not satisfactorily encompass their ever-changing, diverse identities, and particularly not when we cannot *saga* a name at all.

Writing Riddles with Birds

Murphy's solution for Riddle 57 points us to my final suggestion about the ways in which birds make their presence felt in the intellectual challenges of the Old English riddles. For him, the birds exist as a metaphor which reveals the true solution (alphabetic letters) via a tradition which connects birds with writing. In this last part of Chapter Two, I seek not to pursue solutions, but to examine more closely how birds in this ultimate sense become a crucial and integrated aspect in formulating wonder in the Riddles. I focus in particular on Riddle 51, which deftly foregrounds the active presence and mystery of living birds even as we are reminded that the birds serve a perfunctory, technological role.

In the riddle's depiction of a pen and fingers writing we are aware of the material association of feather and quill evident in OE *feþer* (as in Lat. *penna*). The three senses of 'feather', 'wing' (plural

---

[70] Dailey, 'Riddles, Wonder and Responsiveness', p. 464.
[71] Trevisa, XII.i (p. 596).

feðra) and 'pen' are all incorporated into the metaphorical and literal flights that take place.[72]

> Ic seah wrætlice   wuhte feower
> samed siþian;   swearte wæran lastas,
> swaþu swiþe blacu.   Swift wæs on fore,
> fuglum framra;   fleag on lyfte,
> deaf under yþe.   Dreag unstille
> winnende wiga   se him wægas tæcneþ
> ofer fæted gold   feower eallum.[73]
>
> (Riddle 51)

[I saw four strange creatures travel together; dark were the paths, the tracks very black. It was swift in course, stronger among birds; it flew in the air, dived under the waves. The struggling warrior worked tirelessly, who pointed the ways over plated gold to all four.]

As Murphy notes, there are similarities with Riddle 57: an emphasis on a defining blackness in both texts, references to *lyft*, and the tendency of both birds and fingers clutching a quill to travel together. I would add that there is the same alliteration on /*sw*/ that appears in Riddles 8 and 57, denoting a typically aerial or vocal swiftness or dexterity, and that, like the swan and the barnacle goose, the diving bird in Riddle 51 inhabits three ecological realms.[74] As in Riddle

---

[72] Bosworth-Toller, s.v. (n.) *feðer/feþer*, senses 1–3. For other riddles to do with writing, see Riddles 26, 60, 67 and 93.

[73] The precise meaning of line 4a has never been confirmed and editors have varied widely in their readings. Tupper amends to *fultum fromra* 'the support of the swift ones', noting that *fultum* is used elsewhere to describe birds' wings; Frederick Tupper, ed., *The Riddles of the Exeter Book* (Boston, MA: Ginn and Company, 1910), p. 184, n. 52.4. For further discussion, see Williamson, *Old English Riddles*, p. 294. Some, like Williamson, prioritise the feather's movements in the scribe's hand, so that the guided quill is stronger *than* birds. In contrast, others choose to make the feather 'more swift among the birds', placing more emphasis on the feather's original environment; Mitchell and Robinson, *Guide to Old English*, p. 238. The latter translation has the benefit of positioning the feather's swift action as part of the bird against the tiresome efforts of the scribe, which is further supported by the metaphoric *wiga* who battles against the exercise's tedium. Either reading reminds us of the riddle's metaphoric strategy – a feather, transformed into a human implement, is re-envisaged in its original form so that we move between the different meanings of *feþra*, and the purposes it serves to both bird and human.

[74] Terrestrial habitation is implied in the *lastas* 'tracks', *swaþu* 'trails' and *wægas* 'ways' left on the vellum, although the last could also feature a pun on *wægas* 'waves'.

57, then, we encounter the familiar transformative traits that have made birds in other riddles strange and unfathomable creatures. In Riddle 51, a text predominantly concerned with the act of writing, these traits strike a curious and vivid presence. The materiality of a quill and fingers depicted as a flying and diving water bird (OE *dopened ~ duce ~ dufedoppe*), I suggest, should focus us on how this riddler is sensitive to a complex, interlaced relationship between writing and birds in a *scriptorium* riddle that masks itself as a bird riddle.

Whoever he was, the author of Riddle 51 could draw upon a long-lived literary convention represented well in the Anglo-Saxon riddling context which associated quills and their inky marks with birds, feathers and flight. Given the closeness of the riddle to Aldhelm's quill enigma, it seems likely that he did:

> Me dudum genuit candens onocratulus albam
> Gutture   qui   patulo sorbet de gurgite limphas.
> Pergo per albentes directo tramite campos
> Candentique uiae uestigia cerula linquo
> Lucida nigratis fuscans anfractibus arua.
> Nec satis est unam per campos pandere callem
> Semita quin potius milleno tramite tendit
> Quae   non errantes ad caeli culmina uexit
>
> (Enigma 59)

[The bright pelican, which swallows the waters of the sea in its gaping throat, once begot me (such that I was) white. I move through whitened fields in a straight line and leave dark-coloured traces on the glistening path, darkening the shining fields with my blackened meanderings. It is not sufficient to open up a single pathway through these fields – rather, the trail proceeds in a thousand directions and takes those who do not stray from it to the summits of heaven.]

Here, too, we have a water bird, there is talk of murky paths, and the final sentence may metaphorically associate the inky trails with the aerial locomotions ('thousand directions') of birds, particularly when the product of all this pen work directs us to 'the summits of heaven'.[75] Other Anglo-Latin riddles employ this conceit: along sim-

---

[75] Cf. Aldhelm's Enigma 29, in which the letters of the alphabet are created by 'the feather of a bird flying in the sky' (4).

ilar lines, there is Symphosius's Enigma 26 which envisages letters written in the sky by a formation of cranes, and Tatwine's Enigma 6 which mirrors Aldhelm's Enigma 59 in its focus on the feather's scrawling journey from the skies to the 'fields' of the page.[76] There is a striking parallel, too, with another of the Old English *scriptorium* riddles. In Riddle 26's description of manuscript production, the quill features part way through:

> ... ond mec *fugles wyn*
> geond speddropum   spyrede geneahhe,
> ofer brunne brerd,   beamtelge swealg,
> streames dæle,   stop eft on mec,
> siþade sweartlast.
>   (Riddle 26, 7b-11a)

[... and the *bird's joy* scattered success-drops over me, journeyed often over the bright brink, swallowed tree dye, a part of the stream, [then] stepped again on me, travelled a dark path.]

The components of Riddle 51 are all here – a feather envisaged as animate bird, journeying, immersion, dark tracks.[77]

What is evident in the passage from Riddle 26 is the innovation Riddle 51 gives to the feather-quill trope. As the sources above show, whilst it was common in the Latin riddles for the inky letters themselves to be portrayed as marks produced by birds, Riddle 51 focuses more on the material object itself, not just as a singular subject, but a metonymic imagining of the implement's former existence which metaphorically reunites bird body and *feþer*. The disembodied agent of flight bound to terrestrial labours in Latin riddles is reconfigured here as a living, diving water bird in a coordination of fingers and feather guided by a meticulous scribe and animated by the physicality of a bird's movements. The metaphorical bird's vivid presence in the depicted act of writing endows it with an indispensable avian value that is enhanced when we remember that a quill, barely re-worked from a plucked or

---

[76] Welsh mentions Symphosius's crane enigma in relation to Riddle 57; Welsh, 'Swallows Name Themselves', p. 93, n. 11.

[77] Cf. Riddle 93, in which the quill is the *hiþende feond* 'preying fiend' who once *wide bær* 'carried far' the *wulfes gehleþan* 'wolf's companion', i.e. the eagle (28b–29).

moulted feather, is quite literally part of a bird, not metaphorically linked. Riddle 51 does not reduce the quill to an inanimate, utilitarian form and purpose. On the contrary, this riddler powerfully restates birds' material contribution to the technology of writing. The intimate association of birds and writing in Riddle 51 imbues the physical construction of knowledge with the mysteries of these aero-aquatic creatures. In a deeply material sense, birds' shifting forms not only frustrate but also collaborate in the transformative, linguistic performances implied in writing and responding to the actual riddles themselves.

That physical construction, though, is inseparable from the epistemological formulations to which birds have proved so richly troublesome. Those dark tracks on the white page inscribe wisdom, learning, categorisation, as in Aldhelm's Enigma 59 where the pen mark's 'thousand directions' lead diligent scholars to divine knowledge. But implicit in those myriad, changing trails is also the possibility of misdirection for those who do 'stray' (a distinct, even likely possibility in the case of the Exeter Riddles). The bird riddles, as we have seen, threaten misdirection in numerous ways through birds' unique evasions. Tracks are consistently linked with an inky avian progress in Latin riddles, a conceit which is invigorated in Riddle 51. The influence of these early Anglo-Saxon enigmas may mean, then, that the frequent trails in the Old English riddles are always accompanied by the shadow of a bird, particularly when those paths seem aimless or uncertain. In Riddle 29, we are left with the ominous revelation that no *wera gewiste þære wihte sið* 'men knew the journey of that creature' (14), and Riddle 95 ends with *lastas* 'tracks' (11b) that are keenly sought, but also an admission from the enigmatic speaker: *ic swaþe hwilum / mine bemiþe monna gehwylcum* 'sometimes I conceal my tracks from every man' (12b–13).[78] With the obstacles of pursuing these bird-marked trails up front, we might be prompted to remember the limitations in trying to know birds acknowledged by other Anglo-Saxon writers, particularly

---

[78] Riddle 29 is usually solved 'sun and moon', but birds have also been recommended as solutions. See Williamson, *Old English Riddles*, pp. 226–9 (Riddle 27 in his edition).

the 'pathless ways' by which Isidore names the category of birds. To return to Dailey's concept of reinvestment, birds work well as riddle subjects because their diversity and metamorphoses naturally 'reinvest the object[s] with a found strangeness and mystery' that blurs species categories, muddles the process of metaphorical transformation and resists naming. In the specific context of riddling, however, if 'the riddle transforms the object', then birds are a part of this self-reflexive manoeuvre, too, inscribing and erasing the paths to knowledge both physically – because we cannot ignore the feathered materiality of birds in writing – and cognitively, because they partake in the wondrous renewal of all other subjects.[79]

---

[79] Dailey, 'Riddles, Wonder and Responsiveness', p. 470.

Plate 3 **Little owl** *Athene noctua*
© Brian Lawrence
Þu wenest þat ich ne miȝte iso / Vor ich bi daie noȝt ne flo 'You think that I cannot see because I do not fly by day'
(*The Owl and the Nightingale*, 371–2)

3
A Bird's Worth: Mis-Representing Owls in *The Owl and the Nightingale*

> Seie me nu, þu wrecche wiȝt,
> Is in þe eni oþer note
> But þu hauest schille þrote?
> Þu nart noȝt to non oþer þinge,
> ...
> Wat dostu godes among monne?[1]

[Tell me now, you wretched creature: is there any other purpose to you, other than that you have a shrill voice? You mean nothing to any other being ... What good do you do among mankind?]

> Heruore hit is þat me þe shuneþ
> An þe totorue & tobuneþ

[So it is that people shun you, and pelt and beat you to pieces.]
(*The Owl and the Nightingale*, 556–63 and 1165–6)

THE OWL'S VITRIOLIC WORDS in the first epigraph above remind us of the central theme of this poem's 'plaiding suþe stronge' [very strong debate (12)] – an owl and a nightingale contend aggressively on the usefulness of their voices, apologists for their own, and lambasters of the other's. In one respect, this is a generic feature, a recognisable component from a number of the possible Latin or Anglo-Norman debate-poems which are likely sources for *The Owl and the Nightingale*: people, abstractions or creatures debate their individual merits, or those of another whom they

---

[1] *The Owl and the Nightingale: Text and Translation*, ed. by Neil Cartlidge (Exeter: Exeter University Press, 2001); hereafter *O&N*. All references to the text are to this edition.

represent.² On this simple basis, Neil Cartlidge comments, the poem certainly qualifies as a debate-poem, and the adept treatment the author makes of so-called debate-poetry characteristics in itself may point out an important aim for a text whose exact purpose has famously baffled scholars: 'it could reasonably be described both as a self-conscious summation, and a self-conscious surpassing, of received literary possibilities'.³ In this skilled 'summation', however, we are alerted to how those 'received literary possibilities' mesh with other medieval literary discourses in which being useful bears significance. The cut and thrust of *disputatio*, dealt with more simply or superficially in *The Owl and the Nightingale*'s sources, does not exist as a frivolous display of wit, or even just as a comment on rhetoric itself, but to press debating the subject of nonhuman worth to much more provocative ends. The poem is not only the first surviving English example, but also the most sophisticated debate-form treatment of a theme that had increasing cultural relevance in the twelfth and thirteenth centuries – the purpose and value of the natural world, as represented by natural philosophy and literary texts, such as the popular bestiaries. The matter of species, in one significant sense, comes down to culturally-assigned worth: as the owl asks, 'Wat dostu godes among monne?' I ask in this chapter what it means to be a medieval owl or a nightingale by exploring the tangle of cultural and natural species in the poem's taxonomy of avian kinds. Poetic birds and their designated anthropocentric worth in this debate open out to engage and affect wider species conceptualisations.

Indeed, the force of cultural representations that define according to human-assigned values is so persuasive, it seems, that this particular owl and nightingale are very often utterly convinced by

---

² For likely debate-poetry sources for *O&N*, see Neil Cartlidge, 'Medieval Debate-Poetry and *The Owl and the Nightingale*', in *A Companion to Medieval Poetry*, ed. by Corinne Saunders (Oxford: Wiley-Blackwell, 2010), pp. 237–57. Other ME debate-poems involving nonhuman characters who argue for their uses to mankind (or do good by representing particular social groups) include the near-contemporary *Thrush and the Nightingale*, Clanvowe's *Cuckoo and the Nightingale* (*Boke of Cupid*) and Lydgate's 'Horse, Goose and Sheep'. Cf. also 'The Debate of the Carpenter's Tools' (c. 1500).

³ Cartlidge, 'Medieval Debate-Poetry', p. 245.

their literary uses as innate aspects of species-ness. In this pluralistic vision, we are repeatedly reminded that cultural presumptions and expectations about nonhumans are arbitrary and unwarranted, but, nonetheless, persist as taxonomic indices that are inextricably part of a creature's 'cunde' (88), affecting the ways that humans perceive and interact with the actual creatures themselves, and, in this poem, how the birds themselves behave. The poem engages self-consciously, that is, with the very processes of cultural appropriation that perceive birds as particularly useful vehicles for metaphoric transformation, a procedure that the birds get involved with, comically mediating these transformations for their own purposes. As we will see in the final part of the chapter, however, amused contemplation of taxonomies in this poem can lead to more disconcerting realisations. As the second epigraph above denotes, the cultural determinations that seem to carry such weight in the owl's words do not remain benign, or playfully separate, but bring owls (and nightingales) into contact with a set of wider, real-world implications that can turn nastily on the creatures themselves.

The Book of Nature – A Purposeful Existence

When the owl asks if the nightingale has 'any oþer note', or the nightingale queries to the owl 'Wi dostu so?', they align themselves with a familiar and enduring medieval belief. The birds' insistent preoccupations with nonhuman worth reveal the specific cultural principle with which the poem rigorously engages – nothing less than the belief that there is value assigned to each and every nonhuman kind in God's divine scheme for the practical and intellectual uses of mankind. Both birds proudly define themselves by making a great deal of their own instructive and practical 'god' (329), and denigrating the 'unwurþ' (339) capabilities or qualities of the other. The owl claims her song calls people to work in the morning (329–30); aids Christmas cheer (480–4); assuages winter solemnity (531–2); prompts penance (873–4, 887–92, 927–32); warns against bodily indulgences that the nightingale's song encourages (924–6) or impending disasters (1219–22); and comforts neglected or lonely wives (1519–20, 1567–70, 1593–97, 1601–2). Her body is also of use: she can rid man and church of unwanted pests and watch over human dwellings (603–8), and in death will serve as a scarecrow (1612–16) and hunting lure (1624–30). The nightingale argues that her voice heralds spring (433–5); contributes to clerical plainchant (729–35); urges people to remember eternal life (741–2); brings tidings of Christian love (1033–6); promotes honourable love between a lady and her husband (1347–8); cheers young women led astray by adulterous love (1445–8) and teaches them of this type of love's brevity (1449–50) through the short life of her own vernal song.[4] At times, the birds' songs and their uses are brought together in rhyme: 'note', the most commonly used term for 'use' or 'service', is collocated with 'þrote' (329, 558, 1033), associating the birds' dominant attribute and the functions it can perform. There may even be a pun intended on 'note' itself, conflating the musical voice and its services in one word.[5]

This heavy foregrounding of avian *utilitas* takes to comic extremes the idea of assigning a series of cultural purposes to nature. Non-human creatures could, of course, be categorised according to their practical, bodily worth. Clean and unclean creatures for the purposes of eating are delineated in Leviticus (including the owl), and beasts of burden are arranged and discussed in Isidore according to their primary use for labour, utilities that impact very considerably

---

[4] The owl comments on the nightingale's uselessness in the following lines: 337–40, 559, 565, 575, 849–53, 913–16, 1622, 1633–4. The nightingale insults the owl in the same way at lines: 805–8, 971–6, 1127, 1137–8. See also lines 997–8, 1025. Many of the examples outlined in the main text above contradict Monica Brzezinski Potkay's statement that 'never does either bird hold up animal behaviour for humans to imitate'; Monica Brzezinski Potkay, 'Natural Law in *The Owl and the Nightingale*', CR, 28:4 (1994), 368–83 (p. 374).

[5] For other uses of 'note', see lines 330, 557, 1122, 1033, 1034, 1624. Numerous other words meaning 'use' (v. and n.), or relating to it, occur frequently in the poem. See, for instance, 'gode' (1631), 'meoster' (924) and 'wike' (603). Terms which denote the opposite, uselessness, also appear: see 'forworþe' (575) and 'unwurþ' (339). The musical sense of 'note' is not explicit in the poem, although it seems implicit at one point: 'Is in þe eni oþer note / But þu hauest schille þrote?' (557–8); see *MED*, s.v. (n.) *note*, sense 2. Cf. the 'note' of the French roundel at the end of *PF* (677).

on attitudes towards these animals and their treatments.⁶ The impressive range of practical uses the owl and the nightingale recount or dream up for themselves attests to these types of valuation. Even these physical uses of the nonhuman, though, presuppose conceptualised hierarchies. They are part of the *scala naturae* 'chain of being' that understood the natural world as a 'Book of Nature': in Alan of Lille's famous expression, *Omnis mundi creatura / quasi liber et picture / nobis est, et speculum* 'All of creation, like a book and a picture, is a mirror for us'.⁷ Nature's value exists as a form of intellectual property in the idea that humans might learn moral lessons about themselves or perceive aspects of God's divine scheme through scrutinising nature's book.

In the century span in which *The Owl and the Nightingale* is agreed to have been written, the fictions which fostered and perpetuated these ideas were enjoying considerable popularity, particularly in the bestiaries and beast fables.⁸ In one study of the animal in medieval thought and culture, Joyce E. Salisbury goes so far as to suggest that the vogue for beast literatures represents a 'radical departure', 'a new vision of animals and humans' beginning in the late twelfth century and forming part of the burgeoning developments

---

6   See *Etym.*, XII.i. Isidore was a key source for the bestiaries. The list of creatures in Leviticus was integrated into sources across the medieval period, including the bestiaries.
7   From *De incarnatione christi*, cited by Nona C. Flora, ed., in *Animals of the Middle Ages* (New York: Garland, 2000), p. ix. Cf. also, Hugh of St Victor (c. 1096–1191): 'the whole sensible world is like a kind of book written by the finger of God' (*De tribus diebus*); cited in B. T. Coolman, *The Theology of Hugh of St. Victor* (Cambridge: Cambridge University Press, 2010), p. 86. The concept dominated for centuries, such that Keith Thomas can write of the sixteenth century: 'the long established view was that the world had been created for man's sake and that other species were meant to be subordinate to his wishes and needs'; Keith Thomas, *Man and the Natural World: Changing Attitudes in England, 1500–1800* (London: Penguin, 1984), p. 17.
8   The most recent studies on the poem's date suggest a later origin towards the end of the thirteenth century, rather than early thirteenth or late twelfth century. See Neil Cartlidge, 'The Date of *The Owl and the Nightingale*', *MÆ*, 65 (1996), 230–47. For a summary of the main types of beast literature that flourished in the twelfth and thirteenth centuries in Britain which are likely influences on *O&N*, see Jill Mann, *From Aesop to Reynard: Beast Literature in Medieval Britain* (Oxford: Oxford University Press, 2009), pp. 1–27.

in intellectual thought at this time.⁹ Salisbury rather overstates the point (treating animals metaphorically long pre-dates the twelfth century), but she usefully draws attention to the fact that literary activities in the twelfth and thirteenth centuries popularised the Book of Nature vision amongst the laity as well as the clergy. With the production of the First- to Third-Family bestiaries and the rediscovery of the classical fable form and its proliferation in works by writers such as Marie de France and Odo of Cheriton, 'animals served well as creatures from whose actions human lessons might be extracted'.¹⁰ Species, in these terms, are conceived anthropocentrically and behave anthropomorphically to serve largely didactic purposes. Thus, in Odo's fables, the crow teaches us the shame of pride, the cuckoo of traitorous ambition, and in bestiaries the turtle dove's fidelity instructs us on widowhood, and the pelican reminds us of Christ's resurrection.¹¹ The owl's vituperative words to the nightingale indicate this doctrine well, speaking as though with bestiary authority; to lack instructive or practical merit is to 'be noȝt to non oþer þinge' (a troubling status to which I will return).

The striking presence of birds in texts such as the bestiaries and fables, in fact, may suggest why the author of *The Owl and the Nightingale* fastened on avian characters in the first place. They constitute a very significant portion of bestiary manuscripts, but are singled out for particular treatment in two popular religious manuals dating from the approximate period in which the poem is likely to have been written. The first of these is an avian bestiary: Hugh of Fouilloy's twelfth-century *Avarium*, a possible source for *The Owl and the Nightingale*, enjoins readers to *Ecce qualiter per naturam volucrum doceri potest vita religiosorum* 'Observe how the life of religious [sic]

---

⁹ Joyce E. Salisbury, *The Beast Within: Animals in the Middle Ages*, 2nd edn (Abingdon and New York, NY: Routledge, 2011), p. 100.

¹⁰ Jeffrey Jerome Cohen, 'Inventing with Animals', in *Engaging with Nature: Essays on the Natural World in Medieval and Early Modern Europe*, ed. by Barbara A. Hanawalt and Lisa J. Kiser (Notre Dame, IN: University of Notre Dame Press, 2008), pp. 39–62 (42). For an introduction to the bestiary form, see *A Medieval Book of Beasts: The Second-Family Bestiary*, ed. and trans. by Willene B. Clark (Woodbridge: Boydell Press, 2006), pp. 7–33.

¹¹ For Odo's fables, see *The Fables of Odo of Cheriton*, trans. by John C. Jacobs (Syracuse, NY: Syracuse University Press, 1985).

can be taught through the nature of birds'.[12] The choice suggests that birds, in all their various transformative guises and manoeuvres, are the ideal paradigm for pious guidance towards spiritual conversion, and appropriate public and monastic habits. Birds are the most heavily imbued group of animals, purveyors of morally and intellectually instructive worth 'bequeathed to us ... for our edification'.[13] The *Avarium* proceeds in bestiary form, constructing layers of exegesis which attribute symbolic value to the properties of specific birds. Thus, the dove is anatomised (eyes, feet, colour ...) and considered 'mythically' and 'allegorically'.[14] The owl is represented by two species, a fact that becomes particularly significant in *The Owl and the Nightingale*.

The second text is the early thirteenth-century *Ancrene Wisse*, a guide for anchoresses. Although the agenda of the instruction is not specific to the natural world in the way the *Avarium* is, the third part is devoted to enlisting *anes cunnes fuheles þe Dauið i þe Sawter euened him seolf to as he were ancre, ant hu þe cunde of þe ilke fuheles beoð ancren iliche* 'birds of a particular kind that David compares himself to in the Psalter as if he were a recluse, and how the nature of these same birds are like recluses'.[15] The owl, as one of the birds treated in the Psalms (*nycticorax*), makes an appearance just like *nycticorax* in the *Avarium*:

> Þe niht-fuhel i þe euesunges bitacneð recluses, þe wunieð for-þi under chirche euesunges þet ha understonden þet ha ahen to beon of se hali life þet al Hali I Chirche—þet is, Cristene folc—leonie ant wreoðie upon ham, ant heo halden hire up wið hare lif-halinesse ant hare eadie bonen.
> ...
> On þer half, þe niht-fuhel fliþ bi niht ant biyet i þeosternesse his fode. Alswa schal ancre fleon wiþ contemplation ... .[16]

[12] *The Medieval Book of Birds: Hugh of Foilloy's Aviarium*, ed. and trans. by Willene B. Clark (Binghampton, NY: Center for Medieval and Early Renaissance Studies, 1992), II.xliv (pp. 204–5). The text was circulated widely, included in ninety-six extant manuscripts. For discussion of its production and transmission, see *Medieval Book of Birds*, pp. 24–30.
[13] Ibid., Prologue, ii (p. 119).
[14] Ibid., I.i–xi (pp. 122–3 and 124–5).
[15] Millet, *Ancrene Wisse*, vol. 1, Preface, viii (pp. 167–9).
[16] Ibid., III.xiii.325–9.

[The night-bird in the eaves betokens recluses, who live, therefore, under the eaves of the church that they understand that they ought to lead such a holy life that all the Holy Church – that is, Christian folk – can lean upon and be supported by them, and that they shall hold it up with their holiness of life and their blessed prayers.
...
Furthermore, the night-bird flies by night and gathers its food in darkness. Likewise, an anchoress should fly with contemplation ... .]

The nightingale is not well represented in bestiary-type materials, but certainly was in the Latin and French lyric tradition.[17] As a pair, the poem's birds embody a panoply of attributes that demonstrate a cultural fascination with birds' didactic and symbolic worth in both religious and secular contexts, making them ideal candidates for the poem's dealings with cultural value in the matter of species. Because the owl more fully demonstrates the ramifications of these acts of valuation and use, however, it is the multiple and conflicting literary forms of this bird that concern me here. As implied from the start of the poem, owls in the medieval Latin West already had a broad and deep cultural history which affected people's reactions to them. Envisaged as *turpissima avis* 'the worst bird', then as in modern times, owls 'carry upon their backs the whole weight of English folklore'.[18]

The Persuasion of Cultural Species

The Owl and the Nightingale's exploration of the implications and effects of cultural species is reliant, of course, on that aspect of the poem's birds with which critics have been repeatedly occupied, because it alerts us to the fact that literary avian species are placed

---

[17] For discussion of the nightingale's romantic role in these lyrics, see Wendy Pfeffer, 'Spring, Love, Birdsong: The Nightingale in Two Cultures', in *The Mark of the Beast: The Medieval Bestiary in Art, Life and Literature*, Garland Medieval Casebooks, 22, ed. by Debra Hassig (New York, NY and London: Garland, 1999), pp. 88–95.

[18] Clive Fairweather, a contributor to Mark Cocker's *Birds Britannica* (London: Chatto and Windus, 2005), p. 281. For general discussion of British owl folklore, see Cocker, *Birds Britannica*, pp. 281–5.

under scrutiny and suspicion. Indeed, whilst few of the text's critical responses have focused chiefly on ornithological or taxonomic matters, there has always been a need to address or accommodate the birds' 'distinctly avian presences'.[19] The poet understands very clearly that owls and nightingales exist outside the pages of books: the details of the birds' natural characteristics and their habitats do genuinely reflect their real-world existence, not the selective or fantastical *naturas* descriptions that pass for natural history in the bestiaries.[20] The owl's 'swore is smal' [neck is squat (73)], her eyes 'col-blake and brode' (75), and her bill 'stif & scharp & hoked' (79) with which she 'clackes' just 'on' (81) of her calls.[21] The nightingale receives specific attention to her plumage – 'dim and of fule howe' [unattractive colour (577)] and her preferred habitat 'Among þe wode, among þe netle' (593). The vocabulary of song is particularly rich – the birds variously 'schrichest' and 'pipest' (503) with 'chokeringe' [clucking (504)], 'writelinge' [twittering (48)] and 'huing' [hooting (1264)], 'lude & so sharpe' (141). Indeed, these strikingly accurate observations constitute one aspect that has united critics; all agree that 'the poem is certainly grounded in avian behaviour'.[22]

---

[19] Mann, *Aesop to Reynard*, p. 170.
[20] Broadly speaking, bestiaries are understood to prioritise allegorical significances over the biological, but for a revisionist approach to bestiary hermeneutics in the context of animal studies, see Crane, *Animal Encounters*, pp. 69–100.
[21] Cf. tawny owl in *BWP*, vol. 4, pp. 526 (appearance); 529–6 (food); and 537 (roosting pose and habitat). The purposeful blurring of bestiary owl species in the *O&N* specimen makes it difficult to ascertain if a particular species is intended, but the description suits both the barn owl and the tawny owl, the two most commonly encountered British species. One of the poem's most recent commentators prefers the tawny owl: see Carolynn Van Dyke, 'Names of the Beasts: Tracking the *Animot* in the Medieval Texts', *SAC*, 34 (2012), 1–51 (p. 24), and Van Dyke, 'Touched by an Owl: An Essay in Vernacular Ethology', *Postmedieval: A Journal of Medieval Cultural Studies*, 7:2 (2016), 304–27 (p. 323, n. 18). The poet's references to the owl's location in an 'old stoc' [tree stump (25)] and her 'huing' (1264) may well suggest *Strix aluco*, but, as I argue, the confusion between species is important. ME *huing* is cognate with *hule* (cf. Old French *hüer* 'hoot' and *hüant* 'owl'), and fits well the typical 'hoot' of the tawny owl, but, as Eric Lacey has pointed out with reference to OE *ule*, 'as the Tawny Owl is nocturnal and rarely seen … *ule* could plausibly lend itself to a range of nocturnal birds'; Lacey, 'Birds and Words', p. 91.
[22] Van Dyke, 'Names of the Beasts', 23.

On one level, these details mean that *The Owl and the Nightingale* consciously exposes and ridicules the anthropomorphic meaning-making that goes into the medieval Book of Nature through a process of deflation, consistently drawing our attention to wider species conceptions, to birds that exist 'out there'. Real owls and nightingales are able, at times, to pull away from their textual counterparts. But whilst these tactics persistently remind us that these meanings are arbitrary and inconsistent, they also reveal just how pervasive and influential cultural representations can be, because these two birds are deeply affected by such treatments. The incongruities that result are not simply a clever bit of genre bending; they run deeper to suggest species concepts in which the various real and fictive 'subspecies' are not so easily separated or distinguishable. Much work in the field of animal studies has emphasised this permeability in modern depictions and treatments of the nonhuman. In concepts that attend to the large-scale impact of the human on the earth, the natural world is, paradoxically, the 'product of ... civilisation ... [which] could hardly be contaminated by the very stuff of which it is made'.[23] And yet, when we are dealing with the stuff of nature itself, the material 'phenomena of being-in-the-world', in Paul Matthews's phrase, we cannot deny contamination.[24] Human perceptions of, and responses to, in-the-world species are shaped and affected by anthropomorphism and other forms of representation; whilst one can be 'wild, unpredictable, uncontrolled, aloof', the other is often 'tame, dependent, dependable, neutered, civilized, humanized and sanitized', and the two do not remain apart.[25]

The mockery of the poem achieves some of its most potent effects because the birds (who at times admit that they are just birds)

---

[23] William Cronon, 'The Trouble with Wilderness; or, Getting Back to the Wrong Nature', in *Uncommon Ground: Rethinking the Human Place in Nature*, ed. by William Cronon (New York, NY: W. W. Norton & Co., 1995), pp. 69–90 (p. 69).

[24] Paul Matthews, *The Revelation of Nature* (Aldershot and Burlington, VT: Ashgate Publishing, 2001), p. 6.

[25] Elizabeth Lawrence, 'The Tamed Wild: Symbolic Bears in American Culture', in *Dominant Symbols in Popular Culture*, ed. by Ray Brown, Marshall Fishwick and Kevin Browne (Bowling Green, OH: Bowling Green State University Popular Press, 1990), pp. 140–53 (150). Lawrence's comments here refer to the teddy bear, a good example in modern times of how cultural simulacra can affect human responses to the creature itself.

highlight these incompatibilities themselves, as if recovering and vindicating the intrinsic value of their own species against human re-conceptualisations. What makes the poem particularly sophisticated, however, is the intricate, at times untraceable, manner in which natural and cultural species fold back into one another, so that, in effect at least, there is no difference between the two. Whilst the birds do at times behave in ways 'wittily at odds ... with the way in which we as human beings perceive them', it seems to me that the bigger joke of the poem involves a double-undercutting; the avian self-awareness capable of puncturing inflated literary impressions is then undercut by the birds' own willingness to accept 'culturally falsified version[s]' of themselves or of the other bird, and even to invent these.[26] What occurs in the course of the birds' arguments about their respective uses is that they meet with humanised, distorted incarnations of their kind, ironically presented by the birds to each other, but un-ironically acknowledged by them as true of the first person self, or a broadly defined species. This is particularly evident in the case of the owl because the various species of owl in the bestiary cause a deal of confusion and misunderstanding about owl kind and owl behaviour. Avian diversity comes to the fore once again in these moments, but it does not work in the birds' favour here because cultural treatments merge species difference into a fractured, conflicting and damaging homogeneity to suit a more governing depiction of owlish being. Monica Brzezinski Potkay has suggested that the bird is presented by the poet as singular 'abstract generic': the 'owl is the very type of owl nature'.[27] The birds certainly do seem to accept species singularities, and there are key moments when an 'abstract generic' is central to the effect, but the

---

[26] Alexandra Barratt, 'Avian Self-Fashioning and Self-Doubt in *The Owl and the Nightingale*', in *Individuality and Achievement in Middle English Poetry*, ed. by O. S. Pickering (Cambridge: D. S. Brewer, 1997), pp. 1–18 (1), and Arnold Arluke and Clinton R. Saunders, *Regarding Animals* (Philadelphia, PA: Temple University Press, 1996), p. 17, respectively. Cartlidge perceives a 'lack of self-knowledge', which is certainly evident, but I argue a more nuanced misconception: the birds are, in fact, highly self-knowing, but this self-knowledge is often distorted by the conflicting amalgamation of the natural with various cultural representations; *O&N*, p. xxiv, n. 53.

[27] Potkay, 'Natural Law', 372.

poem, more pertinently, emphasises the disjunctive consequences of birds that are actually multi-species, the meeting of the natural and various cultural forms, all of which together undermine any essential nature. Indeed, with the owl this effect is doubled because she not only acts, or is expected to act, according to overlapping literary species of owl, but literary species that purport to represent a whole range of actual owl species. It is hardly surprising, under these circumstances, that both birds seem defensive or confused about their identities. They speak up for misattributed traits, but they are also fooled by them.

A Fabled Owl

An excellent example of the birds confronting their own cultural types involves the first exemplum to be offered as an attack by the nightingale: a 'cuckoo' owl chick is reared in a falcon's brood (a strange confusion of species in itself: owls are, and were, not known for laying eggs in other birds' nests), but betrays itself by fouling the nest. The falcon chicks inform on the owl, and the mother immediately ejects it to be eaten by scavenging crows and magpies (101–26). The nightingale's purpose here is to exploit a perceived avian trait, fostered in humanised depictions, in use against the owl. To this end, it is telling that she selects a familiar tale as though it illustrates owl kind quite evidently, not only to humans, but to birds as well. Precisely which version of the fable is behind its appearance in *The Owl and the Nightingale* is not known, but a multi-version is particularly effective: the owl comes face to face with one, specifically selected account of a pluralised fable species whose particular trait in question (innate uncleanliness) is recorded in bestiary sources.[28] Of the five extant versions of this fable, four

---

[28] These associations stretch back to the Bible. The *bubo* appears in Leviticus (XI. xvii) and again in Deuteronomy with the *nycticorax* (XIV.xvii); both are listed as unclean birds that should not be eaten. In the bestiaries, the trait is particularly associated with *bubo* (eagle owl): *foeda esse dicitur, quia fimo eius locus in quo habitat commaculatur, quia peccator illos cum quibus habitat exemplo perversi opens dehonestat* 'It is said to be a filthy bird, because the place where it lives is

include an owl chick as the culprit, but Odo of Cheriton's features a buzzard.[29] Marie de France and Nicholas of Bozon's Anglo-Norman texts give *huan*, a general term for owl (cognate with ME *hule*), but the Romulus tradition specifies a particular owl that was identified in some bestiaries – Latin *noctua* (not a species, incidentally, that was traditionally labelled with messy habits). In *The Owl and the Nightingale*, the hawk (common to all non-English versions) becomes a 'faukun' [falcon (101)].

These small distinctions are not insignificant; the nightingale herself, in rendering her example of the fable, makes changes that have much to do with intentional representation and reveal the way that these categories of owls inflict unfairly on the specific individual that appears in the poem. The nightingale unwittingly draws attention to the possibility that what she says about the owl may not be entirely reliable: she tells us that this is a 'bispel / Þoȝ hit ne bo fuliche spel' [fable, though it is not completely fiction (127–8)]. The difficulty lies in this confusing blend, for the nightingale has explicitly veered into fable and exposition, modelling the metaphorical systems we find in popular beast literature, but treats it as a genuine aspect of owlish kind. The apparent authority of this owl species represented in the fables is indicated by the nightingale's directly instructive manner; she draws attention to the 'uorbisne' [proverb (98)], and the sententious feel of the passage is enhanced with a further reference to another related and apparently well-known proverb: 'Dahet habbe þat ilke best / Þat fuleþ his owe nest' [Cursed be that same beast that fouls its own nest (99–100)].[30] The nightingale here speaks with something that may be taken for approved authority, but we should be aware that proverbial truths in this poem are often suspect, particularly when it is the birds themselves that treat them as axiomatic. Literary, homespun, or spuriously attributed to King Alfred, the validation of fables and

---

befouled with its dung, because a sinner by the example of his wayward action dishonors those with whom he lives'; *Medieval Book of Birds*, xlix (pp. 218–19).

[29] The sources for this fable (and the proverb embedded within) are listed in Appendix D in *O&N*, pp. 99–101. For a translation of Odo's fable of the buzzard and the hawk's nest, see Odo of Cheriton, *Fables of Odo*, p. 75.

[30] There are various sources for this proverb; see *O&N*, p. 50.

proverbs' construction of nonhuman moral worth is as questionable as the reputed jurisdiction of Nicholas of Guildford which, significantly, we do not get to hear. All this self-conscious repetition and adaptation of various influences highlights the crafted literariness in this particular avian representation, which both humours the trend for treating animals as illustrative metaphors and also foregrounds the unstable multiplicity of responses potentially involved in glossing nature as a metaphor, each reflecting the interpreter's individual agenda. Thus, the nightingale, in her zeal to vilify the owl, disposes of the friendship between the birds in Marie's fable so that the owl is conveyed as a despicable infiltrator in the falcon's nest.[31] The conclusions alter as well; the sorrowful outcome for the poor owlet does not mirror the endings of either Marie's or Bozon's renditions, in both of which the moral is drawn without any harm to the bird at all. The sense of the apple proverb, too (separated and used to elucidate the proverb, unlike the integrated versions in the sources) which achieves positive meaning in Marie's fable, is distorted to suit the nightingale's purposes.[32] The owl is not *De la pum del duz pumer / Si ele cheit desuz le fust amer* 'a sweet apple from a sweet apple tree that feel beneath a bitter tree'; instead the fruit is pejoratively read as 'þan ungode' [the bad person (129)] and 'þan adel-eye' [the addled egg (133)].[33]

The fable, then, tellingly reveals the extent to which real and fictitious birds are entangled. Some tensions do exist between these natural and cultural versions; the owl subsequently defends herself against these particular character assassinations by detailing the intricacies of her nest-making and insisting that her young do not, in fact, foul the nest:

> Mi nest is holȝ & rum amidde.
> So hit is softest mine bridde,
> Hit is broiden al abute.
> Vrom þe neste uor wiþute,

---

[31] The birds are not depicted as close friends in Bozon's version, but they are amiable and helpful to each other.
[32] Cf. Bozon, where the moral concerns ignoble birth, but the owlet is not reviled. The case is similar in the Lat. translation.
[33] *O&N*, p. 100.

> Þarto hi god to hore node:
> Ac þat þu menest ich hom forbode.³⁴
>
> (643–8)

[My nest is hollow and roomy in the middle. So that it is soft for my chicks, it is broidered all around. From far beyond the nest, that's where they go to do their deeds; but what you are suggesting, I forbid them.]

But she makes no issue about owls laying their eggs in other birds' nests, and both individuals seem entirely comfortable with the fact that birds' behaviours exist to provide moral lessons to humans. When the nightingale completes her exemplum with the apple proverb, it is a tale that 'men segget' [say (127)] about bad types who mix with 'fro monne' [respectable men (131)]. The birds are indoctrinated with the human-imagined lore pertaining to their kind to the extent that they are embroiled in a meta-game of sign-making. In this instance, a nightingale tells a fable in which other (talking) birds feature as a *significacio* for humans. Jill Mann has written convincingly of how the nightingale dismantles the effects of metaphor by misunderstanding how it works; when men talk of proverbial foul nests (99–100) 'they are of course not objecting to the filthy behaviour of birds—why should men care?—but implicitly correlating it with a human situation'.³⁵ In the case of the apple proverb, too, we might well be fooled momentarily into thinking that the nightingale is 'implicitly correlating' the metaphor with a 'human situation', until we remember that she is unaware of any human narrator or audience, and is speaking only to another bird. In the framework of the fable mode, drawing moral significance from animal behaviour, the nightingale plays the human role. But she is not human, of course. What occurs here is another example of literalism undermining textual constructions to expose a gap between real and figurative birds; when birds are involved, surely, the brood, egg and nest can only function literally because the apparatus of the metaphor is left meaningless.

---

³⁴ Cf. *BWP*, vol. 4, 442.
³⁵ Mann, *Aesop to Reynard*, p. 179.

This is not quite so, however. For these disputing birds, the metaphor is not meaningless. The poet's layered treatment of the episode does indeed reveal the fabrication of making birds morally useful, but it also registers the pervasive force of such fictions that take hold so thoroughly that even the birds themselves commit to cultural self-representation, or, more precisely, mis-representation. These birds, that is, participate in a continual and unstable species re-creation, codifying and legitimising their own moral and practical usefulness through a process of extoling and denigrating. The result is that human-attributed species worth, appropriated by the birds themselves, is presumed to be innate to *cunde*, not superimposed: nightingales apparently *do* sing with all sincerity and empathy for beleaguered aristocratic wives (1337–9); owls *do* have remarkable powers of prescience (1189–207); or, in the instance above, a nightingale is blithely convinced that owls serve as meaningful proverbs about moral filth and unchangeable kind. She collapses real and fabled owls so that they become one and the same. The second person 'þu' is not simply one of owl kind, but specifically the very owl whom the nightingale addresses from her hedge, an act which seems all the more mistaken because the narrator at the poem's opening designates 'An hule and one niȝtingale' (4). The owl perpetuates this confusion when she defends herself against the fable later on. Despite refuting the accusation, she identifies herself with the owl in the fable because she employs a possessive pronoun to label the chicks in the nest specifically as 'mine briddes'.[36]

As it turns out, in these convoluted performances of speciation, the faecal details pertaining to the owl have a complicated effect. When the nightingale makes direct reference to the owl's 'unclene' (91) qualities we encroach upon familiar bestiary territory – the owl's proverbial unclean nest, a metaphor for the sinner in the mire of his or her own filth, as apparent in the nightingale's recounted proverb (99–100). But the nightingale also refers to a literal dirtiness, the nest and the owl's brood ('Bi þine neste ich hit mene' [92]) which

---

[36] Other readers have made similar observations about this confusion of pronouns, most recently Van Dyke, 'Names of the Beasts', 25, but see also Potkay, 'Natural Law', 372.

culminates in the 'loþ viste!' [loathsome fart (115)]. A humanised cultural perception has corrupted the nightingale's understanding of natural bodily functions to the extent that literal and metaphorical have become indistinguishable – moral besmirchment is now intrinsic to actual faeces. It turns back unfairly on the nightingale's opponent, so that a habit of bestiary *bubo* (eagle owl), manipulated in the fable form, is aimed against another owl species who is not only wrongly accused of literal uncleanliness but also 'contaminated' by a most unfortunate moral value.[37] The nightingale herself has equally unsanitary habitation (an observation which does, in fact, have some factual merit) and the owl quite understandably draws attention to this (584–96). The nightingale lives closely with excrement and is no more 'clene' (584) than the owl, a comparison that reveals an inconsistency in the Book of Nature. Both birds, as all creatures, can be said to be filthy in one way or another, but one is lumbered with the unfortunate role of being a negative *figura* of the sinner, and the other is attributed more positive associations.

Confused and Confusable Birds

This confusion of metaphor and reality is characteristic of the debate. The birds themselves are embroiled in the game of assimilating and distancing, though often without clarity or logic. What was affective in *The Seafarer*, or intellectually revealing in the Riddles, is ludicrous and comic in *The Owl and the Nightingale*. The fable episode involves a nightingale employing a traditional perception of owls to misrepresent another bird. But the deep influence of cultural avian versions affects the way they choose to represent themselves, too. The inconsistencies evident in the Book of Nature

---

[37] There is no evidence in the bestiaries' known sources (nor, indeed, in modern ornithological accounts) for owls defecating in their nests. The emphasis in the case of the barn owl and tawny owl is, on the contrary, quite the opposite. This popular characteristic of *bubo* in the bestiaries is adapted from the biblical vision of the unclean owl, perpetuated in the *Physiologus*. Although Isidore makes use of a passage from Ovid which does refer to the owl as dirty (*Metamorphoses*, V.549–50), he does not make explicit mention of this himself.

are mirrored in the birds' debating strategies which involve them in explaining their individual worthiness through a curious miscellany of identity traits that not only confirms the weight of cultural types persuasive enough to affect their own sense of species – what exactly is natural for an owl or a nightingale? – but concurrently exposes the arbitrariness of these falsifications. In a sense, these birds are made to suffer from the self-conscious delusion that humans foster to legitimise a paradigmatic separation between themselves and animals: 'Faced with a constitutive and irreparable disparity between themselves and their human self-image, humans assert that animals lack what uniquely afflicts humans'.[38] The owl and the nightingale are faced with something like this disparity between themselves and their self-images.

At times, the birds resort to their natural selves. The best example of this is the owl's insistence that she is fierce because she acts only according to 'hauekes cunne' [hawks' kind (271)]. How can any man 'schende' [blame (274)] a creature for merely possessing 'cliuers scharp & longe' [talons (270)]? The true reason why small birds fear and mob the owl during the day is simple – she is a predator.[39] The owl roosts during the day, not because she sins or rejects Christ, but because she behaves instinctively as a bird, according to her 'riȝte cunde' (276). She only wants to 'sitte stille in min neste' (282) and avoid retaliation, just as the hawk does in the owl's ornithological analogy (303–8). In her first run of insults, the nightingale also mentions the owl's proverbial blindness in daylight.[40] The owl rationalises this piece of nonsense with ease, once again through comparison to another detailed piece of animal behaviour which intensifies the effect of placing the answer, as it were, in the field:

---

[38] Steel, *How To Make a Human*, p. 5.
[39] Pliny mentions that night-birds have crooked talons, and that *noctua* is assisted by *accipiter* (goshawk) in its battles against other birds (*HN*, X.xvi and xix), but the association by the owl might be a further example of distorted self-representation.
[40] No doubt this belief developed quite rationally from owls' nocturnal activity and the fact that they roost with eyes closed as though sensitive to and avoiding light (*BWP*, vol. 4, p. 537), but it was allegorised as an indication of sinfulness, and concerned *noctua* particularly. See *Medieval Book of Beasts*, lxix (p. 178). Cf. *Etym.*, XII.vii.39–42.

> Þu liest: on me hit is isene
> Þat ich habbe gode sene;
> Vor nis non so dim þusternesse
> Þat ich euer iso þe lasse.
> Þu wenest þat ich ne miʒte iso
> Vor ich bi daie noʒt ne flo.
> Þe hare luteþ al dai,
> Ac noþeles iso he mai:
> ʒif hundes urneþ to him ward,
> He gengþ wel suiþe awaiwart,
> & hokeþ paþes sviþe narewe;
>
> (367–77)

[You lie: it is clear in me that I have good sight, for there is no darkness so dim that I ever saw the less. You think that I cannot see because I do not fly by day. The hare hides all day, but nevertheless he can see. If hounds run towards him, he veers very swiftly away and jinks down very narrow paths.]

The problem, however, is that 'riʒte cunde' has become a suspicious and blurry concept. In the examples above, the owl explains away undesirable species values through real-world animal behaviour analogues. But this tactic is employed in a contradictory manner. Cited here in literal terms, the more usual response is to treat these behaviours as moral exempla for humans, as we saw clearly in the fable. The owl's attempts to neutralise her proverbial ferocity and blindness do not entirely escape humanised reasoning, and in this case the owl provides the gloss herself. In the first of these, she inventively explains her diurnal sleeping as a prudent exercise in self-preservation: she hides (384) away in the day (another bestiary anthropomorphism that she overtly accepts) to avoid the unpleasant and uncouth business of hurling profanities (281–8). She then proceeds to moralise her own behaviour through reference to a series of proverbs on the good sense of keeping out of trouble's way which, indirectly, codify her own patience as a model for human practice. In the second, a straightforward rejection of her mythic blindness leads, ultimately, to a further piece of apparently invented – and irrelevant – species characterisation whereby she claims empathy with courageous soldiers because she flies 'bi niʒte in hore banne' [by night in their army (390)]. The processes of exegesis are both endorsed and dismissed by the owl; characteristics attributed by lore that are literalised by quotidian justifications are re-codified as morals or conscious assistance for humans in other ways.

We sense at moments like these that anything goes when it comes to interpreting how nature might best serve a lesson for mankind. The whimsies the birds create for themselves demonstrate the unpredictable character of sign-making; there is nothing intrinsic, only the interpretations that best suit at a given moment or for a specific purpose, and which must be accepted for it to carry meaning. If, as Alan Fletcher notes, 'many subscribed to the serious belief that the "truth" was out there and could be accessed dialectically', the poem implies that systems (the Book of Nature being one) for accessing that 'truth' could be fallible, even though these indeterminate significations are intimately and stubbornly involved in species identity.[41] This valuation is pinpointed nicely when the nightingale acknowledges that there is nothing stable about the way her voice is interpreted or considered useful: 'Þah heo beo god me hine mai misfonge,/ An drahe hine to sothede / An to oþre uuele dede [Though it is good itself, people can misuse it, and turn it to lechery and to other evil deeds (1374–6)]. The nightingale performs this misuse elsewhere, as when she interprets the natural rhythms and pitches of her own song as a lesson on the transience of adulterous love (1459–62), or justifies her constant singing in religious terms (739–42).

Comically, these birds are also shrewd enough and quite ready to pull each other up on fictive personas. When the nightingale's self-assigned ecclesiastic duties (1033–7) and preacherly bombast become too much, the owl retaliates by exposing the ridiculousness of her opponent's claims:

> "Wat!" quaþ ho, "Hartu ihoded
> Oþer þu kursest al unihoded?
> For prestes wike ich wat þu dest:
> Ich not ȝef þu were ȝaure prest!

---

[41] Alan J. Fletcher, 'Middle English Debate Literature', in *Readings in Medieval Texts: Interpreting Old and Middle English Literature*, ed. by David F. Johnson and Elaine Treharne (Oxford: Oxford University Press, 2005), pp. 241–56 (249).

>   Ich not ȝef þu canst masse singe—
>   Inoh þu canst of mansinge!"
>   (1177–82)

["What!" she said, "Are you hooded (like a priest), or do you curse completely unhooded (without authority). For I know what you do is a priest's office: I don't know if you've ever been a priest before! I don't know if you can sing masses – you know enough about excommunications (though)!"]

The birds' evaluations of their own and the other's usefulness demonstrate the legacy of cultural types. At times with complete sincerity, at other moments with an apparent self-reflexive awareness for the indeterminate signification of these types, the owl and the nightingale inconsistently but persuasively interpellate their multi-species, misfit selves.

Bird Like a Man

Species confusion is not restricted to avian kind; the owl and the nightingale's convictions in their own moral statuses at times induce a belief that they somehow exist beyond their own kinds.[42] In responding to their literary counterparts, the owl and the nightingale come to imagine themselves as humans at moments in the poems, transforming themselves into those Christian human types we encounter in the Book of Nature tradition: the sinner, the humbled, the virtuous, the abstainer. They appoint themselves superior positions in the natural hierarchy of beings to sit alongside or above man, who is responsible for the birds' elevated allegorical values in the first place. The narrator at one point draws our attention to their species delusions, reporting that the nightingale 'Mid sworde an mid speres orde, / Ȝif ho mon were, wolde fiȝte' [would fight with sword and a spear's point, if she were a man (1068–9)]. The enclosed subordinate clause with its foregrounded conjunction pokes above

---

[42] For another discussion of taxonomic ambiguity in *O&N*, see Van Dyke's 'Touched by an Owl', in which she employs an ethological perspective to examine how '"human society" overlaps with the nonhuman, both beyond and within its individual members' (324).

the metaphor to remind us of the obvious – that a bird cannot take up weapons. Conditionals, however, are not always obvious to the owl and the nightingale. Just as examples of avian second person singular and plural blur, conflating with the birds' own senses of first person being, so, too, nouns distinguishing mankind become less distinct, expanding at times to function as cross-kind signifiers. Thus, the owl is able to define herself in relation to the variety of 'hauekes cunne', but moments later implicitly associates herself with 'wise monne dome' [wise men's judgements (289)] as though, on a moral plane at least, she abides in man's realm. In a similar manner the nightingale allies herself with a collective who despise the owl's voice:

> Þu miȝt mid þine songe afere
> Alle þat ihereþ þine ibere.
> Þu schrichest & ȝollest to þine fere
> Þat hit is grislich to ihere.
> Hit þincheþ boþe wise & snepe,
> Noȝt þat þu singe, ac þat þu wepe.
> (221–6)

[You might frighten with your song all that hear your outcry. You shriek and you yell so to your mate that it is grisly to hear. It seems to the wise and foolish (to all) not as if you sing, but that you weep.]

'Alle' and 'wise & snepe' here appear to include herself, as a nonhuman species who interprets the owl's singing in human ways. The extensive vocabulary relating to *man* is very evident in the poem, principally because the birds are engaged in debating their usefulness to mankind (which implies that they are perfectly aware of species distinction), but the continual references to *man* make it easy to overlook that both birds often overlap or dissolve boundaries all together. In her defence of the erroneous myth about her species' mucky nests, for instance, the owl defers to an all-kind responsibility for instinctive defecation (628–35), and despite her owlish pride in the species-specific details of her nest, admits that it is modelled on 'manne bure' [man's dwellings (649)]. In this case, the Book of Nature model is turned entirely on its head so that the birds take human behaviour and treat it as a model against which to measure themselves, such is the level of disruption to species discreteness.

A Bird's Worth

The birds' inflated self-perceptions about their species status are perhaps most precisely demonstrated and satirised at the point when they move towards their most vituperative and sustained attacks on who 'mai do gode note' (1624). The nightingale delivers a speech on the rational incapabilities of beasts and man's ultimate supreme intelligence which gives him dominion over all other earthly things:

> An hors is strengur þan a mon,
> Ac for hit non iwit ne kon,
> Hit berþ on rugge grete semes,
> An dra3þ bi suore grete temes;
> An þoleþ boþe 3erd & spure,
> An stont iteid at mulne dure;
> An hit deþ þat mon hit hot;
> An forþan þat hit no wit not,
> Ne mai his strenþe hit ishilde
> Þat hit nabu3þ þe lutle childe.
> Mon deþ mid strengþe & mid witte
> At oþer þing nis non his fitte.
> Þe3 all strengþe at one were,
> Monnes wit 3et more were:
> Vor þe mon mid his crafte
> Ouerkumeþ al orþliche shafte.
>
> (773–88)

[A horse is stronger than a man, but because it cannot know intellect, it bears on its back great loads, and drags by its neck great ploughs; and suffers both yard and spur, and stands tied at the mill door; and it does whatever man asks of it. And all because it has no understanding, nor can its strength shield it from submitting even to the little child. Man acts with (such) strength and with intelligence that no other creature is his match. Even if all strength were one, man's intelligence would still be more: for the human with his wit overcomes all earthly creatures.]

The speech is unequivocally anthropocentric in content and tone, authoritative in its denouncement of all nature to its rightful position below mankind where it shall serve his every command and meet his every use. As a treatise in itself, it chimes a central medieval doctrine on nature – that man's intelligence sets him apart from other creatures, placing them at his disposal – and reads as though from the work of a medieval scholar on the topic of *natura rerum* 'the nature of things', or *de scala naturae* 'the chain of being'.[43] The *auctoritas* with which the nightingale speaks contributes to this effect because it reveals a complex layering of voices which hint at the species confusion that I identify above. The bird speaks with something like human authority; indeed, there is the sense that the words come from beyond her own voice, as though she paraphrases familiar scholastic thought. Here is a bird which not only voices human ideas, but at times seems to place itself outside of the hierarchy to which it refers. The nightingale equates herself ('Also ich do' [789]) with 'Monnes wit', nightingale 'crafte' and human 'crafte' alike, and the owl with the mindless horse who 'non iwit ne kon' and must do what 'man hit hot'. The owl, too, is prone to these inconsistencies: a talking, sententious bird who superciliously derides man for his bestial actions amongst all other beasts in summer which 'eurich upon oþer rideþ' [each climbs upon the other (494)] and yet positions herself with 'hauekes cunne' (271) elsewhere in the poem (an avian family with which she bears resemblances, but is not grouped with in the bestiaries or encyclopaedic texts). These are birds that simultaneously accept and flaunt their *utilitas*, subservient to mankind, whilst ironically speaking from beyond their *cunde*.

Of all the birds' derogations, the one to carry most leverage as an indicator of taxonomic disintegration and in conveying the messy tangle of natural and cultural species is the very first utterance spoken by either bird. To the nightingale, the owl is an 'Vnwiȝt' (33), an insult she repeats soon after (90). The general sense of this word in Middle English – unnatural creature, mutant, evil being, devil – is used by the nightingale as an easy term of abuse to denounce the owl's negative values to mankind; the owl's key uses result from unnatural characteristics and are, therefore, less worthy than the nightingale's own abilities. The construction of this word, however, and its prominent position in a text that deals broadly with

---

[43] For a brief outline of Bernardus Silverstris and the Neoplatonic concept of the Great Chain of Being and its influence on medieval perceptions of the natural world, see Richard Jones, *The Medieval Natural World* (Harlow: Pearson, 2013), pp. 22–3.

taxonomic interests, suggests that its power as invective is greater than we might first suspect. In the nightingale's possession, *vnwi3t* reveals the extent to which these birds confuse identities. Each time the nightingale employs the word, including the comparison she makes to other 'unwi3tis' (218), she objects to owlish characteristics that we would surely call natural: her 'vule lete' [foul expression (35)], that she 'sittest a dai & fli3st a ni3t' (89) and 'singist a ni3t' (219).[44] The owl is in an impossible situation: accused of bird-eating (83), and yet regarded as unnatural because of her more typical diet, what 'Boþ þine cunde & þine ri3te' [is right and natural to you (88)]. She is equated with her food; both are 'fule wi3te' (87). The nightingale's perceptions of owls, confusing numerous species, is so affected by human perceptions that she interprets owl innateness as unnatural, a transference of understanding that the narrator highlights immediately before the nightingale's opening salvo: she 'þu3te wel vul of þare Hule, / For me hi halt lodlich & fule' [thought most scornfully of the owl, for she is considered very loathsome and foul by people (31–2)]. The owl is made to exist paradoxically, her unnatural naturalness defines her as the very essence of owl, but also denies her owl status because what is proper to real owls is undermined, mutated, by the cultural visions upon which the nightingale constructs her attack. Vocative *vnwi3t* enacts this simultaneous owling and un-owling.

The term may go further than this, even. Literally meaning 'un-being', it may also amount to a reversal of meaningful existence entirely.[45] Carolynn Van Dyke has commented that *vnwi3t* does not equate to 'non-existent', but it seems to me that there is a sense in which the word does mean this in the context of the poem.[46] The owl never uses *vnwi3t* against the nightingale, but, as seen in the opening epigraph, she does claim that her opponent is 'no3t to non

---

[44] The nightingale conveniently overlooks the obvious irony that her species, too, sings at night.
[45] The word is derived from OE (*un-* + *wiht*). The very common ME prefix *un-* could mean 'not', or could express reversal or deprivation, all of which are apparent in *O&N*'s use of *unwi3t* to varying degrees. See *MED* s.v. (pref.), *un-*, senses 1–2, and Bosworth-Toller, s.v. (pref.) *un-*, senses 1–3. Cf. also with Bosworth-Toller, s.v. (n.) *nawiht*, sense 1a.
[46] Van Dyke, 'Names of the Beasts', 23.

oþer þinge', and elsewhere 'bute on forworþe þing' (575), a 'useless thing' who should not bother to 'briest þi brod' [bring up your brood (1633)]. The owl uses the nightingale's natural characteristics against her, not to level the accusation of unnaturalness, but in order to work a revised interpretation of the nightingale's features that, in her poetic subspecies, are credited with a romantic and largely positive symbolic power. To the owl though, she is nothing more than a pathetic 'lutel soti clowe' [little sooty ball (577–8)], and the songster's famous voice leads to a flippant perversion of her name: she is re-titled 'galegale' (256), literally 'sing-sing'.[47] To the owl, the nightingale is not unnatural, but what is equally reprehensible, entirely useless, which in the framework of discourses that define according to instructive worth, is to say 'noȝt'. Species confusions have led to a great deal of uncertainty about what even constitutes an owl and a nightingale.

The Death of an Owl

Of all the cultural representations that distort avian identity in the poem, the bestiary form is arguably the most responsible, largely because it depicts various owls, with accompanying negative interpretations. All the owls to be found in the bestiaries (or bestiary sources) are present in the poem, some of which we have encountered already: *noctua* and *nyticorax*, night owls who fly by night and cannot see in the day (221–52); *bubo*, the horned owl who befouls its nest (101–26); and *ulula* and *strix*, screech owls known for their wailing or unpleasant calls (220, 223). The nightingale's knowledge of strigine habits is well informed, though clearly confused, when she launches a multi-species attack upon the owl:

> Vor eurich þing þat schuniet riȝt,
> Hit luueþ þuster & hatiet liȝt;

---

[47] This neologism repeats the second part of the OE name. Cartlidge (*O&N*) conveys the owl's mockery by translating the word more loosely as 'nightingabble'.

& eurich þing þat is lof misdede,
Hit luueþ þuster to his dede.⁴⁸

(229–32)

[For everything that shuns righteousness, it loves darkness and hates light, and everything that is fond of misdeeds, it loves darkness for his actions.]

From all the owl species in one form or another, man shall learn and be warned of the sinner who delights in dark evil and despises the light of Christ. The poet alerts us to the accumulation of diverse sources and their influence by the nightingale's slick mimicking of bestiary discourse, enhanced by King Alfred's proverb (235–6) and her own analogy in which the owl is broadly the 'ungode, / Þat noȝt ne suþ to none gode / & is so ful of vuele wrench' [no-gooder who never seeks good, and is so full of evil tricks (245–6)]. From owls' habits, 'Þarbi men [and birds] segget a uorbisne' [Thereby men speak a proverb (244)].

The nightingale's confusion of different bestiary owls, rolled into one to hold up to her opponent as a mirror image, is not without reasonable cause, however, for even the bestiary entries customarily display some level of uncertainty about which owl is which.⁴⁹ Indeed, the tradition is not even consistent in its treatment of specific species. In contrast to the more usual negative associations relating to *bubo* and *noctua*, there are interpretations of *nycticorax* – whose

---

⁴⁸ This association was commonplace across owl species in the bestiaries. See *Medieval Book of Birds*, where the *bubo* owl *in tenebris peccatorum deditos, et lucem iustitiae fugientes significat* 'signifies those delivered into the darkness of sins, and those fleeing the light of righteousness' (xlix, pp. 218–19). Hugh cites Hrabanus Maurus's *De rerum naturis* (XXII.vi). See also the entry for *De noctua et nycticorace* in *Medieval Book of Beasts*, pp. 178–9.

⁴⁹ Cf. Oxford, Bodleian Library, MS Bodley 764, in which 'the night-owl is the same as the screech-owl [*bubo* in this instance], but the screech-owl is bigger. The night-raven (*nycticorax*) is the same as the night owl'. For the text, see *Bestiary*, p. 147. Cf. Isidore: 'The night owl is not the same as the horned owl, for the horned owl is bigger'; *Etym.*, XII.vii.40. *Ulula* in Bartholomaeus's description is also confused: 'vlula and þe owle is alle one' and 'herby it semeþ þat vlula is a myredromble'; Trevisa, XII.xxxvii (p. 644). Imprecise distinctions of owl species stretch back to antiquity: in *HA*, Aristotle makes a similar identification of owls via comparison between species: 'The eared owl is like an ordinary owl, only that it has feathers about its ears; by some it is called the night-raven' (VIII.xii.597b, p. 934).

status is least stable in the owl family – which envisage the bird in entirely contradictory, Christ-like, terms. This portrait occurs in the *Ancrene Wisse*, but is best known in the *Aviarium*: *Mystice nycticorax Christum significat qui noctis tenebras amat* 'Spiritually interpreted the *nycticorax* signifies the Christ, who loves the darkness of the night'.[50] The *Avarium*, in fact, includes both interpretations of the *nycticorax*, an example of contradictory representation that is mirrored in the owl and the nightingale's 'chopped logic, false analogies, *non sequiturs*' as they inconsistently present themselves and defame each other.[51] As is now well recognised, it is this more unusual interpretation that is likely behind the culminating image in the debate proper.[52] The owl's final defence (which unexpectedly leaps back to an attack made by the nightingale much earlier on in the debate) fastens on the violent death she suffers at the hands of peasants, pelted to death. In the hatred, violent persecution and final hanging of her kind 'in one rodde' [on a stick (1123)], the owl interprets herself allegorically. The standard metaphor that depicts *nycticorax* as a light-shunning Christ is augmented so that it aspires to transubstantiation. The owl mimics the Eucharist by transforming her bodily use to quasi-divine sacrifice: 'ich do heom god / An for heom ich chadde mi blod. / Ich do heom god mid mine deaþe' [I do them good and I shed my blood for them. I do them good by my death (1615–17)]. The moment is critical, not because it brings a triumph, but because it features as the climax of avian misrepresentation. In this lofty manoeuvre, the owl falls in with a falsified hybrid

---

[50] *Medieval Book of Birds*, xxxix (pp. 172–3). Cf. *Ancrene Wisse*, III.xiii–xiv. *Nycticorax*'s status (night-raven, night-heron) has a legacy of difficult translation and identification. In Aristotle, Isidore and the bestiaries it is sometimes grouped with owls because it shares their nocturnal habits, and sometimes assigned owl status itself. Cassiodorus, in his interpretation of Psalm 101:7, remarks that '*Nycticorax* in Greek means "night-raven" (*noctis corvus*), which some have said is the horned owl (*bubo*), others the little owl (*noctua*); others that in size and colour it is more like the raven (*corvus*)'; Cassiodorus, *Expositio Psalmorum LXXI–CL*, ed. by M. Adriaen, Corpus Christianorum: series Latina, 98 (Turnhout: Brepols, 1953–), p. 903.

[51] Cartlidge, *O&N*, p. xxv (italics original).

[52] Mortimer J. Donovan was the first to suggest the relevance of positive readings of the *nycticorax* to this moment in the poem. See Mortimer J. Donovan, 'The Owl as Religious Altruist in *The Owl and the Nightingale*', *Medieval Studies*, 18 (1956), 207–14 (pp. 209 and 211).

self, accepting that 'manne loþ' (1607) her – 'hit beo soþ' [it is true (1615)] – but then re-modelling herself in the most bold example of self-identification in the whole poem by playing the human exegete upon herself. Once again, singular and plural categories are collapsed so that the owl manages to talk about herself as an absurd, eternally resurrecting specimen, a present, talking 'Ich' who talks of her own deaths. It is hard under these circumstances not to laugh at the owl, even in her pitiable condition, and, moreover, not to direct our laughter at the arbitrary, self-serving literary premises which have led an owl to re-orientate her identity to this extent.

Impressive owlish martyrdom aside, even if the primary scholastic view was to 'look upon animals first and foremost as objects … designed to remind human beings of the spiritual reality lying beyond the material world', it may be the material world, the bodily owl, that most strikes us in the end.[53] The palpability of the 'fule codde' [rotten corpse (1124)] is conspicuous. Rather like excremental habits, the grisly and pitiful image of the mangled owl returns us to an anatomical creature which jars with pompous allegorical identifications. The absurdity of a beaten, mangy owl sacrificing itself for the good of mankind invalidates any figurative impact. This bodily owl, though, is never entirely unattended; it is always invested with some degree of humanised purpose. Convinced to the end that a bird's role is to 'do gode note', the owl ends with two matter-of-fact examples of the domestic, practical uses for her imagined demise: a scarecrow (strung up like vermin), and a concluding image that depicts her in a macabre version of mobbing:

> Me mai upone smale sticke
> Me sette a wude ine þe þicke
> An swa mai mon tolli him to
> Lutle brides & iuo;
> An swa me mai mid me biʒete
> Wel gode brede to his mete.
>
> (1625–30)

---

[53] David Salter refers here specifically to Saint Francis and his followers; David Salter, *Holy and Noble Beasts: Encounters with Animals in Medieval Literature* (Cambridge: D. S. Brewer, 2001), p. 51.

[People can set me upon small sticks in the thickest part of the wood, and so may man lure little birds towards him and catch them. And so can men with me get very good meat for their food.]

Before now, the nightingale has anticipated the owl's self-portrait in equally gruesome terms:

> Nis noþer noȝt, þi life ne þi blod,
> Ac þu art shueles suþe god,
> Þar nowe sedes boþ isowe.
> Pinnuc, golfinc, rok, ne crowe,
> Ne dar þar nuere cumen ihende,
> Ȝif þi buc hongeþ at þan ende.
>
> (1127–32)

[Neither your life nor your blood are worth anything, except that you are a very good scarecrow where seeds now are sown. The dunnock, goldfinch, rook, nor the crow never dare come near there if your carcass hangs at the boundary.]

The owl's final attempts to raise herself beyond the completely useless (by a form of individual and species suicide, it seems) echo both aspects of the familiar belief, that, in Thomas of Chobham's words, the 'Lord created different creatures with different natures not only for the sustenance of men, but for their instruction.'[54] The debate proper, then, closes with a reminder of the two principal ways in which nature was regarded as useful in medieval European thought. The owl satisfies herself by assisting man's 'sustenance', reminding us that for most (the 'heme' [peasants (1115)] who by necessity 'had to work with and not against nature, to understand its rhythms and cycles') this was a fundamental way in which the natural world served a purpose.[55]

A vivid sense of rusticity is evident throughout the poem, which well emphasises the relevance of vernacular, not institutional, schemes of valuation.[56] In the wider passages from which the

---

[54] Thomas of Chobham, *Summa de arte praedicandi*, trans. by D. L. Avray, in his *The Preaching of the Friars: Sermons Diffused from Paris before 1300* (Oxford: Clarendon Press, 1985), chapter 7, pp. 232–3.
[55] Jones, *Medieval Natural World*, p. 111.
[56] Cartlidge suggests that at least part of the birds' evidence is 'drawn from the observable facts of nature ... widely current traditions, stories and sayings'.

nightingale and the owl's words above are taken, the agricultural location is significant to the overall impression: the owl is suspended above 'manne corn' [man's corn (1126)], where her body participates in arable routines, 'Þar tron shulle a ȝere blowe / An ȝunge sedes spring & growe' [Wherever trees shall blossom each year and young seeds spring and grow (1133–4)], which wild 'dore' [animals (1126)] and 'fuȝel' [birds (1135)] would attempt to eat were it not for the owl's feared presence. There are the vermin '[mag]pie an crowe' (1613) scavenging the farmland worked by the 'chorles' [churls (509)]; the 'uox kan crope bi þe heie' [fox (who) knows how to slink by the hedge (819)]; the 'hen a snowe' (413); and the 'hei-sugge, / Þat fliȝþ bi grunde among þe stubbe' [hedge-sparrow that flits on the ground amongst the stubble (505–6)]. This real-world context establishes a distinctive background in which birds exist as noticeable elements of everyday life for many, and in which their existences perform genuine and important functions to mankind. The owl and the nightingale, that is, can exist as natural species beyond their literary representations, even if the natural bird, as in the case of the owl, is still conceived in utilitarian terms.

Such 'homely details of everyday life ... designed to give the poem the widest possible appeal' go much further, though.[57] Crucially, the practical uses of birds are not necessarily distinguished from cultural conceptualisations of species in this poem. Just as we have seen the natural and cultural intertwine in complex patterns that determine the birds' identities, so, too, metaphorical applications of the nonhuman, which define according to moral, instructive purposes (both good and bad), can be seen to impinge upon and inform wider understandings of species and how they are treated in the real world. There is, I contend, an uncomfortable ethical dimension to defining and 'using' species in *The Owl and the Nightingale*, which can go unrecognised beneath the generally comic register and pomposity of two birds arguing their worth in a mock judicial debate.

The birds might even be seen, he says, as 'literary representations of country people living outside the circles of literacy and education'; *O&N*, p. xxxix.
[57] Ibid., p. xxvi.

As the most obvious victim of species misrepresentation, the owl continues to be my central focus here, but the nightingale is by no means unaffected. As she recognises herself, a nightingale's voice, in Jill Mann's words, can be 'created afresh in the responses of each human hearer'.[58] Despite the centuries of accumulated poetic significance which attribute largely positive symbolism, it can, if desired, be put to 'oþer uuele dede' [another deceitful deed (1376)]: a woman 'mai do bi mine songe, / Hwaþer heo wule wel þe wronge' [can signify by my song, whether she intends good or wrong (1361–2)]. There is the potential, of course, for this to occur in any act of arbitrary signifying, however fixed or innate the signified might seem. The bestiary owls demonstrate well how negative attributions can, in a twist of interpretation, be put to fully contrary moral use. The debate stages these ethical quandaries in the second half when the owl, ingeniously, turns the nightingale's song to pejorative effect, loading her opponent with moral culpability for the sexual weaknesses of noble women. Part of the poem's joke, of course, is that the birds happily accept responsibility when it suits them, but at other times seem fully aware that they are maligned, that their species are defined according to unwarranted associations that may prove harmful: 'Schal ich þaruore beon ibunde?' 'Hwitistu me hore misdede?' [Shall I therefore be blamed? Do you blame me for their misdeeds? (1354, 1356)]. In the lai the owl likely adapts from Marie de France's *Laüstic* – another example in which a present individual is lumbered with the reputation of a transhistorical species – the nightingale does, in fact, suffer violent consequences as the result of her unfortunate associations with a courtly couple. As in the example of the fable aimed against the owl, the owl engages a like-for-like strategy and manipulates her source for 'uuele dede'.[59] Marie's account imputes no motive or character to the nightingale. We understand that the vindictive husband has

---

[58] Mann, *Aesop to Reynard*, p. 154.
[59] The notion of variation in species perceptions is hinted at the beginning of *Laüstic* when Marie introduces us to the different names by which readers might know the bird in different languages: 'Laüstic', 'russignol' and 'nihtegale' (3–6); *The Lais of Marie de France*, trans. by Glynn S. Burgess and Keith Busby, 2nd edn (London: Penguin, 1999), p. 156.

erred in taking vengeance on a bird that cannot be held responsible for the fact that it is made to function as a poetic symbol by human listeners. In *The Owl and the Nightingale*, the bird is made the central character, with full, deceitful agency. She 'woldest lere / Þe lefdi to an uuel luue' [would incite the lady to an immoral love (1050–1)], and is punished by death, this time by equine quartering. This last example is too ludicrous to be taken seriously (given the size of the bird), but in both cases the nightingale comes to a violent end because of moral convictions that hang on culturally-prescribed values.

The nightingale's grisly death, as far as we know, remains in the bounds of fiction; for the owl, however, death in the poem can reflect real-world implications for species conceptions, and responses to these conceptions. We are aware that the owl has not actually died, but the manner in which owl deaths are related in the poem is grimly disturbing (unlike the preposterous demise of the lai nightingale). The owl has, after all, met a vicious end because of superstitions associated with her kind. The metaphorical bird does not stay harmlessly in its abstract category, but infects the real bird, dangerously instructing the ways humans act upon nature. The persistently present folkloric customs and beliefs proceed along similar lines to those of institutional traditions, overlapping and sharing in a general hatred which burdens owls' appearances, voices and habits with pernicious meanings. They are the target of witchcraft (1301–4), despised as foretellers of doom (1257–8), immediately 'lodlich and fule' (32) from the beginning of the poem: 'eauereuch chil þe cleopeþ "fule" / An euereuch man "a wrecche hule"' [every child calls you 'foul', and every man a 'wretched owl' (1315–16)].[60] This defamation, moreover, manifests itself in

---

[60] See also lines 1111–44, 1150–1, 1165–72, 1607–34, 1641–8. Hume claims that hanging a dead owl's corpse as a scarecrow (1127–36) 'reflects actual farm practices', but fails to provide support for this; Hume, *Owl and Nightingale*, p. 21. Edward A. Armstrong writes, 'The custom of nailing owls to barn doors or walls, which has only recently been abandoned in England, was too widespread to have arisen through literary influence. Ignorant countryfolk thus disposing of owls explained that they were merely getting rid of vermin, but their actions were really determined by ancient, probably prehistoric, precedent'; Edward A. Armstrong, *The Folklore of Birds: An Enquiry into the Origin*

violent, sustained persecution. As this chapter's second epigraphy confirms, the owl's cultural legacy of doom and gloom directly prompts attacks ('Heruore hit is' [1165]). The nightingale reports elsewhere on this lynching with distinct familiarity:

> Vor children, gromes, heme & hine,
> Hi þencheþ alle of þire pine.
> 3if hi muʒe iso þe sitte,
> Stones hi doþ in hore slitte
> An þe tortorued & toheneþ,
> An þine fule bon tosheneþ.
>
> (1115–20)

[For this, children, servants, peasants and farm-hands all intend your demise (pain). If they happen to see you sitting, they put stones in their pockets, and they pelt you and stone you, and smash your horrible bones to pieces.]

These practices are legitimised in a further sense, through the frequent references to mobbing owls by small birds.[61] The premise of the poem's debate, in fact, can be said to exist upon this common

---

and *Distribution of some Magico-Religious Traditions* (London: Collins, 1958), p. 118. Mark Cocker also refers to the 'superstitious persecution that the barn owl suffered until the late 1950s: birds nailed spread-eagle to barn doors to ward off storms'; Cocker, *Birds Britannica*, pp. 283. For discussion of negative cultural connotations in ibid., see especially pp. 281–5. For barn owl, see pp. 285–6, and tawny owl, pp. 289–91. The *O&N* bird is killed for practical use, rather than ritual, but these deaths still seem to be prompted by superstitious beliefs. The connection between witchcraft and owls, like much lore surrounding these birds, has little substantial evidence from the medieval period, but seems to have persisted as part of an ancient tradition stretching back to classical times, and forward to the early modern period. In *Macbeth*, for example, the owl's wing is an associative ingredient in the witches' cauldron brew (IV.i.17). Perhaps more telling, for pre-modern associations, is that witches could bear the Lat. names of owls (*strix, scobax* [from Greek *scops* – the scops owl]); see Jeffrey Burton Russell, *Witchcraft in the Middle Ages* (Ithaca, NY and London: Cornell University Press, 1972), p. 15. For general observations about the 'evil owl' in culture, see Desmond Morris, *Owl* (London: Reaktion Books, 2009), pp. 36–45.

[61] Mobbing is referred to frequently in the poem, alongside human violence: see lines 63–70, 277–80, 1139–44, 1625–8, 1658–64. For a typical bestiary-type exegesis of this behaviour, see *bubo* in *Medieval Book of Birds*, chapter xlix (p. 219). The image of small birds mobbing an owl appears in numerous manuscripts and on the carvings of misericords. For manuscript images depicting the apparently common practice of exploiting owl-mobbing to trap small birds through staking an owl, dead or alive, as a decoy, see Brunsdon Yapp, *Birds*

piece of avian behaviour; it is, after all, what has apparently drawn the narrator's attention to the birds in the first place. Mobbing is made explicit at the end when the nightingale summons the passerine troops (1654–64) to signal her self-granted defeat. Avian mobbing, however, is interpreted in the poem in the way it commonly is in bestiary texts and illuminations. It functions as a vindication of human hatred towards owls by locating this response as a 'natural' phenomenon in the nonhuman environment. The metaphor which reads bird behaviour as a moral indication for human action is turned back on itself to project human reasoning onto the birds so that all species join in endorsed victimisation:

> Vorþi þu art loþ al fuel kunne,
> & alle ho þe driueþ honne,
> & þe bischricheþ & bigredet,
> & wel narewe þe biledet;
> & ek forþe þe sulue mose
> Hire þonkes wolde þe totose!
>
> (65–70)

[For this you are loathed by all bird-kind, and they all drive you away, and screech at and protest against you, and very closely mob you; and also for this reason the titmouse would willingly tear you to pieces!]

In the events described above, birds (or some birds, at least) are included in the broad and entrenched cultural vision that legitimises and employs violence against the nonhuman as a system for prioritising and justifying human worth. Defining nonhuman species according to practical or instructive purposes contributes to this violence in insidious ways. As we have seen, confusion and misrepresentation of avian identities results in abusive species concepts, perversely staged as comedy in *The Owl and the Nightingale* by birds that exact these abuses upon each other. But these abuses are also realised in extra-literary contexts with greater unease through the physical violence suffered by the birds at the hands of humans. As the birds discover, configuring an homogenous species

---

in Medieval Manuscripts (London: British Library, 1981), p. 37. For mobbing behaviour, see also *BWP*, vol. 4, p. 443.

from cultural types that is perpetuated and confirmed by proverbial truth risks injurious results; if one believes, that is, 'veirs est dis ten engleis: *Stroke oul and schrape oule and evere is oule oule*' ('It's true what the English say: *Stroke an owl or scrape an owl but always an owl's an owl*')[62] In all its forms, the consequences of species-making in this poem register with the more overt forms of violence that Karl Steel identifies as central to medieval human attitudes towards the nonhuman; it shows a 'recognition of the constructedness of the categories of human and animal' and a 'consideration of the categories' real effects'.[63] It is well known that there were indeed social realities to these categories; most famously, of course, in the late medieval animal legal trials, in which creatures could be held morally culpable and sentenced for crimes ranging from bestiality to crop destruction, or even homicide.[64] Birds do not seem to have suffered in the way that domesticated mammals did, but literary accounts of 'hauekes cunne' may reflect a more widespread vernacular characterisation of these species as vermin. In the Anglo-Norman *Petit Plet*, for instance, a proverb that closely matches the apple proverb in *The Owl and the Nightingale* depicts the moral turpitude of despicable kites and buzzards ('you'll never make a good hawk out of a kite or a buzzard' [837–8]), and Alexander Neckam recounts a tail of a goshawk hanged for treason because it killed an eagle in self-defence, its social better in human terms.[65]

Pejorative impacts on the nonhuman could also turn on the human, though, not as a positive affirmation of supremacy, but as a further, elite manoeuvre that exploits the instability of species conceptions and hierarchies to re-conceive humans in nonhuman

[62] From Nicholas Bozon's *Contes*. Text cited in full in *O&N*, p. 100.
[63] Steel, *How To Make a Human*, p. 13. Steel's text deals extensively with these legitimised forms of violence upon the nonhuman. See especially, pp. 61–6.
[64] These trials were a European phenomenon and have been much mythologised. However, as Anila Srivastava states, although some are likely to be 'licentious', it is 'far less likely that all of the accounts … are wholly invented'; Anila Srivastava, '"Mean, Dangerous and Uncontrollable Beasts": Medieval Animal Trials', *Mosaic*, 40:1 (2007), 127–43 (p. 130).
[65] For the *Petit Plet*, see *Le Petit Plet*, ed. by Brian S. Merrilees, Anglo-Norman Texts, 20 (Oxford: Oxford University Press, 1970). For the goshawk anecdote, see Neckam, *De naturis rerum*, p. xxiv (summarised by Wright in the preface, p. xxi).

terms. Or, more precisely, *some* humans. In *Man and the Natural World*, Keith Thomas argues, with reference to the early-modern centuries, that distinctions between human and nonhuman had a palpable effect upon certain categories of humanity: 'Most beast-like of all were those on the margins of human society ... [and] Once perceived as beasts, people were liable to be treated accordingly'.[66] Some human social groups were (or are) genuinely treated according to their attributed overlapping proximity to irrational beasts, the victims of negative species assimilation. As Karl Steel has demonstrated, though, such habits were already deeply entrenched in medieval culture. I discuss above how the poem's multiple and confusable avian species produce two birds who are both highly conscious of their constructed and disparate identities, exploiting and configuring owl- and nightingale-kind as it suits, and thoroughly deluded, because they often speak from beyond their species, locating themselves alongside, or even above, mankind. These moments are layered with comic irony, such as when the owl disdains to use 'schitworde' [shit-words] as 'herdes doþ' [shepherds do (286)], and surely encourage us to perceive the birds as 'pompous, unprincipled, egotistical'.[67] But in light of the more serious implications that I have suggested adhere to the ethics of species representations in the poem, human-aspiring birds can also reveal the troublesome ambiguities of species boundaries, and how these can be misused, not only against the birds themselves (saddled with human moral or immoral attributes) but also against certain deprived human social groups whose worth is judged akin to animality.

This is apparent when the nightingale sermonises on the *scala naturae*, particularly because we might sense that this bird has somehow adopted that 'crafte' (787) by which mankind 'Ouerkume al orþliche shafte' [overcomes all earthly creatures (788)] to speak condescendingly elsewhere about certain humans that do not apparently qualify for full species status; 'those "primitive" peoples who lacked the same attributes as those in which the animals

---

[66] Thomas, *Man and the Natural World*, pp. 41–50.
[67] Cartlidge, *O&N*, p. xxiv.

were deficient'.[68] Northern British peoples are deemed incorrigible by the nightingale in another extended harangue that reflects contemporary attitudes towards heathen populations:

> Þar lond is grislich & unuele
> Þe men boþ wilde & unisele.
> Hi nabbeþ noþer griþ ne sibbe.
> Hi ne recceþ hu hi libbe.
> Hi eteþ fihs an flehs unsode
> Suich wulues hit hadde tobrode.
> Hi drinkeþ milc & wei þarto.
> Hi nuteþ ells wat hi do.
> Hi nabbeþ noþer win ne bor,
> Ac libbeþ also wild dor.
> Hi goþ bitiȝt mid ruȝe uelle,
> Riȝt suich hi comen ut of helle.
> Þeȝ eni god man to hom come—
> So wile dude sum from Rome—
> For hom to lere gode þewes
> An for to leten hore unþewes,
> He mite bet sitte stille,
> For al his wile he sholde spille.
> He mitȝe bet teche ane bore
> To weȝe boþe sheld & spere,
> Þan me þat wilde folc ibringe
> Þat hi me wolde ihere singe.[69]
>
> (1003–24)

[Wherever the land is grisly and unpleasant, the people are wild and unfortunate. They have neither peace nor friendship. They do not care how they live. They eat fish and raw flesh, as if wolves had torn

---

[68] Thomas, *Man and the Natural World*, p. 42.
[69] Cf. Gerald of Wales's words on the Irish: *gens silvestris, gens inhospita; gens ex bestiis solum et bestialiter vivens; gens a primo pastoralis vitæ vivendi modo non recedens* 'a wild and inhospitable people; a people living only on animals and living like animals; a people who have not developed from living a primitive, pastoral way of life'; *Topographia hibernica et expugnatio hibernica*, in *Giraldi Cambrensis opera*, Rolls Series, 8 vols, ed. by James F. Dimock (London, 1861–91), vol. 5, III.x (p. 151). Translation from *O&N*, p. 73. For a detailed study of the nonhuman human in this context, see Jeffrey Jerome Cohen, *Hybridity, Identity and Monstrosity in Medieval Britain: On Difficult Middles* (New York, NY: Palgrave Macmillan, 2006).

it apart. They drink milk and also the whey. They don't know what else they do. They have neither wine nor beer, and live like wild animals. They go about clothed with rough pelts, just as if they had come out of hell. Even if any good man came to them – as someone from Rome once did – to teach them good habits and relinquish their vices, he might better have sat still, for he would waste all his time. He might more easily teach a bear to use both shield and spear than could anyone bring those wild folk to want to hear me sing.]

The image of teaching a bear to use a shield and spear anticipates the narrator's reminder to us soon after this passage that the nightingale herself is unable to use a sword and spear, because she is not a man (1068–9), although here she despises primitive peoples as less worthy than animals and, thus, not deserving of her edifying song. The nightingale's scorn comically exploits oblivious misconceptions again – a supercilious bird deprecating northern pagans highlights that it is human perceptions of the nonhuman in the first place that have paradoxically led to categories of human defined as nonhuman, but here this understanding is treated as so self-evident that it is natural for a nightingale to expound these values, too. Focusing on the human in these instances does not establish an anthropocentric agenda, but, rather, an awareness of the far-reaching effects of suspect species representations which manifest in undesirable outcomes for parties on either side of the metaphorical equation.

The nightingale herself experiences these abuses in the poem, but it is the owl that can truly be said to suffer such consequences. In fact, the persecutions that she encounters as the result of superstitions may also have called to mind for some readers one particular late medieval example of a mutually harmful nonhuman-human association that had a shocking and prevalent social reality. The Jews were one group that were most certainly on the margins in late medieval England, and the owl was a well-known nonhuman representative.[70] In a city like Norwich, anti-Semitic riots

---

[70] Traditionally assigned to *nycticorax* in the *Physiologus*, thirteenth-century bestiaries applied the analogy to other owls, so that texts and illuminations confuse and merge species definitions with apparent ease. For *nycticorax* in the *Physiologus*, see *Physiologus: A Medieval Book of Nature Lore*, trans. by Michael J. Curley

and persecutions escalated in the thirteenth century, and Mariko Miyazaki proposes a correlation between these tumults and the relatively high numbers of owl portraits in the city's cathedral: 'The identification of the owl with the Jews was probably stronger in places with a long history of the Christian-Jewish hostility, like Norwich, where the imagery of the owl mobbed by small birds had become a symbol of the righteous indignation of Christians against the wickedness of the Jews.'[71] Miyazaki's study of Norwich Cathedral's three misericord and three roof boss carvings of owls recommends an 'anti-Jewish visual commentary' which records popular sentiments even in the centuries after the particularly tense relations that existed in the city in the twelfth and thirteenth centuries.[72] There is no evidence that owls themselves suffered as a consequence of this specific association, but if the images Miyazaki considers were in fact linked in cultural perceptions to a prevalent fear of or disdain for Jews, we might speculate that this unfavourable pairing could well have increased traditional beliefs in the owl's reputed 'lodlich and fule' character.

(Chicago, IL and London: University of Chicago Press, 2009), pp. 10–12. For thirteenth-century bestiary examples of the Jewish owl, see *nycticorax* in Guillaume le Clerc's *Bestiaire*, the Aberdeen bestiary (MS 24), and Oxford, Bodleian Library, MS Bodley 764. In Bodley 764, *ulula* is connected to the Jew (indirectly through reference to the destruction of Babylon, for which cf. *nycticorax* in Oxford, Bodleian Library, MS Bodley 602). In British Library, MS Harley 4751, the Jew-*nycticorax* pairing is given to *noctua* (as it is in the Aberdeen bestiary as well) and the illustration for *bubo* seems clearly designed to recall the Jew stereotype with its humanoid hooked nose (cf. the *bubo* illustration in the Wesminster Abbey bestiary). Although *bubo* was not explicitly correlated with the Jew, illustrations often exploited the 'horned' ears of this species to recall the supposed diabolism of the Jews. The traditional references to its uncleanliness and its mobbing by small birds must also have encouraged the transfer of characteristics. *Bubo* in Bodley 764 is also depicted being mobbed by small birds. The Aberdeen bestiary illustration of *bubo* appears to blend owl physiology – the white and sandy plumage suggests a barn owl, but the bird is also given horns. For an edition of Bodley 764, see *Bestiary*.

[71] Mariko Miyazaki, 'Misericord Owls and Medieval Anti-Semitism', in *Mark of the Beast*, pp. 23–50 (33).

[72] The roof boss and misericord carvings were not produced until the fourteenth and fifteenth centuries, but Miyazaki perceives them as a response to the legacy of anti-Semitism in a city where such feelings 'died particularly hard'; ibid.

Considering how comprehensively *The Owl and the Nightingale* surveys medieval owlish being in its numerous cultural guises, there is a curious absence of Jewish signification in the poem. It is not one of the insults or accusations the nightingale flings at the owl, despite the conspicuous and frequent references to both avian and human mobbing, and the emphasis on the owl's filthiness. Perhaps the contemporary association attracted too much opprobrium to suit the poem's more general levity, but, as Debra Higgs Strickland has remarked of muddled bestiary image owls, the association was so consistent it may be that readers would have recognised the anti-Jewish theme in *The Owl and the Nightingale*'s portrait nonetheless, just as the familiar mobbing depiction in illuminations 'may have … functioned as an allegorical reference to actual physical assaults on Jews', whether this outcome was intended or not.[73] To be sure, the strange conflation of species in owl bestiary entries that deal specifically with the Jewish allegory is a recognisable misrepresentation, too, in the poem. In literary depictions and in reality, these are entwined victims of blurred metaphorical similarity and real difference.

An explicit Jewish connection may be absent from the poem, but the mechanisms of metaphorical association that attend and may have contributed to actual violence in this specific example are reflected in the attacks that do occur in the poem for more general reasons. The broad extension of particular species' traits to others meant that owls generally in the late Middle Ages could be indiscriminately hated for their negative instructive worth, and a ubiquitous, homogenising imagery, borne out by a genuine superstitious distrust of nocturnal birds, could be used to promulgate an aversion to human sin and sinners. In *The Owl and the Nightingale*, most prominently, it is birds that suffer. Particular social events or narratives that engage definitions of birds' worth as reminders of morally reprehensible types can afflict certain human victims, but

---

[73] Debra Higgs Strickland, 'The Jews, Leviticus, and the Unclean', in *Beyond the Yellow Badge: Anti-Judaism and Antisemitism in Medieval and Early Modern Visual Culture*, ed. by Mitchell B. Merback (Leiden: Brill, 2007), pp. 203–32 (224). Owls are discussed on pp. 223–4.

the connection also vilifies the birds themselves, with potentially violent ramifications. Cultural depictions of 'fule and lodliche' owls were bound up with some alarming social realities (as was the nonhuman more broadly) but *The Owl and the Nightingale* also shows us how corrupted species conceptions also produce and affect avian realities.

Plate 4 **Turtle dove** *Streptopelia turtur*
© Brian Lawrence
'I am a seed-foul, oon the unworthieste'
(*The Parliament of Fowls*, 512)

4
'Kek Kek':
Translating Birds in
The Parliament Of Fowls

> The biosemiotic view that there exist signs, *per se*, in animal communication, or in any other communication among living systems, poses the question about the translatability of these signs, both by humans and by other organisms.
>
> Kalevi Kull and Peeter Torop[1]

THERE IS NO EVIDENCE that Chaucer ever came across *The Owl and the Nightingale*, but given the remarkable similarities between this squabbling pair and the dissenting avian gang in his own bird-debate, you might think he had. Once again birds find themselves fruitful subjects for anthropomorphic conversion and so, too, do their habits resist these procedures, so that birds view themselves in both natural and cultural terms. Chaucer, however, adds a further dimension to the vociferous voices in *The Parliament of Fowls*: there is a moment when three of his talking birds suddenly drop human speech and revert to 'birdspeak', forcefully reversing anthropomorphic tactics and foregrounding the issue of birds' voices. As we have seen in previous chapters, avian vocality presents a particularly compelling and troublesome example of birds' strange familiarity. At once alike and unlike the human voice, it suggests and defies categories equally. In *The Parliament*, the din of birds from 'every kynde that men thynke may' (310) is transformed into human voices by the turn of allegory, but these birds are capable of re-translating themselves.

---

[1] Kalevi Kull and Peeter Torop, 'Biotranslation: Translation Between *Umwelten*', in *Translation Translation*, ed. by Susan Petrilli (Amsterdam: Rodopi, 2003), pp. 313–28 (315).

Lévi-Strauss's remarks on birdsong reminded us in my introduction that birds' apparent 'articulated language' (*langue articulé*) is central to parallels that humans across cultures often seem to have drawn between themselves and birds.[2] His choice of words, though, echoes a particularly medieval debate on the nature of the articulate, rational voice, in which birds were prominent precisely because their human-sounding vocalisations foregrounded and reified a central worry for medieval theologians: the distinction between rational man (*animal rationale*) and irrational beast (*animal irrationale*). Paradoxically, birds' voices were ubiquitously compared to or depicted as human speech in various discourses because they display vocal abilities, even whilst being rigorously denied this likeness. Avian vocality, that is, could plausibly be considered discrete and articulate, sophisticated and adaptable, but such possibilities were hard to reconcile with mainstream doctrines that sought to secure the identity of the rational, vocalising human. Read within this familiar medieval context, *The Parliament* can be seen to treat birds' voices in particularly imaginative ways; it not only moves beyond typically superficial comparisons with human articulated language, but, I suggest, imagines the potential for translatability between species.[3] The interspecies communications and translative acts in this poem make birds' utterances 'richly problematic' in the way that Peter W. Travis argues for in his discussion of Thomas's reverberating fart in the *Summoner's Tale*. The 'cultural proscription' that claims 'certain sounds are insignificant noises' is problematised to produce voices that might be read not as unreasonable nonsense, but as legitimate 'counter-harmonics' which, moreover, have significant impact upon our

[2] Lévi-Strauss, *Savage Mind*, p. 204, and *Pensée sauvage*, p. 270.
[3] This poem has received surprisingly little attention in this regard, perhaps because it does not involve explicit human-nonhuman discourse or bird mimicry. For a study that does approach *The Parliament* with an eye for birds' voices, see Emma Gorst, 'Interspecies Mimicry: Birdsong in Chaucer's "Manciple's Tale" and *The Parlement of Fowles*', *New Medieval Literatures*, 12 (2010), 147–54. Gorst says very little on *The Parliament*, however, focusing mostly on the *MancT*. See also Wendy Matlock, 'Talking Animals, Debating Beasts', in *Rethinking Chaucerian Beasts*, ed. by Carolynn Van Dyke (New York, NY: Palgrave Macmillan, 2012), pp. 217–32, in which she recognizes that 'animals talk ... mooting the question of whether animals have reason' (p. 221).

understanding of the dizzyingly complex allegory.[4] The birds and their voices are responsible for a great deal of complication in our attempts to read the poem figuratively, but they also might be key to understanding how we can approach these complications. If *The Parliament*'s allegory, as so many readers have discovered, refuses to settle, there is some reflection of this in Chaucer's vociferous assembly of squabbling birds who do not conform to wholesale figuration, whose vocal and symbolic meanings slip in and out of coherency.

This chapter gives full attention to birds' voices per se through a detailed analysis of the well-known, intrusive bird calls line (499) to argue how Chaucer engages with issues of translation, an act which invests the birds' voices with meaning that is traditionally denied to them in the contexts of both allegory and scholastics. The moment occurs when the lower birds – the seed-eaters and water fowl – erupt into outcry at the lengthy and tedious protestations of love from the eagles which last from 'morwe ... / Tyl dounward went the sonne' (489–90):

> The goos, the cokkow, and the doke also
> So cryede, "Kek kek! kokkow! quek quek!" hye,
> That thourgh myne eres the noyse wente tho.
>
> (498–500)

Impatient to get on with the business of pairing, certain birds take matters into their own hands, and the debate rapidly disintegrates. In this poem about which voices do and do not count, I propose that Chaucer asks us to consider real birds' voices at line 499 (or, at least, human attempts to replicate their real utterances) because they momentarily take us by surprise, crying forth in a strange semiotic mode. In my view, linguistic translation is brought forcibly to our attention here because it momentarily breaks down, raising queries about categories of species and voice, and places the Middle English spoken by the narrator (and the birds) throughout the poem under scrutiny. It confirms both language barriers and species' differences, but can also function as a form of sympathetic

---

[4] Peter W. Travis, 'Thirteen Ways of Listening to a Fart: Noise in Chaucer's *Summoner's Tale*', *Exemplaria*, 16 (2004), 323–48 (p. 324).

interspecies translation, a procedure that I will ultimately parallel with the concept of 'biotranslation' outlined in my epigraph to explore what this movement between human and nonhuman languages suggests about meaningful avian utterances, and how this can affect our perception of the poem's allegory at work. Linguistic translation, in other words, has profound implications for the wider forms of translation that allegory performs upon the animal figure.

Allegory – the Bird Is Not a Bird

The category of voice persistently announces its importance in the poem: the word itself (382, 558, 638, 545) – along with 'tonge' (514, 570, 521) and the associated faculty of 'resoun' (564 568, 591) – occurs throughout. Allegorically speaking, though, the problem is that these are not birds' voices at all; the bird-debate genre only asks us to entertain the illusion that birds share our linguistic abilities. For scholars arguing the case for nuanced category definitions (what medieval texts might have to tell us about species similarity, or how difference is not so easily sustained) in the face of texts which co-opt the nonhuman for human purposes, allegory is both vexing and fascinating, a mode necessarily embroiled in the ethics-driven project of representation. When birds speak in allegory, who speaks? Correctly speaking, are we dealing with birds' voices at all?

In this respect, *The Parliament* stands as a typical, but particularly difficult, text. A 'correct' reading of this allegorical dream vision understands that the avian debate is actually a human debate, and that this premise inflects any birdy attributes we might be tempted to read more literally. From a traditional stance, human socio-political interests are double-filtered through the kaleidoscope of both a dream and a bird-debate to a human narrator who relates the matter to a human audience. That birds express reason in articulate language is not of interest in itself, because they are not really birds, only transparent signifiers. Articulate speech from birds is implausible; it only reflects a human ability, and orthodox doctrine tells us as much.⁵ In this sense, avian language serves as the perfect tool 'to make us think of the bird world as a metaphorical human society', a convenient balance of assimilation and distance (as in Lévi-Strauss's totemic paradigm) that nicely suits the allegorical model.⁶ Here we have a communication that is remarkably comparable to human speech, but which is most emphatically not, and, therefore, does not run the risk of confusion.

The fraught history of *The Parliament*'s interpretation should give us pause for thought, however (as might *The Owl and the Nightingale*, which has a similar critical legacy). Scholars have never been convinced one way or the other about the extent to which *The Parliament* functions as allegory. It is a poem beset with hermeneutical problems. Coherent translations between one level and another are consistently thwarted. With its inconsistent allegorical figures, unresolved ending, and hapless narrator who never discovers 'that thyng that I wolde' (91), here is an allegory that will not easily be read allegorically. In Van Dyke's phrase, it is 'misaligned with its allegorical principles' to the point that it might even be read as a 'mock allegory'.⁷ *The Parliament*'s birds have repeatedly avoided satisfactory interpretation, because they 'behave as if they were *somewhat* stylised human beings'.⁸ As much as readers are tempted by allegorical principles to identify birds with human agendas, we cannot dismiss the fact that in this poem birds do all the things that birds should do, to the point where it becomes difficult to know,

---

5   As Augustine states: '[E]ither you would be forced to say magpies, parrots and crows are rational, or you have been pretty rash in calling imitation by the name of art'; Saint Augustine, *On Music*, trans. by Robert Catesby Taliaferro, in *The Immortality of the Soul, The Magnitude of the Soul, On Music, The Advantage of Believing, On Faith in Things Unseen*, The Fathers of the Church: A New Translation, 4, ed. by Ludwig Schopp (Washington, D.C.: Catholic University of America Press, 1947), pp. 151–379 (178). Dante proposes, similarly, that 'their act is not speaking, but rather an imitation of the sound of the human voices'; Dante Alighieri, *De vulgari eloquentia*, ed. and trans. by Stephen Botterill (Cambridge: Cambridge University Press, 1996), pp. 4–5.
6   Lévi-Strauss, *Savage Mind*, p. 204.
7   Carolynn Van Dyke, *Chaucer's Agents: Cause and Representation in Chaucerian Narrative* (Madison, WI: Fairleigh Dickinson University Press, 2005), pp. 55 and 52.
8   Paul Olson, 'The *Parlement of Foules*: Aristotle's *Politics* and the Foundations of Human Society', *SAC*, 2 (1980), 53–69 (p. 59) [italics mine].

at times, whether we are talking about birds or humans because parallel levels of figuration cross over. As Van Dyke has usefully noted, '[i]f Chaucer intends to exploit his avian agents to advance a human message, he is an inept imperialist'.[9] I return to the issue of allegory later; for now, it will suffice to note that the critical to-do surrounding the mechanics and agenda of this allegory suggests the continued need to re-examine the importance of birds' voices that are at the heart of this poem's 'translations'.

Birds and Medieval *Vox*

In representing birds' voices in his poem, particularly ones that squawk at line 499 as though from the pages of a grammar treatise, Chaucer engages another obstacle to credible birdspeak – the considerable body of scholastic writing on the category of *vox*. On the face of it, in fact, it would hardly seem to matter even if we do accept Chaucer's birds as genuinely avian, because by and large these institutional discourses emphatically dismissed nonhuman voices as meaningless. The excellent work achieved by current scholars on the nonhuman in medieval culture has familiarised this extensive practice of distinguishing the human from nonhuman, or, more specific to the threat that birds presented, excluding nonhumans from the logocentric standpoint in order that inarticulacy could be taken as a sign of innate irrationality.[10] Birds were a particular case because their vocal abilities, most of all, forced medieval scholars

---

[9] Van Dyke, *Chaucer's Agents*, p. 75.
[10] Examples abound from patristic authors to writers in Chaucer's own century. Specific to the category of voice, typical statements noted that 'the human voice is distinct, and animal indistinct' (*articulata hominum, confusa animalium*); Thomas de Cantimpré, *Liber de natura rerum: Editio princeps secundum codices manuscriptos*, ed. by Helmut Boese (Berlin: W. de Gruyter, 1973), I.xxvi. For further examples and discussions on the topic of distinguishing human rationality in medieval thought, see Steel, *How To Make a Human*, especially chapter 1. For a concise summary, see Crane, *Animal Encounters*, pp. 49–54. For birdsong and rationality, see Elizabeth Eva Leach, *Sung Birds: Music, Nature, and Poetry in the Later Middle Ages* (Ithaca, NY and London: Cornell University Press, 2007), especially chapters 1 and 2. For Aristotelian principles, see, e.g., *On the Soul*, II.viii.420b 5 to 421a, 1–5, or *HA*, IV.ix.535a 27–535b, 1.

to defend against uncanny similarities with the human that also fascinated them. The poly-vocal jay in Exeter Riddle 24 has already demonstrated to us the challenging possibilities of certain mimicking species who perform the most transgressive language acts of all. To repeat Isidore's remark on the magpie and the parrot: 'if you did not see the bird you would think a human was speaking'.[11] In Alan of Lille's *De planctu naturae,* a key source for *The Parliament,* we encounter a human-mimicking parrot who even fools another bird species.[12] Such examples might strike a difficult chord with those aiming to segregate species; there are times when avian *vox* is too close for comfort. Through rigorously appropriating anomalies into orthodoxy, these authors assuage their fears, but also unavoidably expose them, and the possibility that human categories and systems might not be accurate or sufficient. As Elizabeth Eva Leach notes, 'Theorists would not be at such pains to stress the rationality that must inform human ... practice if the sound of birds' songs were not ostensibly musical'.[13]

Because songbirds and mimicking species do something which, at the least, seems considerably more sophisticated than just producing noise, it comes as no surprise that medieval grammarians and music theorists were the scholars who most fully confronted birdsong in tackling the tricky category of voice. Music, closely allied to grammar in medieval schools, relied upon long-lived Latin traditions from the likes of Probus and Priscian that differentiated

---

[11] He refers to the magpie and the parrot; *Etym.,* XII.vii.46 and XII.xii.24. It was birds' voices such as the magpie's that prompted writers to argue that 'the apparently rational and articulate linguistic properties of spoken language may also be a deception if the listener just relies on aural data'; Leach, *Sung Birds,* p. 42.

[12] Alan of Lille, *The Plaint of Nature,* trans. by James J. Sheridan (Toronto: Pontifical Institute of Medieval Studies, 1980), p. 94.

[13] Leach, *Sung Birds,* p. 40. I am indebted to Leach's text for my knowledge of medieval music theory and the relevant distinctions of human/bird voice. For an example of the sort of theoretical anxiety regarding rational animals to which I refer above, see Aelred of Rievaulx, who asks, 'If sparrows and crows had the dictates of reason to tell them what to do, where to do it, and what precautions to take, how many cities and castles could they not burn down?'; Aelred of Rievaulx, *Dialogue on the Soul,* trans. by Charles H. Talbot (Kalamazoo, MI: Cistercian Publications, 1981), p. 81.

between *vox articulata* and *vox confusa*.¹⁴ Singing, to be correctly defined as such by medieval theorists, required articulate language, the property unique to humans: 'meaning is defined as verbal or linguistic in content, and thus melody, for all its numerical rationality, is meaningless without text'.¹⁵ Birdsong, in these terms, is meaningless, nothing more than instinctive imitation.¹⁶

But birds could slip this net, too. If linguistic discreteness, specifically writeability, is key, then birds presented 'an embarrassing situation', to borrow Umberto Eco's phrase for the barking dog phenomenon (that other tricky nonhuman utterance well known amongst medieval logicians).¹⁷ Some birds' voices can plausibly be written down, which incorporates them back into the realm of meaningful. The crow was the usual example (*'cra cra'*), but the cuckoo – a key dissenter in *The Parliament* – also produces discrete pitches which can be written down, as, indeed, can the duck and the goose in Chaucer's rendition at line 499. There was potential, therefore, for blurring between meaningful human noises which could not be written down, and meaningless animal sounds which could be written down. As Leach explains, 'This would mean that

---

14 See Probus, *Grammatici latini*, ed. by Heinrich Keil, 7 vols (Leipzig: Teubner, 1857–80), vol. 4, p. 47. By the late Middle Ages, the influence of Aristotle's animal texts was complicating definitions and categorisations – *vox* was both precise in many ways, and impossibly broad. As Christopher Cannon notes, *vox* could refer to both the 'voice, sound, tone, cry, [or] call' of a living thing, and a 'word, saying, speech, [or] sentence'; Christopher Cannon, *The Grounds of English Literature* (Oxford: Oxford University Press, 2007), p. 116. Cannon cites Carlton C. Lewis and Charles Short, *A Latin Dictionary* (Oxford: Oxford University Press, 1879), s.v. (n.) *vox*. Aristotle defined voice as 'a kind of sound characteristic of what has soul in it'; *On the Soul*, II.viii.420b.5–6. Cf. Isidore, who states that 'Properly, voice is a human characteristic, or a characteristic of unreasoning animals'; *Etym.*, III.ixx.1.
15 Leach, *Sung Birds*, p. 40.
16 Although medieval writers focused on the mimicry of human voices, they also must have experienced birds' imitation of nonhuman species, a skill which involves no human contact or tutoring. Medieval grammarians are noticeably silent on this matter. Exeter Book Riddle 24 offers one example, and Chaucer's *ManT* includes a crow that not only copies a human word, but a cuckoo's song (243).
17 This familiar example came down to medieval grammarians through Boethius's commentary on Aristotle's *De interpretatione*. See Umberto Eco, *The Limits of Interpretation* (Bloomington and Indianapolis, IN: Indiana University Press, 1990), chapter 7, especially at pp. 114–16.

although whistling and groaning have discreteness ... because such sounds do not contain discrete pitches they would rank below not only spoken or sung language but also below the languageless, nonrational, but musically ratioed song of birds'.[18] Alan of Lille's description of the lark in *De planctu* seems aware of these potential concerns: the bird performs 'not from a study of the technique but from Nature's teaching ... She separated tones into subtle particles, kept dividing semitones until they reached indivisible units'.[19] Even in Priscian's more discriminating four-part model, although human sounds are privileged above birdsong, birds still contain their own category above other creatures and human sounds like grinding teeth, indicating their more troublesome position in attempts to classify *vox*.[20]

Although orthodox opinions dominated, then, the inconsistences described above meant that it was possible to entertain contradictory paradigms.[21] Recent work on medieval translation theories has begun to pay closer attention to texts which tease out these interstitial voices between orthodox categories and taxonomies, such as fourteenth-century hunting treatises, or animal-sound lists. Texts such as these have been said to 'effectively thwart the idea that an inarticulate beast occupies a state of linguistic understanding

---

[18] Leach, *Sung Birds*, p. 35. Human singers, too, could end up in this murky middle ground: players who produced music simply by rote or instinct, lacking the rational application of theory, were considered inferior; see ibid., pp. 45–6.

[19] Alan of Lille, *Plaint of Nature*, p. 94.

[20] It was because of difficult examples like certain birds' calls that a more rigorous four-part model was required; writeability could not be the prime indicator of rationality. Priscian identifies *vox articulata literata* (intelligible, writeable speech), *vox articulata illiterata* (intelligible, unwriteable speech), *vox literata inarticulata* (writeable, unintelligible speech) and *vox illiterata inarticulata* (unwriteable, unintelligible speech). For more detailed discussion of Priscian's model and rational song, see Leach, *Sung Birds*, chapters 1 and 2.

[21] Albertus Magnus, e.g., who was able to deny animals rationality in his *De animalibus*, and yet also present a physiological study of the shared faculty of natural voice in humans and birds. Albertus Magnus, *On Animals: A Medieval Summa Zoologica*, trans. by K. F. Kitchell Jr. and I. M. Resnick, 2 vols (Baltimore, MD: John Hopkins University Press, 1999), vol. 1, pp. 480–1. For unorthodox opinions in music, see Leach, *Sung Birds*, pp. 65–7. Robert Stanton explores how some Skeptic philosophers may have influenced the construction of birds' voices in some Exeter Book riddles in his 'Mimicry, Subjectivity, and the Embodied Voice', pp. 29–43.

entirely apart from that of the rational, speaking human'.²² When Chaucer draws our attention to both the vexations and illuminating potential of translation processes, *The Parliament of Fowls* reveals its own curiosities with inter- or trans-species. Chaucer may begin with a well-established topos in which birds' voices function as metaphor for human speech, but the figuration blurs so that divisions between articulate and inarticulate utterances do not necessarily pertain, and language takes on a cross-species valence. 'The road is open', to adapt Eco on dogs' barking again, 'for a significant' call of the bird.²³

Translating Birdspeak

Susan Crane has commented how 'birdsong fills the function of human language' in the larger parallel between birds and human society that feature in medieval romance.²⁴ In *The Parliament*, I suggest that the opposite is also possible. The English the birds speak, that is, might be seen as a form of speculative translation, a manoeuvre that Chaucer shows to be fraught with difficulties, but which at least aims to envisage recognition between species and genera (human and nonhuman), despite competing agendas or perspectives that are more concerned with difference than similarity and do not always acknowledge others' points of view. For the philosopher John Berger, a 'lack of common language ... guarantees its [the animal's] distance, its distinctness', but *imaginatively* speaking, at least, this is not necessarily an insurmountable boundary.²⁵

These themes are, in fact, recurring interests for Chaucer. In three of the *Canterbury Tales*, the poet explores exactly this type of

---

22   Hsy, 'Between Species'. Crane examines a fourteenth-century hunting treatise in which 'the hounds' barks and baying are meaningful to humans', and *ad hoc* patois yelled by hunters is construed meaningfully by dogs; Susan Crane, 'Ritual Aspects of the Hunt *à Force*', in Hanawalt and Kiser, *Engaging with Nature*, pp. 63–74 (73).
23   Eco, *Limits of Interpretation*, p. 114.
24   Crane, 'For the Birds', 25. Crane refers to the romance generally here, but in relation to *SqT*.
25   John Berger, *About Looking* (1980; repr. London: Bloomsbury, 2009), p. 6.

interspecies fantasy: there is Phoebus's crow that can 'countrefete the speche of every man' (*MancT*, 134); the eloquent 'nonhuman but man-like rooster' in the *Nun's Priest Tale*, in an age when 'Beestes and briddes koude speke and synge' (4071); and *The Squire's Tale*, with its talk between a falcon and a princess who is enabled to magically understand birdspeak.[26] Recent work on these texts has yielded some rich studies about how Chaucer 'shift[s] the emphasis ... in a way that lets the animal world into the equation' with 'semantic integrity' to reveal or re-orientate complex interspecies discourse.[27] The *Squire's Tale*, in which a bird is explicitly allowed the faculty of species-specific, articulate speech, is a particularly revealing example. It is not that the falcon speaks English in this poem, but that Canacee is able to understand the speech of the bird, to 'knowe his menyng openly and pleyn, / And answere hym in his langage' (151–2), which is then fully and conveniently given as Middle English by the Squire. Chaucer does hint at the otherness of the falcon's speech, though, in his use of the word 'leden' (435–6, 478). It is a striking term which seems to defy preferred distinctions between human and nonhuman voices, by offering a catch-all polysemy; it conveys every type of utterance from the Latin language to an animal cry, and even specifically birdsong.[28] I propose a similar, if less transparent, enterprise at play in *The Parliament* whereby an eternal garden in a dream world, suspending the realities of conscious perception, functions something like Canacee's ring. It is a form of 'animal acts [sic]' akin to that envisaged by Jennifer Ham

---

[26] The description of Chauntecleer is taken from Megan Palmer Browne, 'Chaucer's Chauntecleer', in *Rethinking Chaucerian Beasts*, pp. 203–15 (213).

[27] Kordecki, *Ecofeminist Subjectivities*, pp. 143 and 122. See also Crane, 'For the Birds', and relevant chapters in Van Dyke, *Rethinking Chaucerian Beasts*.

[28] Benson glosses the term only as 'language' in *Riverside Chaucer*, but see *MED*, s.v. (n.) *leden*, senses 1–3. The concerns with cross-species communication in *SqT* seem to justify an intentional ambiguity. In Old French poetry, too, birds frequently sing *en leur latin* 'in their Latin' (*Jehan et Blonde*, 3039); Philippe de Remi, *Jehan et Blonde, Poems, and Songs*, ed. and trans. by Barbara N. Sargent-Baur (Amsterdam and Atlanta, GA: Rodopi, 2001). As with ME *leden*, the Old French term could mean simply 'language' as well as Latin. For further examples, see the glossarial index in *Charlemagne: An Anglo-Norman Poem of the Twelfth Century* ed. by Francisque Michel (London: William Pickering, 1836), p. 100.

and Matthew Senior: 'a quest for another kind of language which merges with the sounds and gestures of animals'.[29] On first entering the garden, the dreamer hears the birds in their usual mode: they 'synge' (190) 'forth to brynge' (192). By the time he exits the temple and encounters Lady Nature, they speak human language, although they still produce mere 'noyse' (312) from time to time. *The Parliament* does not, of course, involve explicit bird-human discourse, nor does it have the magical apparatus which justifies the possibility of cross-species communication. But whilst translation and cross-species communication do not achieve the full and overt status that they do in his later work, Chaucer's earlier poem involving talking birds is already preoccupied with these possibilities, and it does allow us to glimpse another kind of language, with profound implications.

The notion of translation is abruptly brought to our attention at line 499 when we hear what are distinctly avian, not human, utterances. If *The Parliament*'s allegory is intended to efface genuine bird voices, or substitute them for human speech, then this aberrant line brings those voices to the fore to disrupt usual interpretive procedures because human and bird voices are set starkly besides one another. In a text that gives human voice to birds and expects us to maintain faith in this superimposition, a sudden moment in which the birds utter bird calls draws our attention specifically to issues of *vox* categories and translation procedures that otherwise might have been overlooked or lacked relevance. At this point we hear the birds' 'leden', and it alerts us to the potential for meaningful communication that eludes standard grammarians' definitions. As an attempt to represent actual birds' calls, in one sense it engages more intricately with interspecies communications than does *The Squire's Tale* because it confronts the difficulties of translation even as it endorses its potential.

Linguistic slippage between bird and human languages at this point compromises the allegory. How are we to respond to voices that are no longer recognisably human? To those Latin grammarians,

---

[29] Jennifer Ham and Matthew Senior, eds, *Animal Acts: Configuring the Human in Western History* (London and New York, NY: Routledge, 1997), p. 2.

Chaucer's bird calls would be a prime example of the inarticulate form of *sonus* that separates birdsong from human singing, and in this orthodox sense they have been more than once interpreted as evidence that these birds are representative of vulgarity and ignorance. To be sure, elsewhere in the poem Chaucer invests the duck and goose with idiomatic speech that is feasibly designed to suggest human class differences, but this line problematises that particular argument because it drops out of the representative scheme entirely. The slippage, too, reminds us that the narrator's voice is implicated in the reception and transmission of these calls. Are we to imagine that the line stands as his attempt to translate what he denounces as 'noyse', conveyed *verbum pro verbo* or *sensum pro sensu* (to use the terminology known to medieval authors)?[30] In which case, why does he not do so in Middle English? Are we to understand that the dream matrix enables the fantasy of nonhuman to human understanding (a manoeuvre akin to that in *The Squire's Tale*), and that the birds do not actually speak English to each other? Or perhaps the birds' utterances indicate something incomprehensible to the narrator – accurately reported, anomalous bird sounds amongst voices that otherwise genuinely speak English. The line, in fact, both conveys real bird calls, and presents a human mimicking bird calls (a detail with greater comic potential if we envisage a performance context for the poem). The usual procedure of allegory presents human speech through apparent birdspeak, which never actually exists because we only ever hear it as human speech, but line 499 doubles back so that we hear something of that omitted middle voice.

Arguably, we are more acutely aware at this moment than any other that our reception of the birds' voices is dependent on the narrator. Indeed, his unexpected rendition of the birds' utterances reminds us that in other ways throughout the poem he is 'inept', to borrow Van Dyke's term. It is, after all, the human dreamer's words which ultimately recount the birds' discourse, and which shape our

[30] 'Word for word' and 'sense for sense'. For discussion of these issues across the medieval period, see the collection of essays in Jeanette Beer, ed., *Translation Theory and Practice in the Middle Ages*, Studies in Medieval Culture, 38 (Kalamazoo, MI: Medieval Institute Publications, 1997).

perceptions. He is a part of the allegorical scheme, but is remarkably unhelpful in assisting us through the interpretive maze. The role he plays seems as inconsistent or puzzling as many other features of the allegory we noted above: a narrator whose perceptions direct proceedings, and which emphatically do not at the same time; who apparently draws no connection between what he witnesses and that 'certeyn thing' (20); and, indeed, dismisses the dream in favour of books 'som day ... to fare / The bet' (697–9). Without denying the narrator's physical presence, it is also noticeable, in A. C. Spearing's words, that the 'Dreamer drops almost completely out of sight, as if the birds had squeezed him out of the poem', which does, indeed, seem to be the case: the birds take up so much room that 'unethe was there space / For me to stonde' (314–15).[31] His guide, Affrican, is also characterised by non-participation, departing early on, and suddenly (169–70). The enigmatic narrator, then, only creates further interpretive difficulties; on the question about what precisely the birds do signify or represent, he does not comment.

These wider discrepancies impact on the relevance of line 499. When it comes to the bird calls, to what extent do we trust those 'eres' (500) which receive and interpret, most times hearing or narrating articulate speech, sometimes inferring 'noyse'? Whatever our stance, translation issues are at stake. With the human 'translator' engaged, the line is a particularly provocative example of interspecies utterances because it not only plays with bird-to-bird communication (single and plural species), but also an imagined possibility of bird-to-human comprehension.

The phonetics employed in this line only partly or haphazardly transmit voices across the species divide (like terms in a particular human language that cannot accurately carry over into another) and in this manner occupy a fuzzy middle ground. The 'kek[s]' and 'quek[s]' in themselves are the result of a human attempt to translate, to correlate signs from one language to another, akin to modern ornithologists' efforts to articulate birdsong, or, in a

---

[31] A. C. Spearing, *Medieval Dream Poetry* (Cambridge: Cambridge University Press, 1976), p. 96. Other readers have noticed this conspicuous absence, too; e.g., Kordecki, *Ecofeminist Subjectivities*, pp. 59–60.

medieval context, the sounds transcribed as verbs in Latin sound lists or translation texts.³² All three birds are familiar species with calls that are easily transcribable in human letters. The cuckoo, commonly featured in Latin grammar texts as an example of *vox confusa*, is potentially troublesome because its song is writeable and involves discrete pitches. In Middle English, though, *cokkow* was doubly problematic because it forms a near homophone with *cokewold*, a pun Chaucer exploits himself to great effect in *The Manciple's Tale* (243). The calls in *The Parliament* do not so obviously convey the uncanny similarity of mimicking voices, but they do highlight an interspecies vocal convergence: humans can sound like birds, and birds can sound like humans.

Chaucer's phonetics reveal a familiar paradox of translation. Whilst aiming to familiarise, they equally alienate by denoting difference from human language. The line is not and cannot be a full translation, and in this sense attends, however unintentionally, to the ethics of representing alterity. Whilst the phonetics are another form of human representation (closer to the 'original', but still removed from a language that we can fully comprehend), something of the nonhuman is retained in these human attempts at bird mimicry. The limits of our own language are turned against us, a risk that plagues literary human-to-human translations, too, as Chaucer well knew; translating or transcribing always runs the risk of getting it wrong.³³ In one respect, then, such unavoidable strangeness confirms orthodox medieval opinion – birds can be safely and thankfully separated from us, their voices dismissed as *vox confusa*, usefully reinforcing how human rationality makes us superior beings. The voices in *The Parliament*, however, are not so neatly resolved. We are suspended between grammatical categories: the calls are not *articulata* in the anthropocentric sense important to grammarians, but they are not emptied to the status of *confusa*

---

[32] For ornithologists' phonetic renditions of bird calls, see, e.g., 'ahnk-ga-ga' (Greylag Goose); 'quaek-quaek-quak-quah-qua-...' (Mallard); 'goo-ko' (Cuckoo); Lars Svensson, Killian Mullarney and Dan Zetterström, *Collins Bird Guide*, 2nd edn (London: Collins, 2009), pp. 9, 24 and 220.

[33] Cf. *Adam*, in which he berates his scribe for transcribing incorrectly and implies the risks of not writing 'more trewe' (4).

either.³⁴ Indeed, the positioning of the calls, immediately between gripes from the same three birds expressed in Middle English, encourages us to transfer meaning. Here are parallel complaints in two modes, a literal form of doublespeak to be processed simultaneously that recalls the correlation of bird voice and esoteric Latin in the 'Bird with Four Feathers' I note in my introduction. Avian utterance is not empty there, but associable in its alterity with the numinous mysteries of *parce* that the speaker desires to penetrate. Moments such as these, then, should encourage us, in Hsy's words, 'not necessarily [to] follow the lead of Priscian and other medieval Latin grammarians by segregating the "inarticulate" animal *vox* ... from rational human speech that can be set to writing'.³⁵ Rather, the two categories are blurred so that whilst the animal *vox* remains ineluctably remote to human understanding, it is not necessarily meaningless. 'Kek kek', and other such onomatopoeic transcriptions, enact this blurring by producing an unorthodox instance of *vox*: a writeable sound (*literata*) which is *inarticulata* to humans, but *articulata* to birds (or some birds, at least). They might be said to occupy the same territory as tricky, unclassified human sounds, like 'tut, tut', an utterance which, although not a word, is both writeable and meaningful, unlike groaning or sighing (both treatise entries) which are meaningful, but unwriteable. Chaucer's bird calls are deictic in the way that other, human utterances are; the boundary between articulate and inarticulate depends on who speaks, and who listens.

What is more, the fact that the birds in question go on to make salient and convincing arguments about concerns that are as plausibly avian as they are human (the matter of breeding), suggests that we are not meant to gloss over the line as nothing more than proof

---

[34] I contradict Gorst's reading of this line which argues that there is no confusion of *vox* categories; Gorst, 'Interspecies Mimicry', 151.

[35] Hsy, 'Between Species'. Hsy suggests a similar moment in John Clanvowe's *Boke of Cupide*, in which human languages can be seen to function as forms of translation: 'The cuckoo asserts that his language is clear and plain, and his simple English diction conveys this effect; the nightingale – whose sonic performance is considered much more sophisticated – utters a "nyse, queynt crie" [strange, unfamiliar cry] that employs obscure forms of French-inflected vocabulary.'

of unintelligibility (avian or human). The goose offers an obvious solution to unrequited love (567) and the duck contests fidelity to one partner with simple logic that is difficult to deny:

> That men shulde loven alwey causeles!
> Who can a resoun fynde or wit in that?
> Daunseth he murye that is myrtheles?
> Who shulde recche of that is recheles?'
> 'Ye queke,' seyde the goos, 'ful wel and fayre!
> There been mo sterres, God wot, than a payre!'
> (590–5)

If we are to assume that the voices of a goose, a cuckoo and a duck feature allegorically as the nonsensical gobbledygook of an ill-bred human social class, we must also confront the problem that these birds are neither nonsensical nor nonrational. Indeed, they are thoroughly pragmatic. They dispense solid common sense, which reflects back rather well on the supposedly meaningless 'kek[s]' and 'quek[s]' apparently employed in the first place to represent their stupidity.[36] That is, a scheme which aims to derogate idiotic proclamations from a lower social class by association with irrational birds' voices cannot persist when those proclamations are not, in fact, unreasonable, or disparaged and dismissed, except by those characters whose own principles are no more endorsed or justified by Lady Nature, or by the narrator. If anything, it is the collective, heterogeneous voice of the lower birds which receives implicit approval at the poem's end, not the elitism of the raptors. As Alastair Minnis has remarked of another unauthorised and outspoken Chaucerian character who delivers profound wisdom, the Wife of Bath, these birds 'cannot be contained within discourses which would serve to limit ... [their] potency'.[37] The Parliament's birds, in bird terms, do what such discourses emphatically claim they cannot do.

---

[36] Cf. 'goosissh peoples speche' in Tr, III.584. Grammarians' observations on nonhuman voices do not, in fact, denounce content – they only emphasise whether the outward sound that strikes the ear is comprehensible or not, implying, at least, that nonhuman utterances could be meaningful in their own terms.

[37] Alastair Minnis, Fallible Authors: Chaucer's Pardoner and Wife of Bath (Philadelphia, PA: University of Pennsylvania Press, 2008), p. 23

Perhaps then, these calls do mean something. Here is an avian *ratio* of sorts. They are loaded with the volatility and force of all those diverse voices and perspectives that desire to be heard in competition with the birds of prey that are granted priority – an inclusive alterity that can embrace a human *and* avian vernacular. To the birds that make these calls, that is, they are as reasonable, intelligible and functional as any other voice in the parliament, including those that more obviously represent an exclusive, elite human standpoint. So, on the one hand, the strange squawks remind us of differences, but on the other, that they cannot be so easily explained away, because they acknowledge both 'the recognition of kinship in difference and of difference among kin', because their 'language encodes respect for difference, particularly alterity, without repudiating the underlying affinity that is the first prerequisite for knowledge'.[38]

Equating bird squawking with human speech can, then, be a positive way to explore common meaning-making, an imagined opportunity to understand and appreciate what other species might have to say, despite the differences that separate. To return to that recent concept from biosemiotics defined in the epigraph, in the context of *The Parliament*'s coming-together of multiple voices and standpoints, this sort of interspecies project might be read more precisely as a form of 'biotranslation'. In outlining this theory, Kull and Torop borrow from Jakob von Uexküll's concept of the *Umwelt* (species-specific sphere or world which interrelates with others' *Umwelten*) to postulate that sign systems are shared across life forms and that '*Conversation with nature*' is conceivable at conscious and unconscious levels.[39] Biotranslation 'poses the question of ... translatability' between organisms. As a concept, it raises the types of speculative possibilities that biosemiotics does more generally, the notion that 'in some very real sense, all living organisms "know" things and have purposes', that we must 'rethink what we might mean by such things as "interpretation,"

---

[38] Evelyn Fox Keller, 'The Gender/Science System: or, Is Sex to Gender as Nature Is to Science?', in *Feminism and Science*, ed. by Nancy Tuana (Bloomington, IN: Indiana University Press, 1989), pp. 33–44 (44).

[39] Kull and Torop, 'Biotranslation', p. 315 (italics original).

"mind," and "knowledge"'.[40] Kull and Torop employ bird calls as an example of what they term '*interspecific* sign system[s]', in which alarm calls from one species are 'translated' by another.[41] As for medieval scholars – although with rather different reactions – the category of bird voice is evident and illuminating as a correlative to human signs or abilities. Movements between languages, modes and perspectives in *The Parliament* hint at a similar correspondence between and across beings, in confronting the success or failure of different species (including the human) to make individual perspectives compatible. The species-specific alarms of geese and cuckoos and ducks, articulate to them (like their breeding strategies), may or may not be transmitted to eagles, falcons and doves, and may or may not be interpreted by us. There is also the added joke that, taken literally, the imposed linguistic sign system of human speech would not be understood by the birds.

Chaucer's bird call line, however, interrupting the human speech, invites us to bridge the communicative gap. Writing about incomprehensible nonhuman utterances in the Fifteen Signs tradition, Karl Steel argues that there are instances when such utterances produce a 'gap deliberately left open, a space that has not been stuffed with human meaning'.[42] This, I suggest, is the case in *The Parliament*'s famous bird call line. It provokes a speculative 'biotranslation' act from *us* at this moment, a playful invitation to imagine what the birds mean (or fail to mean) amongst their own and other species. We project meaning, yes, but meaning that starts with the birds. This creative guess is still an illusion, but at least it has alternative voices in mind. From this angle, the lively vernacular of the goose and duck ('Al this nys not worth a flye!' [501]) is not just a way of characterising lower social classes in human society,

---

[40] Wendy Wheeler, '"Tongues I'll Hang on Every Tree": Biosemiotics and the Book of Nature', in *The Cambridge Companion to Literature and the Environment*, ed. by Louise Westling (New York, NY: Cambridge University Press, 2014), pp. 121–35 (127).
[41] Kull and Torop, 'Biotranslation', p. 319 (italics original). Certain calls or acts, of course, such as those intended as deterrents, are fully intended to be translated by other avian and non-avian species (e.g., the 'false lapwynge' [*PF*, 347] who deceives predators away from its nest).
[42] Steel, *How To Make a Human*, p. 229.

but an attempt to translate the otherness of particular species, and that of all nature's voices.

The transformative act of poetic 'translation' becomes a creative 'translation technology' of sorts;[43] like Canacee's ring or an imagined time and place in which all 'beestes and briddes koude speke and synge', it opens up the category of *vox articulata*. Chaucer's text contravenes more typical instances of medieval engagements with talking creatures because he offers us a literary key by which we can envisage sonic or perceptive worlds that feasibly exist outside the categorisations of scholarly discourses. Whether it be through a ring, a pre-humanistic world, or a dreamscape, the poet reveals his awareness that he performs translation, demonstrating that, as Leonard Michael Koff has stated in the context of medieval translation theory: 'Language is a medium of being and translation is always possible, despite boundaries of place and breed.'[44] The poetic imagination can slide between those 'kek[s]' and 'quek[s]' and a language that makes sense to us, another species, where it translates as something like 'Have don' (492) and 'Com of!' (494). So, too, when the goose slips momentarily out of human language to quote the duck's 'queke' (594), but the utterance remains grammatically part of the sentence, functioning as a verb, an elision of bird and human voice that echoes the more famous example in *The House of Fame* when the eagle cries 'Awak!' (555). The preferable taxonomic and grammatical boundaries, erected in the first place to achieve the necessary task of proving human exceptionalism, are rendered insufficient in Chaucer's bird calls because human and nonhuman utterances are bound up in ambiguous and interlocking exchange, and we are prompted to imagine, at least, that these calls carry meaning.

---

[43] Jakob von Uekküll, cited in the epigraph to Kull and Torop, 'Biotranslation', p. 315.

[44] Leonard Michael Koff, '"Awak!" Chaucer Translates Bird Song', in *Traduire au Moyen Age, The Medieval Translator*, 5, ed. by Roger Ellis and René Tixier (Turnhout, Belgium: Brepols, 1996), pp. 390–418 (398). Koff's essay uses the example of birdsong to explore wider concepts of translation in Chaucer (particularly *MancT*), the medieval age generally, and beyond.

The Parliament, as all Chaucer's talking bird texts, resonates with Lévi-Strauss's poignant assertion about the impossibility of interspecies communication, that 'no situation seems more tragic, more offensive to heart and mind, than that of a humanity coexisting and sharing the joys of a planet with other living species yet being unable to communicate with them'.[45] Literature is not real life, and Chaucer's poetic translations can hardly be said to compensate for our inability to know the mysteries of nonhuman creatures, but such attempts might be all we have, incomplete and unstable, but still worthwhile. As Sarah E. McFarland has stated, 'To envisage the *umwelt* [sic] or self-world of nonhuman animals is to speculate in terms of human experience and using human languages; the empathy necessary is somewhat illusory because there is no other way to speculate'.[46] *The Parliament* envisages what communicating might be like, and, in doing so, implies that humans are not the only subjective beings capable of meaning. Chaucer's birds inhabit the *langue articulé* and even this imagined possibility suggests that there might be something worth listening to. When it comes to procreation – the reason for the parliament in the first place – for many birds and many humans, why indeed would one 'loven alwey causeles' (590)?

It is perfectly possible, of course, that Chaucer only intended what many have suspected about line 499: that those bird calls are designed, quite simply, to be funny, their silliness emphasising the indignant outburst of three coarse, bourgeois human figures. It is funny, and can indeed point up human traits, but it is also inconsistent. An anthropocentric interpretation of this more orthodox sort, in fact, highlights the resistance or awkwardness of Chaucer's avian material which is not neatly or completely incorporated into metaphorical translation. It is a moment, intentional or not, that turns out to be more than just a throwaway joke. If the line requires

---

[45] Claude Lévi-Strauss and Didier Eribon, *Conversations with Claude Lévi-Strauss*, trans. by Paula Wissing (Chicago, IL: University of Chicago Press, 1991), p. 139.
[46] Sarah E. McFarland, 'Animal Studies, Literary Animals and Yann Martell's *Life of Pi*', in *The Cambridge Companion to Literature and the Environment*, ed. by Louise Westling (New York, NY: Cambridge University Press, 2014), pp. 152–65 (155).

us to overlook a trivial switch between voices for humour's sake, this is not so easily done when readers are sensitive to the poem's focus on valid and invalid voices. Either way, the birds' surprise transformative interjection at this point disrupts the allegory, and this raises important questions about the translation and reliability of voices. The metaphor and the real, or just the right equation of similarity and difference, are not so easily reconciled.

Allegory Revisited – Translating Other Voices

In his now well-known discussion of the allegorical animal, Jeffrey Jerome Cohen concludes that, sometimes, medieval writers 'lead us to a middle space where allegories and moralizations seem insufficient in their power to contain'.[47] *The Parliament of Fowls* creates just such a middle space. As we noted above, the extensive and long-lived critical fuss surrounding the mechanics and agendas of this poem's allegory highlights the need to reconsider how the birds are represented, to see, indeed, whether birds might point us towards the sort of animal allegory that Onno Oerlemans has argued is able to 'simultaneously hide and reveal the contested nature of the boundary between humans and animals'.[48] Rather than aiming for a fully coherent allegorical reading, perhaps we need to consider how the resistances to this approach intentionally demand new ways of conceiving relations between birds and humans that pivot on the blurry contiguities of voice. Amidst the slippage of existing interpretative standpoints, there is a space for considering the birds' voices as something more than anthropomorphised twittering, to give the fowls a little more of their titular prominence in the 'commune profyt' (47) or the 'speaking together' that Olson identifies as the central civic purpose.[49] As Lisa Kiser reminds us in one of the earliest ecocritical studies of *The Parliament*, Chaucer 'reminds us forcefully that there is indeed a nonhuman world …

---

[47] Cohen, 'Inventing with Animals', p. 57.
[48] Oerlemans, 'The Animal in Allegory', 297.
[49] Olson, 'Aristotle's *Politics*', 56.

unrepresented in his poem', or, in the context of biosemiotics, 'that there exist signs, *per se*, in animal communication'.[50] Chaucer's lingustic discrepancies can lead us towards recognising a little more of this world supposedly obscured or ignored by allegory.

The avian catalogue prefacing the debate is a useful example of Chaucer's incomplete allegorisation of the nonhuman, introducing us early on to the gaps in the anthropomorphic patina. In its orthodox, formalised structure this classification hierarchy is often taken to signal clearly the birds' allegorical status, ruled by the bestiary's 'indifference to zoological categories or probabilities'; every fowl must 'take his owne place' (320) according to kind, which is presumed to confer humanised social statuses.[51] But we can, additionally, consider this in bird terms because Chaucer also takes his avian hierarchy from the works of natural philosophers, all of whom ultimately derive their observations from Aristotle.[52] Divisions between genera according to food type, that is, are not simply the stuff of allegory – they can also be serious suggestion about avian taxonomy.[53] There are disquieting instances of bird behaviour, too,

---

[50] Lisa Kiser, 'Chaucer and the Politics of Nature', in *Beyond Nature Writing: Expanding the Boundaries of Ecocriticism*, ed. by Karla Armbruster and Kathleen R. Wallace (Charlottesville, VA: University Press of Virginia, 2001), pp. 41–56 (49), and Kull and Torop, 'Biotranslation', p. 315, respectively.

[51] J. A. W. Bennett, *The Parlement of Foules* (Oxford: Oxford University Press, 1957), p. 149. Cf. Olson, 'Aristotle's *Politics*', 62–3, and Melissa Ridley Elmes, 'Species or Specious? Authorial Choices and *The Parliament of Fowls*', in *Rethinking Chaucerian Beasts*, pp. 233–47. Elmes reviews the 'blend of fresh observation with conventional anthropomorphism', but prioritises a figurative reading – the poem 'anticipates the full development of estates satire' (pp. 244–5).

[52] See *HA*, VIII.vii.592b–593b. Alongside the announced poetic influence of Alan of Lille's *De planctu* (I.216–89), see also Trevisa, XII.i (p. 600); *Etym.*, XII.vii.1–2; Neckham, *De naturis rerum*, I.23–80; Vincent of Beauvais, *Speculum naturale*, XVI.xiv. Of these natural philosophers, only Vincent was definitely known to Chaucer. Pliny, similarly, separates birds into classes such as feet shape/purpose, song birds and plumage-birds (*HN*, X.xiii and xxii).

[53] Consequently, scholars have been unsure how to explain the unpredictable mix of rhetorical topoi and apparent natural history, the fact that despite the obvious symbolism, the birds are 'closer to nature, have a stronger actuality, than those in the lists of other medieval poets'; Geoffrey Chaucer, *The Parlement of Foulys*, ed. by D. S. Brewer, 2nd edn (Manchester: Manchester University Press, 1972), p. 36. There have been numerous attempts to make the avian catalogue stand for human social groups, but, as Charles Muscatine notes, 'whilst it is certain that he [Chaucer] plays in PF [sic] with social distinctions

that conflict with the carefully assigned placement of each species. Numerous birds in the catalogue are depicted as unruly, anticipating the disruption that is to come and placing emphasis more than once on death, rather than the governing life-creating purpose of Lady Nature: the heron is the 'eles fo' (346); the cormorant is 'hote' (362) with appetite; the swallow is depicted as the 'mortherere of the foules smale [bees]' (353) (like the cuckoo, 'mortherere of the heysoge' [612]); and the drake is the 'stroyere of his owene kynde' (360). Potential violence is most evident with the birds of prey:

> ... the goshauk that doth pyne
> To bryddes for his outrageous ravyne.
>
> The gentyl faucoun, that with his feet distrayneth
> The kynges hand; the hardy sperhauk eke,
> The quayles foo; the merlioun, that payneth
> Hymself ful ofte the larke for to seke.
>
> (335–40)

The quail and lark are not listed in their appropriate food categories, but as prey items for other birds. Chaucer emphasises the grisly reality of these killings: the merlin 'payneth' (strives) to hunt the lark, but the word echoes a previous line ending and recalls the 'pyne' that results from the goshawk's 'outrageous ravyne'. Even the falcon, who is not depicted in pursuit of prey, is still a falconer's bird and his talons 'distrayneth', this word conjuring violence in its primary sense of 'grasp', but also the secondary meanings of 'torment' or 'afflict'.[54] In the background of the falcon's description we are reminded of its ultimate, instinctive purpose. There is the impression, too, as its talons grasp the king's hand, that its natural habits are barely concealed by its taming; the bird's ultimate *kynde* is to hunt and kill for itself, far less any aristocratic role it has been assigned. Bestiary or encyclopaedic moralisations are turned against themselves in *The Parliament*'s avian catalogue. If this line denotes the peaceful order desired by an allegorised Lady Nature, or 'discourages social

---

among the birds and thus with socially characteristic attitudes towards love, his four groups—birds of prey, worm-fowl, seed-fowl, and water-fowl – cannot be precisely identified with any medieval social classes or political interest groups'; *Riverside Chaucer*, p. 1000.

[54] *MED*, s.v. (v.) *distreinen*, senses 1 and 4.

mobility' as Kiser puts it, a barely-suppressed movement outside allegorical constraints already seems to be afoot.[55]

This discord is made apparent, too, by the birds named in the list. In response to the differences between Isidore and Chaucer in their encyclopaedic listings, Melissa Ridley Elmes sees an attempt to 'ground the material ... in native tradition', although she says little about how this tradition contributes meaningfully, other than that it shows Chaucer's 'view of the world in which he lived'.[56] Given the consistent manner in which these birds resist allegorical representation or interpretations in the debate, however, the native-ness likely goes further in effect. Although Chaucer includes conventional species, he does omit mythical species found in his likely sources, such as the phoenix, caladrius and memnonides and non-native birds (the hoopoe or ostrich, for instance), leaving a list of birds which could all feasibly be seen in Britain in the fourteenth century. Of these, the starling (348), robin (349) and the fieldfare (364) cannot be traced to any extant bestiary or encyclopaedic

---

[55] Kiser, 'Politics of Nature', p. 45.
[56] Elmes, 'Species or Specious?', pp. 235 and 244. Elmes compares Chaucer's list with the avian catalogues of Isidore, Bartholomaeus and Alan of Lille (pp. 235–8) in the most recent study to focus on the list of birds. There are a number of points, however, to which I offer the following amendments. Elmes states that the parrot is absent from Isidore and that the duck and goose are 'found in neither encyclopaedia' [Isidore and Bartholomaeus] (p. 235). See, however, *Etym.*, XII.vii.24 (parrot) and XII.vii.51–2 (duck and goose). Elmes moderates her remark to say that Isidore 'does include the drake, but not specifically the female duck' (p. 245, n. 9), but Chaucer refers to the drake directly and to the female only obliquely, so if there is a distinction regarding sex in Isidore, Chaucer does not depart from this. There is no obvious indication that Isidore refers specifically to one sex or the other, though: *ans* is the Lat. term for the genus, and does not refer specifically to the drake. Three other birds on Elmes's absent-from-Isidore list (p. 245, n. 7) are, in fact, present: for the crane, see *Etym.*, XII.vii.14; the kite, XII.vii.58; and the raven, XII.vii.43. In total, Elmes identifies twenty-three birds from Chaucer's list absent in the known sources, or whose descriptions do not match these sources. Many of the birds from this list (p. 246, n. 26), however, are present in the known sources or those which Elmes proposes as likely other influences. Vincent of Beauvais's *Speculum naturale* includes, e.g., the swallow and its reputation for eating bees (I.xvi.97); cf. Neckham, *De naturis rerum*, I.lii). In Bartholomaeus's *De proprietatibus* – a 'likely encyclopaedic source' (Elmes, 'Species or Specious?', p. 235) – we find the kite, the dove, the stork, the turtle dove and the raven, all with the associated characteristics that Chaucer gives these birds in *The Parliament*.

sources.[57] Whether Chaucer drew on popular birdlore or unknown sources, the effect remains that these species represent an unusual presence in the list. David Southmayd notes that the cuckoo, goose and duck do not feature prominently in the bestiary tradition and 'none are moralised for good or bad'.[58] Whilst the birds are not exempt from moralisation in the encyclopaedic tradition, the implication remains – these birds form a group which is less burdened with the weight of exegesis, and it is they who perform the most impressive escape from the allegorical demands exacted upon the birds when they fleetingly switch linguistic modes.[59]

The starling, robin and fieldfare, though, convey the naturalism effect too, because they are most free of all the birds from textual, allegorising traditions. Chaucer's starling is given an anthropomorphic gloss (it was clearly known for its mimicking abilities), but the robin and fieldfare each receive only one adjective, which both serve to describe rather than interpret.[60] The thrush might have been familiar on the banquet table, but 'frosty' indicates the bird's grey-headed, white-breasted appearance, and its status as a winter migrant. The effect is easily overlooked, but significant because the 'frosty feldefare' (364) features as the culminating aberrant species

---

[57] All three of these birds do appear as illustrations in illuminated manuscripts, most obviously as very identifiable and named portraits in the Sherborne Missal. Chaucer could not have known this manuscript (its creation is dated 1399–1407) but it does demonstrate that the birds were likely familiar British species. See Backhouse, *Medieval Birds*, pp. 48, 44 and 54. For further examples, see also Yapp, *Birds in Medieval Manuscripts*, although only the robin is unquestionably identifiable in his suggestions.

[58] David E. Southmayd, 'Chaucer and the Medieval Conventions of Bird Imagery' (unpublished doctoral thesis, McGill University, 1980), p. 83.

[59] For moralisation of the cuckoo, see Neckham, *De naturis rerum*, I.lxxii; for the goose, Vincent, *Speculum naturale*, XVI.xxix, and Neckham, *De naturis rerum*, I.lxxi; and for the duck, Vincent, *Speculum naturale*, I.xxvii.

[60] The robin does seem to have a varied folkloric tradition, including an association with Christ. No source on robin lore, however, can offer a date, origin or author. For a brief discussion, see Peter Tate, *Flights of Fancy: Birds in Myth, Legend and Superstition* (London: Random House, 2007), pp. 118–24. If the robin was symbolic in the medieval period, it is not recorded in extant texts, although the association may have circulated in oral form. Chaucer uses the standard medieval name for the species. The bird's tameness is a distinctive trait (*BWP*, vol. 5, p. 605) and there is no reason for Chaucer's adjective to have come from literary tradition any more than general observation or knowledge.

in a list that clearly invokes traditional avian symbolism. It is the cuckoo, duck and goose who will front the attack against the birds of prey (arguably the most anthropomorphised of all the birds), but there are others who are part of the same initiative; their presence in the list announces a resistant alterity more easily because they have more fully escaped a legacy of allegorical representation. Chaucer emphatically invokes textual tradition, holds it firmly in view, and yet allows in a sort of naturalism akin to the authentic 'kek[s]' and 'quek[s]' we will hear later on. Avian voices have already been raised even before the birds begin speaking in the motley, lively throng of species and divergent representations that recall Bartholomaeus's 'dyuers' avian attributes.

These incongruities occur across the debates as species jostle together, distinct and combined in a 'universal epithalamium, in which not only man, but the entire natural world participates'.[61] On the matter of breeding, birds speak earnestly and belligerently on behalf of birds; by their 'owene autorite' (506) they will 'telle oure tale' (560), resisting the demands of other birds, and humans. (It is the human narrator, in fact, who can 'telle no tale' (326), rather comically on the distinctly avian point of eating worms.) A worm-eating, parasitic cuckoo, acting as 'Nature wolde enclyne' (325) is berated viciously by a merlin who behaves like a lofty aristocrat. The cuckoo – a pointed example in the poem – *can* be anthropomorphised, read as a 'mortherere' (612), but it is also idiosyncratically and uniquely a cuckoo, whose habits cannot be easily reduced to other perspectives, human or otherwise. The duck both speaks and quacks (589, 594) and, most famously, is assigned a metaphorical hat, a detail that so conspicuously draws attention to anthropomorphic strategies that it actually undermines the expected effect: we are acutely aware that birds *don't* actually wear hats.[62] Under these circumstances, love, the theme with which the poem commences, takes on a decidedly cross-species relevance, as complex and diverse as species themselves: raptors who uphold

---

[61] Victoria Rothschild, '*The Parliament of Fowls*: Chaucer's Mirror up to Nature?', *ES*, 35 (1984), 164–84 (p. 184).

[62] I disagree with Jill Mann's reading of this detail, which argues that we 'scarcely notice the incongruity'; Mann, *Aesop to Reynard*, p. 99.

a sustained anthropomorphic vision of *fin amour* (which leads to failed breeding altogether) are chided and mocked by those who promote their own breeding habits and cry out 'lat us wende!' (492). The natural or instinctive breeding preferences of the lower order birds can be read allegorically, but they are most certainly the stuff of avian concerns too. As in the famous Boethian caged-bird simile in *The Squire's Tale*, most of the birds do as their instincts urge despite the demands of allegory (which come, ironically, from other birds within the text, as well as the manipulating hand of a human author): they return 'to the wode ... and wormes ete' (*SqT*, 617). Metaphor as it is, even this example undercuts itself, as occurs in *The Parliament*: we must believe that 'A bird imagines that another bird modelled its actions on a comparison of men's behaviour to that of birds'.[63]

As we have seen, birds' voices, as much as their behaviours, tie us in similar hermeneutical and semiotic knots. They, too, gesture at the 'insufficient ... power' of other discourses, prompting us to reconsider the significance of avian vocality in relation to human speech. Attending more closely to these voices can show us how allegory is not only insufficient at times, but is also, more positively, capable of operating in even more nuanced terms than we suspected. Ultimately, the poem's allegory need not hinder us from recognising that birds in the poem can sometimes be actual birds. The discrepancies, in fact, should encourage us to seek more complex and varied aspects of Chaucer's species relationships, so that we do not necessarily or consistently read one species as replacing another, but allow for the possibility of an inter- or cross-species mode. The act of translating birds correlates linguistic translation with the processes of this allegorical dynamic, with the hermeneutical and ethical act that this poem requires us to engage with – how should we, and to what extent is it possible to, 'translate' another species, another subjectivity, whether human or nonhuman?

Moreover, this is not a suggestion that need work against more widespread allegorical hermeneutics. Some recent work (such as that in what has been named the 'religious turn') argues for the

[63] Van Dyke, *Chaucer's Agents*, p. 84.

sort of 'both/and' dynamic inherent to Augustinian allegory in order to recognise how apparent opposites, the sacred and secular, often co-exist in medieval texts, and do not demand that we choose one over the other.[64] Matilda Tomaryn Bruckner, for instance, has remarked in the context of romance that '[o]pposing terms remain present, equally valid, as they interact in a potentially creative tension that neither dismisses nor suppresses either one'.[65] The 'both/and' hermeneutic is, such scholars recommend, far more prevalent than has been previously acknowledged, and can allow audiences to 'choose between meanings'.[66] We encountered this sort of dualistic paradigm in *The Seafarer*, in which the seabirds exist as literal and metaphorical beings in the poem's scheme, and, indeed, there is a 'both/and' aspect in the very nature of birds that 'beþ bytwene', to borrow Trevisa's words again.[67] In applying such thinking to *The Parliament*, we might detect a similar relation between literal and metaphorical elements capable of negotiating or manipulating the movement between referents to reveal a conjectured alterity, leading to that 'place of dispersal, multiple agency, and intercorporeality' recommended by Cohen.[68] If animal allegory has been long understood as casting the nonhuman in human terms in order to explore human matters, sometimes we catch something of the animal terms, too, reversing our attempts to superimpose so that some of that we intend for the human tenor (meaningful voices) rubs off on the feathered vehicle. To re-echo the Boethian caged-bird metaphor, it is possible for allegory to liberate rather than constrain, to be something other than a form that simply converts into humanised symbolic meaning and demands a singular reading.

---

[64] For a useful summary, see Frederick Van Fleteren, 'Principles of Augustine's Hermeneutic: An Overview', in *Augustine: Biblical Exegete*, ed. by Frederick Van Fleteren and Joseph C. Schnaubelt, Order of Saint Augustine (New York, NY: Peter Lang, 2001), pp. 1–32. For an application of the 'both/and' principle, see Barbara Newman, *Medieval Crossover: Reading the Secular against the Sacred* (Notre Dame, IN: University of Notre Dame Press, 2013).

[65] Matilda Tomaryn Bruckner, *Chrétien Continued: A Study of the* Conte du Graal *and Its Verse Continuations* (Oxford: Oxford University Press, 2009), pp. 18–19.

[66] Newman, *Medieval Crossover*, p. 12. Newman describes motets here as a comparison to textual examples.

[67] Trevisa, XII.i (p. 596).

[68] Cohen, 'Inventing with Animals', p. 57.

To extend our understanding of this simultaneity principle, we can think of the parallel between allegorical and vocal transmissions alongside the more obvious translation project that occurs in the poem (and, indeed, across the 'Grant translateur['s]' works).⁶⁹ Chaucer's English – whether deliberating between literal or loose relationships with other elite or institutional languages, or negotiating its way with adopted forms and prosodies – involves itself in another delicate modulation between 'species'. In the broadest sense, *The Parliament* borrows and transposes Italian and French genres, texts, forms and metres to produce a rich 'speaking together' composite.⁷⁰ Rime royal, still a conspicuously new, foreign poetic form in *The Parliament*, allows Chaucer fluently to incorporate and translate whole *ottava rima* passages from Boccaccio's *Teseida* into the description of Venus's temple, and to convey the 'colloquial, "palpable" style, which he had perfected in the eagle's speeches in *The House of Fame* and which he uses here to such fine effect in the debate of the birds'.⁷¹ Translation, in all these senses, facilitates movement between various types of voices, not simply replacing, but assimilating in a 'both/and' (or cross-species) dynamic. Most specifically, though, the final stage of the poem combines birdsong and human song, French and English, in a manner that consciously points up the poem's translation procedures. The 'note' of both birdsong and human song envisages a distinctly human performance and reception, but is also assigned a perfectly natural avian characteristic: that birds 'synge, / … was alwey hir usaunce' (673–4).⁷² The numerous sounds involved here – birdsong, human singing, the spoken utterance, musical notes – all feature in medieval grammatical and musical theories on the articulate voice (the last of these, for instance, is similar to human speech in possessing qualities of discreteness

---

⁶⁹ The phrase is from Eustache Deschamps's *ballade* 'O Socrates plains de philosophie'; Eustache Deschamps, *Œuvres complètes d'Eustache Deschamps*, ed. by A. H. E. Marquis de Queux de St-Hilaire and Gaston Raynaud, 11 vols (Paris: Firmin Didot, 1878–1903), vol. 2, pp. 138–40.
⁷⁰ Olson, 'Aristotle's *Politics*', 56.
⁷¹ Benson, *Riverside Chaucer*, p. 384.
⁷² *Note*, like *leden*, combines human and nonhuman sounds, and can variously mean song, tune, melody, characteristic sound of a bird, the written letter, words, or musical interval. See *MED*, s.v. (n. [3]) *note*, senses 1–2.

and writeability, despite not being language). The effect, though, created by the complex interplay of *voces* at this moment, is not to separate or dismiss categories, but to give further credence to Chaucer's attempts at translating birds through comparison with other validated forms of translation when all come together in one grand utterance. The birds' 'roundel' (675) is clearly identified: it 'imaked was in Fraunce' (677); a foreign song form from a foreign language, but sung in English, the same language that has enacted bird-to-human speech, yet all the while remaining aware of its Frenchness. It is apparently translated for us by the narrator in the same way as I have suggested he translates the birds' *note*: 'The wordes were swiche as ye may heer fynde, / The nexte vers, as I now have in mynde' (678–9). The birds are at the centre of a double translation act that exposes those delicate movements between sounds and voices, without eclipsing either *note*.

The potential intricacies of allegory's doubleness can be richly exploited and productive in the same way. It can be, in other words, a positive form of 'speaking otherwise' in which the processes of anthropomorphising do not simply reflect back the human (as English in the poem does not only reflect itself), but allow us to imagine, to 'translate' other ways of seeing – what I have argued can be seen in *The Parliament* as a speculative 'biotranslation', enacted through artfully conveyed birdspeak. At such times, it becomes difficult to differentiate species traits as specifically human or animal.

The Parliament of Fowls includes a community of pluralistic, competing voices in which the diversity of birds vividly embodies and represents human and nonhuman perspectives incorporated alongside each other. The confusing business throughout the text of reading birds as humans and humans as birds extends to the question of articulate speech, which, on the one hand, reminds us that the birds signify people, but on the other, serve to indicate the force and capabilities of nonhuman creatures who debate some quite specifically avian agendas. *The Parliament*'s debate begins and largely proceeds according to human interests, but it fails to keep out important and determined avian voices.

Plate 5 **Lapwing** *Vanellus vanellus*
© Brian Lawrence
A lappewincke mad he was, / And thus he hoppeth on the gras ('Tale of Tereus', *Confessio Amantis*, V.6041–2)

5
Birds' Form: Enabling Desire and Identities in *Confessio Amantis*

IN ONE FOURTEENTH-CENTURY manuscript of the hugely popular *Ovide moralisé* (Paris, BnF, MS Arsenal 5069, f. 91r), the familiar metamorphoses of the Philomela myth are depicted in an exquisite accompanying illumination. All three characters are shown in their new forms, but the artist has chosen to illustrate hybrid figures, rather than depict the final, fully avian bodies we find in classical and medieval literary versions of the tale itself when Philomela and Procne are transformed into birds by the gods so that they can escape the murderous wrath of Tereus, who himself becomes a bird, too – a nightingale, swallow and hoopoe, respectively. The bottom halves of the characters are clearly avian, but the top halves are unmistakeably the individual torsos of the human characters. Tereus and Procne wear crowns, and the former brandishes a sword. The choice is intriguing, because it clearly asks us to see the appearance of each character not purely as bird, but as a composite of two species; the human still visibly exists as a part of the newly formed creature. This visual representation of the characters post transformation usefully highlights the way that metamorphosis very often works, and does so in another telling of the Philomela myth, that in Gower's *Confessio Amantis*. In the profusion of shape-shifting figures that populate medieval texts from the twelfth century onwards, at least, there is an enmeshment which does not permit total substitution, but a negotiation of bodies at once alike and unlike.[1] The bird-humans in the *Ovide* illustration

---

[1] In approaching hybridity and metamorphosis in this way, I see less distinction between the two than Caroline Walker Bynum observes in her study of

Plate 6
Tereus, Philomela and Procne transformed into birds in a depiction from the *Ovide moralisé*, Paris, BnF, MS Arsenal 5069, f. 91r.

might appear as hybrids, but, in fact, they more accurately remind us of the innate doubleness that exists in metamorphosis. Like the babewyn the *Ovide* figures also recall – that fantastical misfit beast that abounds in the margins of illuminated manuscripts – double-bodies interlace and reciprocate.[2]

> metamorphosis in the twelfth century. Bynum stresses the difference: 'Hybrid reveals a world of difference, a world that *is* and is multiple; metamorphosis reveals a world of stories, of things under way' (italics original); Bynum, *Metamorphosis and Identity*, p. 31. For her summary of the differences between hybridity and metamorphosis, see pp. 28–33. Bynum does acknowledge that 'they are not, of course, completely different', but I suggest that Gower's treatment of metamorphosis in the *Confessio* positions hybridity as an essential feature that continues to accompany the process of being 'under way'.

[2] Babewyns with bird lowers and human heads or torsos are not uncommon: see, e.g., British Library, MS Harley 7026, f. 16, or British Library, MS Stowe 17, f. 58r.

This commingling and assembling of human and nonhuman bodies, I suggest, is what occurs in Gower's version of the antique myth, his 'Tale of Tereus' in *Confessio Amantis*. This text, with its mutations and constructions of bodies which explicitly echo Ovid's *in nova ... mutates ... formas ... corpora* 'bodies changed into new forms' (*Metamorphoses.*, I.1–2), intermingles avian existences with shifting and regenerating human identities, and thus involves human identities alongside treatments of avian species and transformations the most overtly and literally of all the poems I address in this book.[3] The tale of Tereus, principally narrated to depict the sin of sexual rapacity, is typical of Gower's thematic scheme in *Confessio*; it involves the re-telling of a tale from Ovid's *Metamorphoses* (Book 6) in which physical transformations mirror a complex tangle of threatening and subversive 'mutations' relating to the seven sins that Genius purports to exemplify by way of advice to the lovelorn Amans. Birds, creatures of escape and transformation, feature prominently in four of Gower's tales, but most significantly and fully in 'Tereus' as figures of these transgressive sorts of themes.[4] As in Ovid's version, Procne becomes a swallow and Philomela a nightingale, but Tereus becomes a lapwing rather than a hoopoe. For Gower, as for classical poets, birds are curiously compelling emblems of change and his tales re-engage an ancient mythological tradition in which human narratives are often twinned with the aetiologies of bird species.[5] In 'Tereus' human and bird *formes*

[3] P. Ovid Nasonis, *Metamorphoses*, ed. by R. J. Tarrant (Oxford: Oxford University Press, 2004). Translation from Ovid, *Metamorphoses*, trans. by David Raeburn (London: Penguin, 2004). All references to *Metamorphoses* (hereafter *Met.*) are to these editions. Metamorphosis bodies are usually 'hybrid' in Ovid, in that human identity is not entirely lost. See, e.g., Lycaon, who *veteris servat vestigia formae* 'kept some signs of his former self', even in the body of a wolf (*Met.*, I.237–8).
[4] See also 'Ceix and Alceone' (hereafter 'CeixAl'), 'Phebus and Cornide' (II.783–817), and 'Neptune and Cornix' (V.6145–6224). For comparison, see, respectively, Ovid's *Metamorphoses*, XI.410–748 and II.531–632. The tale of Neptune in Ovid is embedded in that of Phoebus. All references to *Confessio Amantis* (hereafter *CA*) are to John Gower, *Confessio Amantis*, TEAMS Middle English Texts Series, ed. by Russell Peck and Lat. trans. by Andrew Galloway, 3 vols (Kalamazoo, MI: Medieval Institute Publications, 2006).
[5] For a catalogue of birds in Greek myths, see Forbes Irving, *Metamorphosis in Greek Myths*, pp. 223–59. Forbes Irving notes that there are 'nearly fifty

interrelate in ways that reveal avian identity through human narrative, but also suggest the indispensable importance of other beings to the construction of human, embodied identities. Most specifically, avian bodies that occur across the poem and culminate in the final act of turning-bird feature not as figurative images, but as powerful mobilisers of individual desire, capacity and being. In 'Tereus', arguably *Confessio*'s most gruesome and horrific narrative, 'briddes kinde' (V.5939) is engaged in the making and unmaking of the human body. As brief metaphorical expressions and finally as literal transformations that envelop the central gory human mutilations, they reflect and recall bodies that come together in disquieting, problematic sexual acts, poignantly resonant with the violence and violations of dismembered body parts and consumed flesh, and are clearly prioritised in the poem's most overt, concluding instance of forms 'set atwinne' (V.5942), in which avian metamorphoses configure the human in new, plural forms.

Birds are bound up with the broad scheme of human embodiment, but in the ultimate metamorphoses that conclude the tale, we are most affectedly engaged with individual characters. Birds in 'Tereus' represent orthodox human types. They are at times figures of female vulnerability and loquacity, or of aggressive male dominance, but Gower's presentation of avian characteristics also contributes to more transgressive considerations of these types; avian identities are part of figuring Tereus's uncontrollable lust, but also responsible for a degree of troubling moral ambiguity surrounding these desires. Bird bodies demonstrate their potency most strikingly, however, when they become kinds of enablement for Philomela and Procne, not by way of comparison or enactment, but because the women actually *become* birds to achieve a liberated expression in bird flight and birdsong which exceeds the boundaries of human form. In the last stages of the tale, narratives double to involve reciprocating human and avian lives that become one and the same. Assimilation enters new territory here: species distances

> aetiological stories of birds and hardly any of animals' (p. 96), highlighting the extent to which avian and human narratives have continuously been associated in mythology. For his discussion of birds in metamorphosis myths, see ibid., chapter 2, pp. 96–127.

are not entirely dissolved or forgotten, but figurative relationships are distorted so that similarities are meaningful in alternative, literal arrangements.

Gower and Metamorphosis

By the time Gower came to write his most extensive work, there was a considerable legacy of texts from the late twelfth century onwards that show a cultural preoccupation with exploring, depicting and representing the shifting boundaries between human and nonhuman, which in large part reflected theological anxieties. This phenomenon has been well studied, particularly with recent interests from the 'animal turn'.[6] Joyce E. Salisbury has written broadly of this 'twelfth-century acceptance of an animal side of people' with a view to examining how beasts became an essential metaphor for evolving conceptions of the human.[7] From the historical perspective, Caroline Walker Bynum summarises that

> what we find is writers returning again and again to worry ... the possibility of species-crossing, body-hopping, metamorphosis. Surely the tremendous intellectual effort devoted to categorizing types of change, to ferreting out its rules, to limiting whilst not denying species-crossing ... suggests the importance of understanding person as psychosomatic unity.[8]

---

[6] In recent critical work on twelfth- and thirteenth-century hybridity and metamorphosis, writers such as Gerald of Wales, Gervase of Tilbury, William of Malmesbury and Marie de France have all received attention, particularly in regard to the popularity of werewolves as a shapeshifting figure: see, e.g., Bynum, *Metamorphosis and Identity*, especially pp. 77–111, and, most recently, Peggy McCracken, *In the Skin of a Beast: Sovereignty and Animality in Medieval France* (Chicago, IL: University of Chicago Press, 2017), pp. 37–67. For a broader survey of these themes, see Jeffrey Jerome Cohen, *Hybridity, Identity and Monstrosity in Medieval Britain*. On medieval embodiment, see, by the same author, *Medieval Identity Machines* (Minneapolis, MN: University of Minnesota Press, 2003).

[7] Joyce E. Salisbury, 'Human Beasts and Bestial Humans in the Middle Ages', in *Animal Acts*, pp. 9–22 (14). See also Salisbury's *The Beast Within*, particularly chapter 6, pp. 121–45. For discussion specifically on monsters and hybrids in marginal illuminations, see Michael Camille, *Image on the Edge: The Margins of Medieval Art* (London: Reaktion Books, 1992).

[8] Bynum, *Metamorphosis and Identity*, p. 110.

Bodies mattered because they are material (despite the popular *contemptus mundi* trope which devalued or despised them as corrupted). In unity with the soul, bodies constituted individual essence, provided the sentient means of experiencing, both on earth and in heaven: 'the resurrection body, reassembled from its earlier physical bits and conforming in every detail to its earthly structure, was a guarantee that ... we will not be, in the afterlife, something we cannot recognize'.[9] For Bynum, the ubiquitous hybrid and morphing creatures in literature and art of the period are bound up with a whole range of scholastic vexations: a response to fears about metempsychosis and fragmentation; ideas about just how real bodily conversion is during the processes of consumption and digestion; natural philosophy debates on exactly how change occurs; or whether corpses ought to be buried intact, or segmented and dispersed.[10] In general, she argues, whilst it provoked wonder, somatic change was frightening and suspicious, particularly because it suggested the 'possibility of slippage of the human body away from soul' which may have worrying soteriological implications.[11] Fascination with transformation and combination, paradoxically, had more to do with delimiting, maintaining and defining boundaries. As Salisbury puts it, 'metamorphosis is about change and about the fear of change. If humans change, can they lose their identity, indeed even their humanity?'[12] Despite the Church's official position on the demarcation between man and beast, animals in metamorphosis narratives insistently force human identities and categories to disperse and reassemble in forms that must include the animal, however disturbingly.

---

[9] Caroline Walker Bynum, 'Why All the Fuss about the Body? A Medievalist's Perspective', *Critical Enquiry*, 22:1 (1995), 1–33 (p. 24).

[10] For discussion of change in a twelfth-century context, see Bynum, *Metamorphosis and Identity*, pp. 22–8. For corpses, see Caroline Walker Bynum, *The Resurrection of the Body in Western Christianity, 200–1336* (New York, NY: Columbia University Press, 1995).

[11] For references to the views of early church fathers on metamorphosis, and rejection of Ovidian metamorphosis, see Salisbury, *The Beast Within*, p. 141.

[12] Ibid., p. 140.

The prevalence of mutating, misfit bodies in Gower's century has received less attention, but it is clear that the fascination persisted.[13] Bynum has remarked that, for the most part, examples of change in the twelfth-century phenomenon actually involved hybridity, rather than genuine metamorphosis. The possibility of physically replacing one appearance with another was horrifying to the point that stories and images depicting the Ovidian notion of mutation were sometimes condemned as heretical.[14] Indeed, Ovidian metamorphosis inverts a classic model of transubstantiation in the late Middle Ages – the substance is permanent, but the accidence changes. That Gower models this metamorphosis in *Confessio*, though, suggests possibilities about how writers approached and represented other aspects of metamorphosis that Bynum does not consider. Gower's transformations, as I read them in 'Tereus' at least, not only present a 'discourse of animality' at the heart of these re-configurations, but also engage with auspicious forms of metamorphosis that solicit non-deprecatory or non-fearful responses.[15]

[13] Marginalia continued to demonstrate an artistic fascination with babewyns. One such example (British Library, MS Add. 42130, f. 175r [Luttrell Psalter]) shows a cadaverous-looking queen with an avian body, and a reptilian, foliated tail, making her a truly multiple body that traverses animal and vegetal forms. Salisbury provides a simple, indicative graph charting the growth of hybrid forms in illuminated manuscripts between the ninth to fifteenth centuries; Salisbury, *The Beast Within*, p. 101.

[14] Bynum, *Metamorphosis and Identity*, p. 178. Bynum concludes that Gerald of Wales's famous werewolf in his *Topographica hibernica* (II.lii) is, significantly, not a full example of metamorphosis because it does not involve metempsychosis – there is always a complete human, with body and soul, inside the wolf's skin; *Metamorphosis and Identity*, pp. 105–9. Examples from the likes of Marie de France are clearly an exception to this theory, although even Marie steers clear of detailed descriptions of the physical changes themselves. Likewise, Gower's examples do enact metempsychosis but do not give explicit or extended detail about the actual change itself.

[15] Salisbury, *The Beast Within*, p. 140. Bynum's study does, after all, confine itself to the twelfth and thirteenth centuries. Even within the centuries on which *Metamorphosis and Identity* focuses, much recent scholarship on shape-shifting in, e.g., Marie's fables and lais, has posited divergent ways of reading how and why transformation is significant. See Miranda Griffin, *Transforming Tales: Rewriting Metamorphosis in Medieval French Literature* (Oxford: Oxford University Press, 2015), pp. 102–19, and Crane, *Animal Encounters*, pp. 42–68. Christine Ferlampin-Acher has suggested that twelfth-century hybrid forms are less evident in the thirteenth century and then reappear as transforming bodies rather than composites in the fourteenth; Christine Ferlampin-Acher, 'Le monstre

The responses to bodily change that Bynum emphasises (suspicion, anxiety) are not absent from Gower's text, but they are not necessarily responses to transformation itself, and, as I demonstrate shortly in another tale of avian transformation, 'Ceix and Alceone', there could be other, more positive ways of dealing with metamorphosis.

As *Confessio* makes clear, of course, the pre-eminent author for ideas and stories about shape-shifting in the late Middle Ages was Ovid, who only continued to grow in popularity. His *Metamorphoses* was prolifically copied in manuscripts across the period, culminating in the best known of Ovidian commentaries, the *Ovide moralisé*, a text that trilingual Gower very likely knew and used.[16] If, as Bynum has warned, the twelfth- and thirteenth-century enthusiasm for Ovid is categorically 'not read as being about body and identity, ... not a revival of interest in metamorphosis', Gower's project in *Confessio* near the end of the fourteenth century presents something less typical, closer to the classical conceptions as expressed in Ovid's vision of fluid, mutable forms and the possibility of metempsychosis. The *Ovide moralisé* continues a tradition of scholastic treatment that sought to integrate and adapt Ovid's works through a dense process of allegorisation and glossing:

> Ovides dist: 'Mes cuers vieult dire
> Les forms qui muess furent
> En nouviaux cors'. Aucun qui durent
> Li'autour espondre et declairer
> S'entremistrent de l'empirier,
> De l'auteur reprendre et desdire ...
> (72–81)

---

dans les romans des XIIIe et XIVe siècles', in *Ecriture et modes de pensée au moyen âge (VIIIe-XVe siècle)*, ed. by Dominique Boutet and Laurence Harf-Lancner (Paris: Ecole Normale Supérieure, 1993), pp. 69–87.

[16] There are twenty-one extant manuscripts of the *Ovide moralisé*, dating from c.1320 to the end of the fifteenth century. Prose versions were also produced. See Ana Pairet, 'Recasting the *Metamorphoses* in Fourteenth-Century France: The Challenges of the *Ovide moralisé*', in *Ovid in the Middle Ages*, ed. by James G. Clark, Frank T. Coulson and Kathryn L. McKinley (Cambridge: Cambridge University Press, 2011), pp. 83–107. On Gower's sources for Ovid, see Kathryn L. McKinley, 'Gower and Chaucer: Readings of Ovid in Late Medieval England', in *Ovid in the Middle Ages*, pp. 197–230. See also C. Mainzer, 'John Gower's Use of the Medieval Ovid in the *Confessio Amantis*', *MÆ*, 41 (1972), 215–29. For discussion of the Ovid revival, see *Ovid in the Middle Ages* generally.

[Ovid says: 'I feel I must tell about the forms that were changed into new bodies.' Some, whose task it was to explain and illuminate the author's meaning, began to make it obscure, correcting and contradicting the author.][17]

In treating the Philomela myth, the *Ovide*, purportedly citing a version by a certain Crestiens, offers an odd, if striking, allegoresis.[18] And similarly, Pierre Bersuire's (Petrus Berchorius) Christianised reading of 'Ceix and Alceone' in *Ovidius Moralizatus* re-casts the narrative in eschatological terms. Gower's treatment of the *Metamorphoses* within his complicated framework (some forty stories from Ovid) bears resemblance to these moralising programmes. The tales function as *exempla* in the context of Amans's confession, each one serving to warn against a particular sin, which Genius makes plain at the beginning and end of each tale. However, despite his likely use of the *Ovide* and, probably, Pierre Bersuire, Gower is noticeably freer of his sources' penchant for allegory. Gower concerns himself with the literal action and what *briddes forme* enables (Genius's interpretative comments following 'Ceix and Alceone' are focused on dreams, not exegesis of birds; IV.3124–31).

Even if the fourteenth century still indulged allegorical interpretation, there is evidence in Gower, then, that metamorphosis could be dealt with in ways that also emphasise and confront real transformation, the 'relationship between shape, story and identity' that Bynum attributes to modern interpretations of Ovid.[19] As Bruce Harbert puts it, Gower shows us that it was 'possible to take one's Ovid neat in the Middle Ages'.[20] The stability of species categories and forms suggested by the Genesis account of creation in which

---

[17] Text and translation from Pairet, 'Recasting the Metamorphoses', p. 89.
[18] Despite the unambiguously bodily nature of the transformation depicted in the *Ovide* illustration, the text itself does provide an allegorical translation. The exegesis presents Pandion as God, Procne variously as the soul and human nature, Tereus as the body, Itys as the fruit of holy life, and Philomela in nightingale form represents the vagaries of earthly love (*OM*, VI.3719–3855).
[19] Bynum, *Metamorphosis and Identity*, p. 100.
[20] Bruce Harbert, 'Ovid and John Gower', in *Ovid Renewed: Ovidian Influences on Literature and Art from the Middle Ages to the Twentieth Century*, ed. by Charles Martindale (Cambridge: Cambridge University Press, 1988), pp. 83–97 (83). For Harbert, Gower demonstrates this more than any other writer.

beings are created in one day by God is troubled by Ovid's vision of matter in flux, in perpetual change:

> omnia mutantur, nihil interit: errat et illinc
> huc venit, hinc illuc, et quoslibet occupat artus
> spiritus eque feris humana in corpora transit
> inque feras noster, nec tempore deperit ullo

[All is subject to change and nothing to death. The spirit in each of us wanders from place to place; it enters whatever body it pleases, crossing over from beast to man, and back again to beast. It never perishes wholly.]

(*Met.*, XV.165–9)

Gower's earlier foray into Ovidian metamorphosis is closer to orthodox treatments of metamorphosis. In *Vox Clamantis*, the terrifying allegorical dream visions of mutating, rioting beasts are best left in the metaphorical realm because they are deeply unnatural and go against man's proper and right use of a distinguishing rational mind to separate himself from abominable acts. God forbid, indeed, that in reality *Deuia natura sic errat ab ordine* 'nature wandered so far from her regular course' (*VC*, I.4.319).[21] Despite the overtly Christian agenda of *Confessio*, it is not allegorical (although it includes allegory within). There is a lesson to be learnt from Tereus's behaviour, but the lapwing is assuredly a lapwing. Bodies in Gower literally change and species combine, such that identities are complicated, extended and inter-translated. These transformed bodies, however, are not *monstra* 'monsters', as in *Vox Clamantis* (I.vi.462), but naturalised, sympathised and legitimised, sometimes perversely so, in ways that expand the relevance and possibilities of combined and changed bodies so that they are less fearsome and condemnable violations against the natural, and more sites of powerful revelation.[22]

---

[21] *Vox Clamantis*, in *The Works of John Gower*, ed. by G. C. Macaulay, 4 vols (Oxford: Clarendon Press, 1902), vol. 4, and *The Major Latin Works of John Gower*, trans. by Eric W. Stockton (Seattle, WA: University of Washington Press, 1962). For the sequence of transforming birds, see I.vii (pp. 61–2 in Stockton).

[22] Genius does not pass judgement when bodies change, but simply describes how a character is 'forschope' (I.370), 'were bore' (I.397), or 'torned' (V.6004).

Ceix and Alceone – Conforming Bodies

In *The Parliament of Fowls,* Chaucer is able to achieve humorous results by mapping incongruous avian and human bodily characteristics onto each other, translations in which ducks can make exclamations involving hats, or—elsewhere in the *Canterbury Tales*—Pertelote queries Chauntecleer's lack of a 'mannes herte, and … a berd' (*NPT*, 2920), or a metaphor conveying a male peregrine's falseness assigns him sandals (*SqT*, 555). Gower, too, is capable of employing a similar tactic to great effect. Like Chaucer, he reminds us that bird bodies are not human bodies, but the dissonance does not lead to laughter. Gower is prepared to recognise and make something of incompatible interspecies bodies, but he is also interested in bodily consonance, not straightforward anthropomorphism which replaces one identity with another, but the creation of a middle zone where newly focused, more complex and comprehensive bodies are possible—bird bodies that function as enablers. The characters of Philomela, Procne and Tereus are all more vividly and profoundly embodied when the natural world comes into play and interacts.

Before I turn to 'Tereus' let us consider a tale from the previous book in *Confessio* involving bird metamorphosis, 'Ceix and Alceone', in which the intricacies of aligned and misaligned bodies anticipate those to come in the later narrative. Human-avian discordance is highlighted persistently by Genius in the final moment of the tale when husband and wife are transformed into kingfishers (halcyons): Alceone's form reminds her of what she has lost, that 'other lif' (IV.3112). Unlike bodies, felt in poignantly actual terms, are clearly an issue here, as is suggested particularly by the verb 'fondeth': Alecone *tries* 'in hire briddes forme':

> And whan sche sih hire lord livende
> In liknesse of a bridd swimmende,
> And sche was of the same sort,
> So as sche mihte do desport,
> Upon the joie which sche hadde
> Hire wynges bothe abrod sche spradde,
> And him, so as sche mai suffise,

> Beclipte and keste in such a wise,
> As sche was whilom wont to do:
> Hire wynges for hire armes tuo
> Sche tok, and for hire lippes softe
> Hire hard bille, and so fulofte
> Sche fondeth in hire briddes forme,
> If that sche mihte hirself conforme
> To do the plesance of a wif,
> As sche dede in that other lif:
> For thogh sche hadde hir pouer lore,
> Hir wil stod as it was tofore,
> And serveth him so as sche mai.
> (IV.3097–3115)

Dorothy Yamamoto has argued that the end of this tale is poignant because of limitation: 'Alceone yearns to do everything for Ceyx that she once did, but there is now no way in which this is possible. Wings are not arms, and beaks are not at all like lips'.[23] For Yamamoto, Gower emphasises incongruence in the simple adjectives that compare lips to beak: 'hire lippes softe / Hire harde bile'. This is true, and the subjunctive mode of the passage certainly highlights incapacity: 'So as sche *mihte* ... sche *mai* suffise ... If that sche *mihte*'. But a comparison with Ovid's telling of this moment reveals that Gower merely describes here; he does not convey grief. In Ovid, she 'vainly attempted / to kiss his lips; the bill was too hard and the kisses were cold' (*Met.*, IV.737–8). Gower's *fondeth* echoes something of these pitiable efforts, but the moment is also active: she 'tok' 'wynges for hire armes' and is quite able to 'serveth him so as sche mai' ('Beclipte and keste') 'in such a wise / As sche was whilom wont to do'. In fact, the overall action of this passage in Gower does not suggest impediment. Whilst difference is acknowledged, having lost her human abilities (3113), Alceone's will is unchanged, such that she acclimatises to her new form quickly to express the 'joie' that she feels, a joy that ignites when she sees her lord 'livende / In liknesse of a bridd'. The sense of 'conforme' is significant here, with the suggestion that she accommodates or moulds her old will and new body in a re-configuration that

---

[23] Yamamoto, *Boundaries of the Human*, p. 40.

corresponds shapes and kinds to enable strange, but not primarily limited, pleasures.[24] The verb 'fondeth' in the previous line, too, adds to this sense. The word is resistant to simple interpretation in its various possible meanings in this passage. Whilst the indications of limitation foreground the sense of 'struggle', the emphasis on Alceone's joy and her ultimately successful efforts to 'conforme' may bring into play more optimistic meanings of 'fondeth' below the surface. That is, this woman in her new avian form does not merely suffer, but seeks and enjoys, particularly with the emphasis on her powerful and persistent 'desport'.[25]

So whilst bird bodies 'make it impossible for them to express their love in fully human terms', the sense of impossibility should not be overstated, nor the superiority of fully human terms.[26] After all, the mutation into bird form is effected in the first place by the gods to turn 'deth to lyve' (IV.3094) in order that the 'trowthe of love' (IV.3090) can be sustained. Another alteration that Gower makes to Ovid is to have both characters turned into birds at the same time. In Ovid's version, Ceix only *fatis obnoxius isdem* 'suffered the self-same fate' (*Met.*, XI.742) of being turned into a bird when the gods take pity on Alceone. The effect of Gower's revision is that birds' bodies are less an endurance or pitiable fate, and more new, curious embodiments that make way for future possibilities. That Ceix becomes a bird at the same time as Alceone heightens the appropriateness of their new beings, together. Their old, human lives are not forgotten, but they are swept up, involved, in new conformations in which their futures – part bird, part human – are played out across time. The impossibility that Yamamoto discerns seems, in fact, more about possibility, for what they are 'wont to do', the 'desport' or 'plesance', is clearly still realised: 'into this ilke day' (IV.3116) 'many a dowhter and a sone / Thei bringen forth of

---

[24] See *MED*, s.v. (v.) *conformen*, senses 1, 3 and 4; also (adj.) *conform* 'similar or corresponding (in shape or degree)'.

[25] See *MED*, s.v. (v.) *fonden*, senses 5–8. For examples of *fonden* in the sense of sexual pleasure or indulgence, see sense 5. In *CA*, Gower uses the word in relation to Venus: 'And sche [Venus] which thoghte hire lustes fonde, / Diverse loves tok in honde' (V.1421). See also OE *fandian* 'to try, tempt, prove, examine, explore, seek, search out'; Bosworth-Toller, s.v. (v.) *fandian*.

[26] Yamamoto, *Boundaries of the Human*, p. 39.

briddes kinde' (IV.3118–19). *Briddes forme* has not prevented, but become an embodied expression of characters' most fervent desires.

The effects in 'Ceix and Alceone' are multiplied and intensified in 'Tereus' where otherly forms are also accommodated and newly fashioned to become, as Hugh White has said of nature generally in the poem, sites of 'enormous poetic power as the focus of contesting energies'.[27] Metamorphoses can seem unnatural and shocking (in some forms horrifying in 'Tereus'), but to be 'stranged' from one's 'oghne kinde' (V.6040) or 'turned out of kinde' (V.6004) can also be desirable; the action accentuates difference, but a difference of species and natural conduct (*kinde*) that can also turn *unkinde* to *kinde*, and reveal compatibility and liberation in these reconfigured avian-human identities.

A Raptor and Ravisher – Vulnerability and Violent Desire

The most distinctive birds to appear before the metamorphoses themselves constitute an innovative re-working of the avian predatory image that Gower inherits from Ovid's description of Tereus's rape of Philomela – specifically a goshawk clutching its small-bird prey:

> [He] hield hire under in such wise,
> That sche ne myhte noght arise,
> Bot lay oppressed and desesed,
> As if a goshawk hadde sesed
> A brid, which dorste noght for fere
> Remue: and thus this tirant there
> Beraft hire ...
>
> (V.5641–7)

Brief though it is, the simile adumbrates the sequence of bodily violations that play across the poem, which culminate in the final fragmentations and integrations of the metaphorphoses. In one of the tales succeeding 'Tereus', Genius uses another bird metamorphosis

---

[27] Hugh White, *Nature, Sex, and Goodness in a Medieval Literary Tradition* (Oxford: Oxford University Press, 2000), p. 47.

to illustrate his point about defiling virginity. Cornix escapes Neptune's lusty force through transforming 'Out of wommanisshe kinde / Into a briddes' (V.6199–6200). There are obvious echoes with the previous tale: a woman, at the point of attack from a male, achieves safety in the form of a bird.[28] This is, of course, what happens in the final scene of 'Tereus', but in the rape scene it is the opposite which is emphasised – limitation and oppression. It has been remarked that Philomela's human, and ultimately defiant, form is registered at the moment she is grasped by Tereus as hawk, that she is not 'subsumed into the dominant image of the hawk swooping down on its victim' because she is unable to 'arise' (V.5642), 'which is inappropriate to a bird seized on the wing—instead it reminds us of her real, human identity'.[29] I suggest that this is not the case, that Philomela *is*, in fact, subsumed into the 'dominant image'. Like some images in manuscript illuminations, the hawk is not depicted in flight at this moment, but pinning its prey 'under' (V.5641) itself on the ground, poised to pluck and tear, making *arise* (or an inability to arise) entirely appropriate.[30] Philomela is incapacitated, 'oppressed and desesed' (V.5643).[31] Envisaged as consumable flesh, her body coterminous with the prey bird, it is her vulnerability that is emphasised at this moment. Defiance comes later.

Gower's simile closely mirrors Chaucer's depiction of Troilus and Criseyde's precursory sexual embrace, in which Criseyde, like Philomela, is implicitly portrayed as a seized bird.[32] The narrator's question, rhetorically unanswered, conveys something of the meta-

---

[28] Chaucer's *SqT* also implies something intrinsic and intimate between birdness and female sufferance; e.g. lines 450–71, where Canace shows great empathy for the grieving peregrine.

[29] Yamamoto, *Boundaries of the Human*, p. 41.

[30] See, e,g., British Library, MS Add. 24686 (Alphonso Psalter), f. 14v; Oxford, Bodleian Library, MS Douce 366 (Ormesby Psalter), f. 38r; and British Library, MS Stowe 17, f. 81v.

[31] The usual glossing of *desesed* gives 'distressed' or 'tormented', but 'dead' is also apparent. See *MED*, s.v. (v.) *disesen*, sense 3; (v.) *decesen*.

[32] Chaucer's immediate source for this image is Boccaccio's *Filicolo*, II.165–6. The act of predation necessarily presumes consumption, which Forbes Irving identifies as a metaphorical relation to sex generally in Greek myth, too, 'particularly between eating one's own family and incest', all of which exists in Gower's version of the Tereus myth; Forbes Irving, *Metamorphosis in Greek Myths*, p. 103.

phor's cultural force, the familiar assimilation of sexual desire and violent predation: 'What myghte or may the sely larke seye / Whan that the sperhauk hath it in his foot?' (III.1191–2). The moment is a disturbing combination of adulation and anxiety ('gladnesse' and 'hevynesse' [III.1196–7]) which resolves 'wo into blisse' (III.1221) but does not shake off the menace of predatory desire. Criseyde ends up singing like a nightingale, but this joy is accompanied by the fact that she 'stynteth first' (III.1234), and because the bird recalls the earlier nightingale in Book II (918–24), which opens with Procne the swallow singing about her sister's plight (II.64–70). The predator-prey motif, in fact, is a foreboding expression of the male-female sexual dynamic throughout Chaucer's poem: both the lovers are variously compared to the hawk, lion, falcon and eagle, and the lark, boar and deer.

Gower inherits a familiar trope, but in his own poem the metaphor is given new impetus because the concerns with bodiliness and embodiment suggest further possibilities for exploring human-nonhuman correlations. Crucially, this first comparison of Philomela and Tereus to birds prefigures further avian references and, finally, the actual transformation beyond metaphor into bird shape. That Gower chooses the avian image more than once in his tale should affect how we read this first dramatic instance. In the case of Philomela, we should not see her casting off the bird appearance to 'register her own [human] experience', but, rather, recognise that this experience is to be specifically understood and conveyed through the intimate joining of human and bird bodies.[33] Like the other women-turned-birds in *Confessio*, Philomela's plight is conveyed through and with avian experience. Distinctions between sexes (marked by violation of female by male) are paralleled in the breach of species distinctions, so that one (metamorphosis) becomes a reaction to the other (violence). These relations suggest weakness and incapacity, but they will also ultimately come to embody power. I shall return later to empowerment, but for now I remain with the predator-prey conjoining to examine how this metaphorical vision of the rape engages the nonhuman

---

[33] Yamamoto, *Boundaries of the Human*, p. 41.

in destructive, though instinctive, forms of desire, and suggests a disconcerting moral ambiguity to Tereus's heinous actions which reverberates across *Confessio*'s anxious queries about kind.

Although the nonhuman imagery in Gower's description of the rape emphasises Philomela's inaction, we should also expect it to reveal aspects of Tereus's character. Gower does, after all, focus on Tereus in his version of the myth to warn against the sin of 'ravine' (V.5549). A likely source for Gower was *Troilus and Criseyde*, and also Chaucer's telling of the myth in *The Legend of Good Women*, but Ovid's version already provides inspiration with its typical predator-prey couplings: the lamb/wolf and dove/hawk (*Met.*, VI.527–30).[34] Gower's Tereus, too, behaves 'riht as a wolf' (V.5633), but it is the hawk that becomes the central comparison, specified as a goshawk (V.5644) – a familiar bird amongst the nobility, prized by falconers for its fierce hunting abilities:

> The goshauk is a real foul and is i-armed more wiþ boldenesse þan wiþ clawes. And as moche as kynde bynemeþ hir in quantite of body, he rewardiþ hire in boldnesse of herte ... he[o] is a coueytous foul to taken oþir foules, and for þe takynge of oþir foules for pray he[o] is icplepid *aucipiter* 'a raptour and rauyschere'.[35]

As Bartholomaeus does here in Trevisa's translation, Gower plays upon the etymological link between birds of prey (raptors) and the act of ravishing: Middle English *ravine* (from Old French *ravine*; Lat. *rapere*) refers to both robbery (including the forcible seizing of a woman), and to beasts or 'foules of ravyne' (*PF*, 323).[36] Gower's

---

[34] The *Ovide* does not include any metaphors at this moment in the tale. Chaucer sticks close to Ovid, without elaboration of the bird metaphor. He mentions the lamb-wolf duo, omits the hawk, and transfers the dove to partner the eagle (*LGW*, VII.2318–19). Both *LGW* and *Tr* are thought to have been written in the first half of the 1380s, and so were, quite conceivably, sources for Gower (*Confessio* was begun in 1386 and revised in 1390).

[35] Trevisa, XII.3 (p. 607). See also Frederick II, *The Art of Falconry*, p. 112.

[36] *MED*, s.v. (n.) *ravine*, senses 1a and 3b, and (n.) *ravinour*, which includes the sense of a predatory beast or bird (sense d). OE *hafoc* 'hawk', related to OE *hebban* 'to raise', is also derived from an Indo-European root meaning 'to seize'. ME had an extensive cluster of terms ultimately deriving from Lat. *rapere* centring around the associated ideas of seizing, stealing and preying; see, e.g. the long list of words that lead on from (n. [1]) *rape*. Not only *ravine*, but *tirannie* (*MED*, [n.]) was associated with the goshawk. Gower may have had in

choice is precise and apt: seizing and violent predation, as the etymology suggested to medieval writers, are the goshawk's ways, but in choosing to focus the tale on 'that tirant raviner' (V.5627) – the very act the tale purports to illustrate and condemn – Gower makes them Tereus's ways, too. He is envisaged as 'a raptour and rauyschere': '[He] hield hire under in such wise, / That sche ne myhte noght arise.' The goshawk's renowned covetousness, though, could also lead to very favourable associations in medieval elite hunting culture, even, in fact, in other texts involving avian metamorphosis. In Marie de France's *Yonec*, the goshawk maintains positive associations: *Gentil oisel ad en ostur* 'The goshawk is a noble bird' (122) who has undergone *cinc mues* [...] *u* [...] *sis* 'five or six moultings' (111).[37] Muldumarec, in fact, specifies what sort of bird he is so that the lady does not fear him: *neiez poür* 'do not be afraid' (121). In the *Ovide*'s version of the Tereus myth, Philomela is skilled in falconry terminology and moult patterns, and the goshawk is mentioned specifically (*OM*, VI.2398–2401). Bartholomaeus describes how goshawks 'beþ iloued of hire lordes', and in *The Parliament of Fowls*, Chaucer thoroughly exploits the association of birds of prey with

mind the *PF*: 'Ther was the tiraunt with his fetheres donne / And grey — I mene the goshauk' (334–5). Alan of Lille makes a similar connection in *De Planctu* (II.150), as does Bartholomaeus, implicitly, in discussing the bird's cruelty (Trevisa, XII.3 [p. 607]). Cf. Trevisa, XII.i.34 (p. 600), *Etym.*, XII.vii.55, and *PF*, in which last text the ferocity and violence of the raptors generally is very apparent in the description of these species in the avian catalogue preceding the debate (323–40).

[37] *Yonec*, in *Lais Bretons (XII-XIII siècles): Marie de France et ses contemporains*, ed. by Nathalie Koble and Mireille Séguy (Paris: Champion, 2011), pp. 308–33; and *The Lais of Marie de France*, pp. 86–96. Miranda Griffin notes that the added plumage detail implies experience, and, therefore, a noble lady's keener interest in the bird for hawking, comparing this detail to similar references in the twelfth-century romances *Erec et Enide* and *Le Bel Inconnu*, in which older birds are desirable too; Griffin, *Transforming Tales*, p. 6. In the translation to this passage, I have amended Burgess and Busby's 'hawk' to 'goshawk' for *ostur*, following Griffin (ibid.). Dafydd Evans also reads *ostur* to mean goshawk, citing the Anglo-Norman verse fragment of Abelard of Bath's *De avibus tractatus* as an analogue; Dafydd Evans, 'The Nobility of Knight and Falcon', in *The Ideals and Practice of Medieval Knighthood III*, ed. by Christopher Harper-Bill and Ruth Harvey (Woodbridge: Boydell Press, 1990), pp. 79–99. See Evans, too, for more extensive discussion of the goshawk in relation to hunting.

nobility, to the extent that the birds, comically, behave just like their human owners.[38]

A straightforward reading of the nonhuman imagery in this scene perceives Tereus as a debased, irrational beast (rather like the allegorical creatures in *Vox Clamantis* who denote a human loss of *innatae rationis* 'inborn rationality' [I.ii.177]). The moral of the tale certainly encourages this analysis: Tereus is a deplorable, 'ruide ... knyht' (V.5638) whose actions are to be understood as condemnable. Gower wants us to be clear on this point: 'Of such Ravine it was pite' (V.5650). In the homiletic introduction to the tale, Genius warns Amans that 'he that wole of pourveance / Be such a weie his lust avance / He shal it after sore abie' (V. 5539–40). Amans's response, too, directs our reaction:

> Mi fader, goddes forebode!
> Me were levere be fortrode
> With wilde hors and be todrawe,
> Er I ayein love and his lawe
> Dede eny thing or loude or stille,
> Which were noght mi ladi wille.
>   (V.6053–8)

And in case we have not got the point, Genius also follows up with the allegory of Robbery who 'tok his lust under the schawe' (*CA*, V.6133), before giving us two more tales on the same theme: 'Neptune and Cornix', and 'Calistona'. Genius also highlights that Tereus does not behave as a man: 'he was so wod / That he no reson understod' (V.5639–40). In line with the usual tradition which differentiates between human and nonhuman, Tereus is described as a beast to signal his abomination. Elsewhere in *Confessio*, too, Gower expresses orthodox sentiments which may reflect upon our reading of Tereus:

> For god the lawes hath assissed
> Als wel to reson as to kinde,
> Bit he the bestes wolde binde
> Only to lawes of nature,
> Bot to the mannes creature

---

[38] Trevisa, XII.iii (p. 609).

> God gaf him reson forth withal,
> Whereof that he nature schal
> Upon the causes modefie,
> That he schal do no lecherie,
> And yit he schal hise lustes have.
> (VII.5372–81)

As has been shown by others, however, Genius's authority is not beyond question in the poem, one of various factors that make us consider 'whether what is said about Nature [and natural acts] is wholly reliable'.[39] The lines above gloss over the implicit conundrum they present, that man is required to *modefie* his nature, but may still be admitted his *lustes*. Even in Genius's instructional prefatory lines to 'Tereus', there is a niggling ambiguity:

> So as it hath befalle er this,
> In loves cause hou that it is
> A man to take be Ravine
> The preie which is femeline.
> (V.5547–50)

There is a noticeable generalisation here, as though to remark proverbially on how men habitually *take þe Ravine*, and the prey is always and necessarily *femeline*. More intriguingly, *ravine* is conducted in 'loves cause', the very subject that hapless Amans has come to Venus and Genius for in the first place, rather than 'lust' identified at the end of the tale (V.6051). The verb *befalle* resounds throughout the tale, as it does in others, sometimes taking on a note of inevitability. This is appropriate for the genre, but just as the pitiable 'sostres, that ben bothe felle' (V.5880), so Tereus falls into his passion, unstoppably. The tragedy is Tereus's, too: 'it befelle of Tereus' (V.6052).[40] Love and lust seem to be confused, such that sexuality is treated as natural and expected, as much in humans as in all other creatures.

This unsettling ambiguity is evident, too, in Gower's presentation of Tereus's character more generally in the tale. The differences

---

[39] White, *Nature, Sex and Goodness*, p. 174. White discusses Genius's unreliability generally in the poem at pp. 174–6.
[40] Cf. Eolus in the 'Tale of Canace and Machaire': 'Anon into Malencolie, As thogh it were a frenesie, / He fell' (III.209–11).

between Ovid's version and Gower's are telling here. A clear modification Gower makes is in the presentation of Tereus before the rape. As R. F. Yeager has also noted, in contrast to Ovid's inauspicious omens betiding tragedy, Gower's opening to the tale proper is without *fausto ... omine* 'propitious note' (*Met.*, VI.448).[41] In fact, Gower's Tereus is a 'worthi king', a 'noble kniht ... / ... kid in every lond' (V.5566–8), who is clearly much loved by his wife Procne. The conversation about Philomela's delivery to her sister takes places in bed, following which 'there as he lay, / [she] Began him in hire armes clippe / And kist him with hir softe lippe' (V.559–92).[42] Tereus's fall into lust is unpremeditated and described as so unavoidable that his culpability is not clear cut:

> And he with al his hole entente,
> Whan she was fro hir frendes go,
> Assoteth of hire love so,
> His yhe myhte he noght withholde,
> That he ne moste on hir beholde;
> And with the sihte he gan desire,
> And sette his oghne herte on fyre;
> And fyr, whan it to tow aprocheth,
> To him anon the strengthe acrocheth,
> Til with his hete it be devoured,
> The tow ne mai noght be socoured.
> (V.5616–26)

The fire and tow (straw) metaphor implies the speed with which sexual desire overcomes Tereus, and, moreover, the impossibility of doing anything about it. The attraction seems to begin innocently enough as well: he is besotted (*Assoteth*) for love of Philomela.

For Yeager, the lack of odious characteristics prior to the attack on Philomela is designed to heighten just how irrational (and therefore unhuman) Tereus becomes – he 'dehumanizes himself completely'.[43] I argue, however, that the conflicting associations attached to the goshawk establish an ambiguous moral middle, in which Tereus

---

[41] R. F. Yeager, *John Gower's Poetics: The Search for a New Arion* (Cambridge: D. S. Brewer, 1990), pp. 153–4.
[42] Cf. *Met.*, VI.439–44.
[43] Yeager, *Gower's Poetics*, p. 154.

is reprehensible, and yet acting by impulses that are natural and unavoidable. Under these circumstances, the goshawk image is less wholly derogative dehumanisation and more potent admixture of two beings driven by instincts that 'mai noght be socoured' and which expresses something of the cross-species behaviour evident in forced or aggressive copulation.[44] As Diane Watt has remarked of other tales in *Confessio*, 'the distinction between the natural and the unnatural, between virtue and vice, becomes blurred'.[45] So, too, the distinction between man and bird. The goshawk is about an embodied expression of the human self as well in which human bodies and actions are associated with nonhuman forms, a 're-evaluation of the role that physical urges play in the human psyche'.[46] In the depiction of the rape, it is not only possible to read the hawk as a traditional image of corrupted or debased humanity resulting from unnatural behaviour, but also as another form to which Tereus is naturally akin, a form that expresses, and in which he performs, his lust. If 'metamorphosis enables love', as Peggy McCracken has remarked of *Yonec*, it also enables sinful pleasures that are, nonetheless, instinctive.[47] Unsettling as the moment might be, as I suggested of 'Ceix and Alceone' in a very different form of sexual union, it still 'suggests the pleasure to be found in the obscure secrets of boundary crossing'.[48] Unlike the example of Muldumarec in *Yonec*, the metamorphosis is not actual, but our reading of the moment is affected by the climax of the tale when real bird transformations

---

[44] The drake in *PF*, taken from Vincent of Beauvais's *Speculum naturale* (XVI.xx-vii), is the 'stroyere of his owene kynde' (360). Cf. modern ornithological descriptions of mallard mating behaviours: '♂♂ also show marked promiscuous tendency; besides maintaining firm pair-bonds, often attempt to form liaisons with additional ♀♀ during communal courtship and will copulate, *usually by rape*, with as many other ♀♀ as possible'; BWP, vol. 1, p. 511 (italics mine).

[45] Diane Watt, 'Gender and Sexuality in *Confessio Amantis*', in *A Companion to Gower*, ed. by Siân Echard (Cambridge: D. S. Brewer, 2004), pp. 197–214 (212).

[46] Jonathan Morton, 'Wolves in Human Skin: Questions of Animal Appetite in Jean de Meun's *Roman de la Rose*', *Modern Language Review*, 105 (2010), 976–97 (p. 976). Morton makes this statement in reference to Jean de Meun's use of wolves, an animal to which Tereus is also compared.

[47] Peggy McCracken, 'Translation and Animals in Marie de France's *Lais*', *Australian Journal of French Studies*, 46 (2009), 206–18 (p. 214).

[48] Ibid.

do occur. Individual wills are, in the end, mobilised through real bird bodies.

Mutilation and Mutation – Incorporating Bodies

The rapacity characteristic of the goshawk is not simply transferred to the tyrant, but a shared trait dispersed and experienced across species: the 'herte on fyre' in lust (V.5622), 'boldnesse of herte' in 'takynge of oþir foules for pray' (Trevisa) are of a kind. As La Vielle states in a very different register in the *Roman de la Rose*, what goes for animals,

> Ausinc est ..., biau filz, par m'ame,
> de tout homme et de toute fame
> quant a naturel appetit.

[is just as true, my dear boy, by my soul, of every man and woman in terms of their natural appetite.] [49]

(*Roman de la Rose*, 14057–9)

As Jonathan Morton has remarked of this passage in the *Roman*, in 'Tereus' there is 'hardly the most radical distinction between humans and the animal kingdom' at times.[50] The sorts of bodily relations implicit in the predator-prey trope that look towards the final metamorphoses might usefully be added to recent critical discussions of the 'moral void' that exists in *Confessio*.[51] Alongside the list of unstable category distinctions produced by the poem's many subversive sexual acts and identities, there is a crucial place for the

---

[49] Cited in Morton, 'Wolves in Human Skin', 994.
[50] Ibid., 995.
[51] Watt, 'Gender and Sexuality', p. 202. In contradiction to the 'firmness and consistency of moral vision' that more traditional readings emphasise, scholars now often focus on how Gower 'fails to make clear distinctions'; Bruce Harbert, 'The Myth of Tereus in Ovid and Gower', *MÆ*, 41 (1972), 208–14 (p. 208), and Karma Lochrie, *Covert Operations: The Medieval Uses of Secrecy* (Philadelphia, PA: University of Pennsylvania Press, 1999), p. 221, respectively. See also, David Benson, 'Incest and Moral Poetry in Gower's *Confessio Amantis*', CR, 19:2, (1984), 100–9, and Diana Watt, 'Sins of Omission: Transgressive Genders, Subversive Sexualities, and Confessional Silences in John Gower's *Confessio Amantis*', *Exemplaria*, 13:2 (2001), 529–51.

poem's human-nonhuman bodies. Given their predominance in the tales of metamorphosis, we can draw associations between the types of boundary crossings involved in shared trans-species bodies and other forms of category violation. From this perspective, Tereus's *ravine* and incest is connected to his metaphorical movements between species (*kinde* frequently means both natural and species in *Confessio*).[52] The conflicting moral ground of human behaviours and actions across the poem suggests further possibilities about the roles and experiences of the human-bird correlations and assemblages in 'Tereus'. If there is unstable clarity about precisely what constitutes moral and sinful acts across the poem, there is a similar and parallel uncertainty about species boundaries, and the extent to which violating these boundaries should be considered unnatural or condemnable.[53] Ambiguous sexuality is mirrored in ambiguous bodies (inclusive of the nonhuman) which are suggestive and revealing, not simply derogatory and detestable. In Tereus's case we might argue, as White observes generally of *Confessio*, that 'the most fundamental meaning of nature excludes the rational, and ... the animal side of human beings is what is most fundamentally natural'.[54]

Having identified this association between types of boundary crossing, the avian figures and devices that appear at either end of the tale take on a further resonance because they frame the more overt, human body violations which are so memorably gruesome in the myth: Tereus commits incestuous rape, he mutilates Philomela's body, Procne performs infanticide, and Tereus is unwittingly cannibalistic. Further atrocities are set to occur (5930–1), but the gods intervene to transform all three characters into birds. Some commentators have remarked that Gower chooses to omit most of the gruesome details from Ovid's original telling so that character,

---

[52] Medieval definitions of incest included sex with any relative, including in-laws. See Elizabeth Archibald, *Incest and the Medieval Imagination* (Oxford and New York, NY: Oxford University Press, 2001), pp. 26–52 and 221–8.
[53] Elsewhere in the *Confessio*, rape goes unpunished; see, e.g., Jupiter's violation of Calistona which passes entirely without judgement (V.6249–53). Ironically, Philomela prays to Jupiter following her defilement (V.5741).
[54] White, *Nature, Sex, and Goodness*, p. 93.

rather than horror, plays a heightened role.[55] The excess and gore of the violence do not fail to make an impact, however, despite the terse description. Gower's violent images achieve their impact as an accumulative sequence, rather than through bloody detail. Moreover, I suggest, it is because Gower makes more of the relevance of the final bird metamorphoses in this tale than Ovid, that this accumulation of violent instances against bodies is particularly effective.

Specifically, those acts which physically violate through dismemberment, mutilation and consumption are to be associated with other forms of anatomisation in which the limits and reaches of bodies are tested and reconstituted through metamorphosis. All, that is, perform a series of un-makings and re-makings which adumbrate and echo each other within the tale, focusing our attention more fully on the related 'fleisshe and blod' (V.5904) components of all bodies, 'the common ground of stomachs, lungs, diaphragms, and hearts'.[56] So at the moment when Tereus cuts out Philomela's tongue, whilst Ovid's gruesome references to the twitching, bloody tongue on the soil are omitted (*Met.*, VI.557–60), we still grimace because Gower emphasises isolated body parts which more fully suggest the motif of fragmented bodies:

> And he than as a Lyon wod
> With hise unhappi hands stronge
> Hire cauhte be the tresses longe,
> With whiche he bond ther bothe hire armes,
> That was fieble dede of armes,
> And to the grounde anon hire caste,
> And out he clippeth also faste
> Hire tunge with a piere scheres.
> So what with blod and what with teres
> Out of hire yhe and of hir mouth,
> He made hire faire face uncouth.
> (V.5684–94)

The violence implicit in the goshawk who has 'sesed / A brid' (V.5644–5) is recalled in Tereus's mutilation of Philomela's tongue,

---

[55] Harbert, 'Myth of Tereus', 208; Yeager, *Gower's Poetics*, p. 132.
[56] Paul Shepard, *The Others* (Washington, D.C.: Island Press, 1996), p. 32.

a bloody act which depicts the girl as prey and consumable flesh, the disseverance of her tongue mirroring the dismemberment of organs in hunted quarry. Tereus enacts, that is, something like the ritual of the hunt *par force* described in hunting manuals known as the 'undoing' or 'unmaking' of the quarry in which the master of the game performs a skilled and detailed dissection of the hunted beast for all to see following the day-long chase and kill.[57] We return to issues of female vulnerability and disempowerment here, but the parallel goes further than this by reflecting other dismemberments which expand the scope of the flesh image to encompass a number of bodily relations. These early examples of disfiguring and severance look forwards to the ultimate, final transfigurations of human characters into birds at the very end. Gower reveals the paradoxical relation between dismemberment and embodiment, the mutilated parts inherent in mutated forms: when the characters metamorphose, 'Here forms are set atwinne' (V.5942). Metaphorically or literally, becoming-bird reminds us of a strongly Ovidian sense of change and combination, in which human and nonhuman are joined fleshly interactions. The characters come to know both the limits of their own bodies, but also the new or renewed possibilities that come with opening that body to new attachments.

Perhaps the most horrifying (though unpunished) act in the whole tale is Procne's murder of her own son, whom she then cooks and serves to Tereus in a stew:

> This child withouten noise or cry
> Sche slou, and hieu him al to pieces:
> And after with diverse spieces
> The fleissh, whan it was so toheewe,
> Sche takth, and makth therof a sewe,
> With which the fader at his mete
> Was served, til he hadde him ete;
> That he ne wiste hou that it stod,
> Bot thus his oughne fleisshe and blod
> Himself devoureth ayein kinde,

---

[57] See Yamamoto, *Boundaries of the Human*, pp. 109–15, and Rebekah L. Pratt, 'From Animals to Meat: Illuminating the Medieval Ritual of Unmaking', *eHumanista*, 25 (2013), 17–30. For a particular example, see *Sir Gawain and the Green Knight* (1607–16).

> As he that was tofore unkinde.
> ...
> To schewen him that the child was ded,
> This Philomene tok the hed
> Between tuo dishes, and al wrothe
> Tho comen forth the sostres bothe,
> And setten it upon the bord.
> (V.5896–5906, 5909–13)

Without the lengthy, gory details of the infanticide and cooking procedure we have in Ovid, our attention is drawn to the sparse details that remain – the dismemberment, but even more so Tereus's unwary consumption of his 'oughne fleisshe and blod'. In the moral scheme for which Genius has selected the tale, we acknowledge the justness of the punishment, *unkinde* for *unkinde*. Of all acts in which bodies incorporate each other, eating (including one's own kind) vividly exemplifies metamorphosis in a real sense because it is 'a series of mutual transformations in which the border between inside and outside becomes blurry'.[58] Unwittingly, and literally, this time around, Tereus once again 'devoureth' (5905), just as he was 'devoured' (5625) by Philomela's beauty (indicated by the fire and tow metaphor), and she herself is figuratively portrayed as devoured prey. Tereus's 'oughne fleisshe and blod' is made quite literally his *oughne* again. Looking forwards, the anthropophagic act is a sickening version of the combinings of flesh that occur in the final metamorphoses.[59] Itys is torn to pieces, but then reassembled in a disturbing but strangely appropriate hybridity with his own father. The bodies in this episode are locked into a violent incorporation of plural bodies as eater and eaten, recalling the predator and prey metaphor, in a macabre Eucharistic-type consumption that

---

[58] Jane Bennett, *Vibrant Matter: A Political Ecology of Things* (Durham, NC and London: Duke University Press, 2010), p. 49. Bennett refers specifically to the processes of eating here.

[59] This particular *unkinde*-ness may have been uncomfortable to medieval audiences for specific reasons. As Karl Steel states, 'The special horror of anthropophagy is ... its impossibility: a human who has been slaughtered and eaten, who has lost the exemption from being eaten through which it defines itself as not animal, may have ceased to be recognizable as an *anthropos*'; Steel, *How to Make a Human*, p. 124. For medieval distinctions between human and animal flesh, see especially pp. 108–17 on the hybridity of flesh.

presents cannibalistic horror as a justified revenge against Tereus's own unkindness. Amans's immediate exclamation at the end of the tale achieves a disquieting flippancy in the light of such horrifying dismemberments: 'Me were levere be fortrode / With wilde hors and be todrawe, / Er I agein love and his lawe / Dede eny thing' (V.6054–7).

Bird Morphology – Escaping and Empowering

In the final metamorphoses these disturbing somatic distortions become inter-body relations that engage the nonhuman fully and literally in the abiding example of bodies 'set atwinne'. The vocabulary of *formes*, of being *schape*, is conspicuous in this passage. Abuses of flesh, the relation which destructively binds suffering female to dominant male, are anticipated again when Tereus 'caughte a swerd anon and suor / That thei [the sisters] scholde of his hands dye' (V.5930–1), but resolve to productive conformations in which avian motion and materiality give identities new energies and potentialities.[60] Gower's punning use of *preie* in the tale points towards this eventual, literal movement from one body to another. Tereus runs at Philomela 'Riht as a wolf which takth his preie. / And sche began to crie and preie' (V.5633–4). And Procne appeals to Apollo:

> And wel thou wost that myn entente
> Was al for worschipe and for goode.
> O lord, that yifst the lives fode
> To every whyt, I prei thee hiere.
> (V.5854–7)

'[W]orschipe' and 'prei' here refer overtly to one particular definition, but the second meaning is not far below the surface; in the rape scene, Philomela has indeed been 'the lives fode'. The female bond(age) to the male is envisaged most intensively as the prey of predatory creatures, but to pray, to invoke intervention from the

---

[60] Cf. also, 'CeixAl', in which the characters are 'schapen into briddes' (V.3095), and *Tr*, where Procne (Proigne) laments 'Whi she forshapen was' (II.66).

more-than-human, will, in the end, translate both women from the former definition (V.5932–4).

It is not only the goshawk image that prepares for the elaborate significance of birds in the last one hundred lines or so. There are numerous briefer avian references which work alongside the initial bird metaphor to expand human experiences outwards to further relations. In fact, whereas Ovid compares Philomela to a range of creatures, Gower sticks to birds. The early metaphorical relations prefigure the final and true symbiosis of bird and human to confirm the sense of innate correlation between forms. Philomela is the 'brid' in Tereus's raptor talons, but will soon make her own reference to birds. The various prayers to the gods that occur in the tale are mirrored in the entreaties Philomela threatens to make to the 'wyde world' (V.5661), which include a number of imagined interlocutors:

> If I among the poeple duelle,
> Unto the poeple I schal it telle;
> And if I be withinne wall
> Of stones closed, thane I scall
> Unto the stones clepe and crie,
> And tellen hem thi felonie;
> And if I to the wodes wende,
> Ther schal I tellen tale and ende,
> And crie it to the briddes oute,
> That thei schal hiere it al aboute.
> (V.5663–72)

Philomela intends to implore the whole materiality of world, assigning even the non-animate a sympathetic complicity in what has taken place and what will. People, stones, trees and birds achieve an equal agency that is to become entwined with Philomela's and others' futures. They are the 'multiple action-makers and materializers' with which the human drama and narrative jostles, overlaps and fuses.[61] The birds come as the last item in the list, marking her future departure away from the singularity of 'poeple', and into the plurality of nightingale, winter and spring, herbs, flowers, fields,

---

[61] Cohen, *Inhuman Nature*, pp. ii–iii.

meadows, the 'bowes thikke' and 'leves grene' (V.5971–3). Human participants, already integrated with other human lives, engage the uncertain externality of multiple genus and species.

In one sense, of course, all of this is an obvious association, because escape can quite easily be related to the most visually characteristic feature of birds, their flight. But Gower is not simply repeating the role of birds in Ovid's version of the tale. A comparison with Chaucer's adaptation highlights the originality of Gower's treatment; unlike Chaucer, who completely dismisses the characters' metamorphosis altogether in his *Legend of Good Women* as extraneous to his purposes, Gower not only retains the birds, but increases their presence and importance throughout.[62] Even if we were to view Tereus's goshawk ravages as nothing more than a conventional indication of depraved animality, it would be difficult to think the same of the final transformations. For Gower, growing wings is not simply a trope to furnish description, nor to produce a symbolic and ethereal departure. It does not dissipate into allegory as the Ovid moralisers have it – a soul's ascension, as in Bersuire's reading of Alceone in his *Ovidius*. Escape, whether from female vulnerability or a bloody death, continues to be an embodied action. Gower's expressions when describing metamorphosis accentuate movement *out of* human shape, of being loosed from 'thastat' (*CA*, V.5941) 'Out of wommanisshe kinde', 'torned out of kinde' (V.6004), 'stranged' (V.6040) from original kind. That *out of*, though, quickly becomes *into* (V.6005), so that escape necessarily involves an immediate second embodiment.[63]

Bird bodies are not simply vehicles for escape, though. In Gower, as in Ovid, Tereus is also transformed, which complicates the purpose of metamorphosis in the tale. Singularly, we can choose to read the transformations as escape or punishment, but the three taken together suggest something more cohesive about change which focuses on the materiality of embodiment. They offer a legitimised version of human-into-bird in which the essence of

---

[62] The metamorphosis in 'CeixAl' is also missing from Chaucer's telling of this tale in *BD* (62–269).
[63] Cf. 'Neptune and Cornix': 'Out of hire wommanisshe kinde / Into a briddes like I find / Sche was transformed' (V.6199–6201).

individual character becomes most fully itself through the incorporation of indispensable other bodies. Gower is clearly dealing with metamorphosis, but he emphasises psychosomatic hybridity, an essential coming-togetherness in which the limits of human flesh are inadequate. Although characters body-hop, they also enact metempsychosis because they continue to think as their human selves:

> For evere upon hir wommanhiede,
> Thogh that the goddes wolde hire change,
> Sche thenkth, and is the more strange.
> (V.5956–8)

Whatever fears existed about metempsychosis, even in the late fourteenth century, Gower's 'neat' Ovid provides serious examples of metamorphosis which do not incur fear or disdain.[64]

For Philomela and Procne, one key enhancement that results from feathered identities is to find voices that are ultimately meaningful in circumstances that have otherwise involved violent oppression and despicable privation of the female subject. Ovid's fleeting reference to the transformation makes no mention of birdsong, but Gower focuses on voice at length:

> Wher as sche singeth day and nyht,
> And in hir song al openly
> Sche makth hir pleignte and seith, 'O why,
> O why ne were I yit a maide?'
> For so these olde wise saide,
> Which understoden what sche mente,
> Hire notes ben of such entente.
> And ek thei seide hou in hir song
> Sche makth gret joie and merthe among,
> (V.5976–84)

> Than fleth sche forth and ginth to chide,
> And chitreth out in her langage
> What falshod is in mariage,
> And telleth in a maner speche
> Of Tereus the Spousebreche.
> Sche wol noght in the wodes duelle,

---

[64] Harbert, 'Ovid and John Gower', p. 83.

> For sche wolde openliche telle;
> And ek for that sche was a spouse,
> Among the folk sche comth to house,
> To do thes wyves understonde
> The falshod of hire housebonde,
> That thei of hem be war also,
> For ther ben manye untrewe of tho.
> (V.6010–22)

These warnings to an imagined future audience of 'old wise' and 'wyves' echo the disquieting references to Procne and Philomela in *Troilus and Criseyde*, intertextual presences that verify the sisters' avian legacy.[65] In Book Two, Criseyde falls asleep to the sound of a nightingale in a cedar tree (II.918–24), an allusion that does not go unnoticed because at the beginning of the book 'the swalowe Proigne' (II.64) wakes Pandarus with 'hire cheterynge / How Tereus gan forth hire suster take' (II.68–9). Here though the birds are given no attention, portentously, and Procne laments 'Whi she forshapen was' (II.66). In Gower, contrarily, avian shape and accoutrements are powerful enablers; that which the women must speak to the world, and which 'al the world therof schal speke' (V.5870), is proclaimed and heeded. Amidst the sorrow, bird morphology is also a cause for 'gret joie and merthe' (V.5984) to the sisters (as it was for Alceone) because of what it permits: 'Ha, nou I am a brid, / Ha, nou mi face mai ben hid' (V.5985–6). Philomela's face is 'hid with leves grene' in the 'bowes thikke' (V.5973, 5971), but it is the bird's appearance as well that aids and assures her: she sings 'al openly' (V.5977) because bird form has rid her of 'chekes rede' (V.5988) that signal the blush of shame.[66]

The importance of bird voice at this final stage in the tale suggests another reason why Gower makes earlier comparisons between Philomela and birds. Noticeably, these initial metaphors convey

---

[65] On Procne and Philomela as birds in *Tr*, see Carolynn Van Dyke, 'That Which Chargeth Not to Say: Animal Imagery in *Troilus and Criseyde*', in *Rethinking Chaucerian Beasts*, pp. 101–12 (101–2).

[66] Cf. 'Sche [Cornix] flih before his yhe a crow; / Which was to hire a more delit' (V.6206–7). Red cheeks appear in *PF* as a comical discrepancy between human and avian form: the formel eagle blushes 'Ryght as the freshe, rede rose newe' (442).

the girl's distinct lack of voice. Philomela is rendered literally speechless by Tereus, only a stump of tongue left with which she manages to utter jibberish. Ovid's vivid comparison of her severed, writhing tongue to a snake (*Met.*, VI.559) becomes a piteous avian illustration of her voicelessness:

> Bot yit whan he hire tunge refte,
> A litel part therof belefte,
> Bot sche with al no word mai soune,
> Bot chitre and as a brid jargoune.[67]
>   (V.5697–5700)

Birdsong has the complete opposite significance at this stage: it renders Philomela inhuman and dumb. Gower employs another commonplace here, alluding to the tradition that Chaucer broaches in *The Parliament of Fowls*, the meaninglessness of birds' voices. Philomela, having lost most of her tongue, can no longer produce meaningful language, only the nonsensical chittering of birds.[68] Like Chaucer, however, Gower shakes free the expected disparaging associations to revitalise the comparison. Ironically, Philomela will transcend the metaphor to become a real bird, in which form she will regain a meaningful voice precisely *because* she is a bird, able to 'makth diverse melodie' (V. 5992) all 'day and nyht' (V.5976). The voices are clearly birds' voices, too: Gower refers more than once to those who can 'understonde' Philomela's song, and Procne overturns meaningless *chitre*, formerly the mark of incomprehensibility, into something that 'wyves understond' (V.6019): she 'chitreth out

---

[67] Birdsong conveys a comparable dual sense of voice and voicelessness in the nightingale motif in *Tr*. The sparrowhawk/lark pairing, like Gower's goshawk/bird simile, explains Criseyde's initial fear as Troilus embraces her: she is 'al quyt from every dred and tene' (II.1226). In the following stanza, though, like the 'newe abaysed nyghtyngale' 'doth hire vois out rynge' (II.1232 and 1237).

[68] Chatter and jargon are usual collocations with birds in ME. Cf., e.g., *CA*, V.4099–4103 ('riht so as hir jargoun strangeth' [103]); Chaucer's *MerT*, in which January is 'ful of jargon as a flekked pye' (1848); and *Tr*, in which Procne, again, is a swallow defined by 'cheterynge' (II.68). See *MED*, s.v. (ger.) *chiteringe*, 1a; and (n.) *jargoun*. See also Louise W. Stone, ed., *Anglo-Norman Dictionary*, 7 vols (London: Modern Humanities Research Association, 1983), vol 3, s.v. (n.) *jargun*.

in her langage' (V.6011).[69] The sisters' new *langage* is not exclusive to birds, either, but resonates across species – humans, too, 'understoden what sche mente' (V. 5981). It seems that the translation conundrum that exercised Chaucer in *The Parliament* presents less difficulty for Gower in this instance. When the nightingale and swallow sing and chitter, they are perfectly understandable, uttering a genuinely trans-species language between those who share communal experiences of suffering. The song and chattering of nightingale and swallow are translatable, presented as human speech by Gower: 'O why ne were I yit a maide?' But whereas Chaucer introduces phonetically rendered bird utterances in *The Parliament* which remind us of the ultimate foreignness of other species, the nightingale and the swallow in 'Tereus' are understood naturally by hapless lovers and betrayed wives.

The Origin of Species – A Double Narrative

Important though these voices are, they are just one integral aspect of general bird *schape* and *forme*. As Gower reminds us in the description of each character's transformation, the emphasis, each time, is on *kinde*, on species' body into species' body. Body and voice, form and form, are intertwined in a manoeuvre which draws our attention fully to a commixture that has been gently present all along in the poem, to a shared ontology of interrelating forms. It is perhaps the extensive descriptions that strike us most, how far Gower goes in describing the characters' new avian habits, particularly Philomela's. We are being signposted to something more than the closure of a tale purporting to illustrate the vice of *ravine*. Gower is also continuing a classical tradition, inherited by and from Ovid, in which birds are the 'heroes of the bird stories [who] live on in the birds around us', a feature of aetiological transformation stories designed to 'explain the creation ... of a whole species'.[70]

---

[69] Cf. *Tr:* Proigne sings meaningfully about her sister and Tereus, but is clearly 'cheterynge' (II.68).
[70] Forbes Irving, *Metamorphosis in Greek Myths*, p. 96.

This sense of origin myth is clearly evident in Tereus's case, when Gower reminds us that 'yit unto this dai men seith / A lappewincke hath lore his feith' (V.6045–6).

But Gower does far more than just include this additional element. He extends this interest in explaining species through a very considerable elaboration upon Ovid's brief reference to the moment of metamorphosis (and upon that which he may have come across in the *Ovide moralisé*).[71] At this point, the poem turns composite itself, doubling focus so that the text's ending becomes something like natural history, aligning fiction with more doctrinal understanding of avian habits and behaviours. The descriptions are akin to various potential sources available to Gower, and establish the feel of pseudo-bestiary or -encyclopaedia entries. These jostle alongside the tragic human narrative in a manner that encourages us to pay as much interest to how three avian species came to be as it does to a gruesome tale's conclusion. In the instances of Philomela and Procne, Gower draws upon the Aristotelian belief that certain birds (because they are not seen in winter) hibernate at the bottom of lakes and rivers:[72]

---

[71] This telling does name the species and elaborates a little, but nothing like the extent to which Gower does (*OM*, VI.3664–9; 3691–3718).

[72] Two traditions seem to have coexisted in medieval thought regarding birds that are absent in winter. Aristotle's notion that certain birds hibernate, such as the swallow (*HA*, VIII.xvi), evidently survived in birdlore, alongside the accurate understanding that birds migrate. In the bestiaries, for instance, it is noted that swallows migrate; see *The Book of Beasts: Being a Translation from a Latin Bestiary of the Twelfth Century*, trans. by T. H. White (New York, NY: Dover Publications, 1984), p. 147, and *Bestiary*, p. 164. Cf. *Etym.*, XII.vii.1. Pliny, a key source for bestiaries, combines both, remarking that swallows migrate, but only locally, where they hibernate in mountain rocks (*NH*, X.xxxiv). That the hibernation theory was genuinely believed by some is demonstrated by its survival well into modern times: it is depicted in a description and accompanying woodcut from the sixteenth-century *History and Nature of the Northern People* by Archbishop Olaus Magnus. Gilbert White still deliberated over the idea in his *Natural History of Selbourne*, as does Samuel Johnson in the same century, who states that swallows 'certainly sleep all winter'; James Bosworth, *The Life of Samuel Johnson*, ed. by David Wormersley (London: Penguin, 2008), p. 291. The swallow's close living with mankind is attested in numerous medieval sources: see e.g., *Book of Beasts*, p. 147, and *Etym.*, XII.vii.1. Its association with the warm seasons appears in Bartholomaeus (Trevisa, XII.xxii [p. 631]) and its chittering is noted by Isidore (*Etym.*, XII.vii.1) and Bartholomaeus, who refers to it as a 'crienge foule' (Trevisa, XII.xxii [p. 631]). As for the nightingale, Gower

> The ferst into a nyhtingale
> Was schape, and that was Philomene,
> Which in the winter is noght sene
> (V.5944–6)

> ... sche was torned out of kinde
> Into a swalwe swift of winge,
> Which ek in wynter lith swounynge.
> (V.6004–6)

In Tereus's case, Gower chooses to follow the proverbial reputation of the lapwing, considered deceitful because it lures away predators from its nest by feigning injury:[73]

> A lappewincke mad he was,
> And thus he hoppeth on the gras,
> ...
> A lappewincke hath lore his feith
> And is the brid falseste of alle.
> (V.6041–2, 6046–7)

The aetiologies in the *Metamorphoses* are only a few lines (VI.668–74), but span over one hundred in 'Tereus'. P. M. C. Forbes Irving has suggested, in response to this typifying feature of bird transformations in ancient myths, that it is not 'ornithological lore but the relations of human beings' that matter. For Gower, this is not quite so. The space given over to describing the species that the characters become heavily foregrounds birdlore and doubles the relations that are important: human relations, yes, but also those between humans and birds. In Gower, aetiology is no quaint addendum, but a substantial feature of the poem's strategy, in which knowledge

---

remarks that the bird 'in the winter is noght sene' (V.5946), the suggestion being that it hibernates – come spring she 'makth hir ferste yeres flyht' (V.5975). Both Aristotle and Pliny allude to the bird's hibernation; see, respectively, *HA*, V.ix.542b.299–30, and *HN*, X.xliii. All sources on the nightingale focus on the voice, whether poetry or prose. Pliny, in particular, discusses the richness and skill of the bird's song.

[73] The lapwing's association with deceit is unrecorded in medieval natural philosophy texts, but its reputation (from its habit of luring away predators from its nest with feigned injury) clearly existed in oral lore: Chaucer refers to the 'false lapwynge' (*PF*, 347). Cf. Shakespeare, *Measure for Measure*, I.iv.32–3; *Much Ado about Nothing*, III.i.24–5; *Comedy of Errors*, IV.ii.27. Cf. *BWP*, vol. 3, p. 261.

of particular avian species – from the pages of natural philosophy texts at least – plays a key role. Ovid's Philomela merely flies to the forest (*Met.*, VI.668), but Gower's is an overtly named species whose habitat, seasonal habits, mellifluous song and elusive nature are described at length. We are required to think in double: in Procne's case we are aware of a woman's lamentation on 'What falshod is in mariage' (V.6012), but equally aware of a 'swalwe swift of winge' (V.6005) of which 'nothing be sene' (V.6007) in winter, but which 'fleth ... forth' (V.6010) in 'Somertide' (V.6009), 'comth to house' (V.6018) and will 'Unto no mannes hand be tame' (V.6026). The relevance of particular species is clearly important enough, too, for Gower to swap the hoopoe for a lapwing, not only a native bird to Britain, but one whose most familiar behavioural trait and distinctive crest (V.6043–4) are best explained by 'so ruide a kniht' (V.5567).[74] In choosing to extend the aetiological descriptions he finds in Ovid, Gower accentuates the importance of characters turning into birds.

The 'just so' element of the tale's closure does not eclipse the human tragedy. We are dealing with metempsychosis because the human element clearly still resides within the bird. This overt and continuous human presence may encourage us to reduce the whole thing to typical hermeneutics. Avian ontology is explained according to human narrative and, thus, the latter is prioritised. But such an approach must also account for the intricate manner in which human lives in Gower's tale are literally interfused with that of nonhumans, the way in which human narratives are no longer self-enclosed but become the narratives of birds too. What results, in fact, through continued reference to the women themselves, but also through extended description of precise bird species, is a heightened sense of the hybridity between forms implicated in

---

[74] The crest presumably resembles the feathered plume or elaborate headpieces worn ceremonially on knight's helmets. See, e.g., the Codex Manesse (Cod. Pal. Germ. 848, dated c.1300 x 1340) which depicts various examples. The association is evident, too, in Trevisa's conflation of *vpupa* and English *lapwynke*; Trevisa, XII.xxxviii (p. 644). An association with Lat. *upupa* and the lapwing seems to have been established from at least the late Middle Ages onwards (see Wright-Wülcker, pp. 640 and 702).

each other's histories. Each exerts an influence that resonates with anthropologist Paul Shepard's statement that 'Personal identity is not so much a matter of disentangling the self or "the human" from nature', but

> a farrago of selected correspondences in which aspects of the self are projected into the dense, external world where they are discovered among a variety of animals who are both similar and different from us.[75]

We may project ourselves, but the resulting image depends upon that 'variety of animals' with whom we correspond. That related and yet independent variety Shepard invokes can be sensed at the moment Gower describes Procne's transformation 'out of kinde / Into a swalwe' (V.6004–5). The syntax, conjunctive *ek*, and the ambiguity of *which* multiply the possible readings here: it is her sister who *ek* slumbers through winter, by comparison, but also the swallow, an independent creature whose idiosyncrasies (as identified in encyclopaedic texts) are suitably to become those of Procne.[76] Whilst the thrust is principally towards defining the cause and beginning of species (the nightingale 'erst was cleped Philomene' [V.5999]), the nuances of these lines allow us simultaneously to see the characters not simply as *the* proto-species, but '*a* nyhtingale' (V.5944), '*a* swalwe' (6005) and '*A* lappewincke' (6046) [italics mine].

Birds do serve in this tale to provide typical warnings to human listeners and observers about betrayal and deceit, but the device cannot be reduced to simple anthropomorphism or moral exegesis because these are not simply birds treated as humans, but also humans treated as birds: species and behaviours must be read reciprocally in terms of each other. Human suffering and tragedy are dispersed across new embodiments which bring, for Procne and Philomela, at least some measure of relief. There is no denying the fact that the birds are, after all, real, and the detailed descriptions of Philomela, Procne and Tereus in their new avian forms make it

---

[75] Shepard, *The Others*, p. 86.
[76] As with Modern English, ME *who* tended to be reserved for persons. *Which* was more general, and could include humans and nonhumans. See *MED*, s.v. (pron.) *who*, and (pron.) *which*, sense 1. Gower uses *which* for both subjects: see V.5633 and V.5810.

difficult to do away neatly with the suggestion that birds in this tale are only good for figuration. Metaphor in itself is insufficient because these humans do actually become birds, not simply like them. The birds are not a mirror for character, but intimately and literally a part of character.

Epilogue

THE BIRDS THAT FLY AND SING through my five chapters have enacted, provoked and evaded transformations. Metaphor – indeed, all forms of human translation – is repeatedly at stake, empowered and limited through its various and tangled involvements with the avian real. In Chapter One, birds mobilised a paradoxical metaphor, aiding those transfigurations most desired in orthodox Christian doctrine. In Chapter Two they mystified scholastic attempts to decode their diversity of kinds that 'be not distinguyd in certayne', escaping or thwarting human transformative designs upon the natural world.[1] Elsewhere, they managed curious frictions between biological and cultural species traits with comic aplomb, manipulating and resisting their assigned roles in literary modes to reverse or redirect humanised taxonomies of species and voice. In the final chapter, we ended with the most substantial and dramatic of all avian transformations, simultaneously dispersive and integrative mutations that 'bringen forth of briddes kinde' (*CA*, IV.3119).

Studies of the sort I offer here run an unavoidable risk. Those who consciously and rigorously attempt to write about the nonhuman are paradoxically forced to recognise that they always do write about the human. As Erica Fudge comments, in these cases 'we read humans writing about animals', and (even if we do claim to address the animal purely as itself) we must process these writings through our own human faculties.[2] To borrow the words of another writer on birds, there is a 'sense in which a book like this on birds

---

[1] Trevisa, XII.i (p. 596).
[2] Erica Fudge, 'A Left-Handed Blow: Writing the History of Animals', in *Representing Animals*, ed. by Nigel Rothefels (Bloomington, IN: Indiana University Press, 2002), pp. 3–18 (7).

is really about ourselves'.³ I do not intend, however, that the title of this book should be misleading. I maintain that birds are, in fact, my proper focus because their materiality is always evident and deeply relevant. Their presence reveals intertwined human–avian histories and existences that can and do suggest an interdependence or compatibility that makes the bird integral, not marginal, to our self-conceptions. It would be entirely false, of course, to suggest that the birds I discuss are not symbolic, metaphoric or anthropomorphic, or that medieval people were not users of birds in the traditional sense. Like other creatures, birds were most certainly employed in intellectual schemes to ratify human exceptionalism, or to serve as dispensable tools by which to examine our own psychologies or morals. I do propose, however, that my five texts acknowledge that it was possible for medieval authors to do far more than 'only ever [look] at the representation of the animal by the human'.⁴

In contemplating the dilemma of representing the nonhuman, Fudge has argued that we must 'place ourselves next to the animals, rather than as the users of animals, and [that] this opens up a new way of imagining the past'.⁵ This book aspires to a reimagining in this spirit. It explores how five poets depict birds that present challenges to human perceptions and cultural procedures, not, of course, as the result of modern environmental anxieties, but most certainly with an astute eye for the ways in which nonhuman creatures are made to function in human narratives, and the potential outcomes of these representations. The realities of birds in each chapter are cast in numerous positions with and within metaphors which engage and exhibit undeniably human interests, but which also call into question human statuses and privileges. At the heart of these poetic operations is a question that chimes with Fudge's discourse, about how the human-nonhuman relation should be rightly or justly managed. In *The Seafarer*, where figurative correlations that draw together human and nonhuman verge between stable and unstable, we are at least aware of how

³ Jeremy Mynott, *Birdscape: Birds in Imagination and Experience* (Princeton, NJ: Princeton University Press, 2009), p. 27
⁴ Fudge, 'A Left-Handed Blow', p. 6.
⁵ Ibid., p. 15.

resistant the natural world can be to neat designs that seek to draw hierarchical or superficial parallels. Christian doctrine and hopeful endeavour are not easily satisfied or served by a nonhuman world. The nuanced, intricate species connections in *The Seafarer*, in fact, emphasise uncertainty and ignorance, even in the face of stoic piety, and the parallel between seabird and seafarer is all the more powerful for this. In the Old English Riddles, too, human knowledge is in question. Intellectual exercises that ostensibly strip away wonder and confer orderly classification turn out to work in the opposite way, where metaphorical layers are redoubled and confused, and mystery is perpetuated.

These delicate negotiations are more overtly ethical in *The Owl and the Nightingale* and *The Parliament of Fowls*. The debates in the former poem over species' usefulness foreground literary simulacra that turn out to have detrimental effects for birds (and certain humans), and Chaucer's text reveals with explosive consequences how similar cultural expectations about avian species clash with the respective birds' instinctive breeding urges. In my reading, it is a small slip in linguistic substitution that pointedly raises questions about the mechanics and legitimacy of allegorical translations. I offer a positive approach to the complex effects of Chaucer's allegory, but more unsettling issues about representing the nonhuman remain. The merlin's hostility towards the cuckoo hinges on an anthropomorphised understanding that the cuckoo is a 'mortherere' (612) – a bird is judged by human standards, but is still acknowledged to eat worms, as is its nature. One of the tercel eagles condemns the duck's rationale about breeding choices, and does so, moreover, by comparing the duck's experience to that old commonplace about owls: 'Thow farst by love as oules don by lyght' (599). There are curious interspecies references here which expose the difficulties of assimilating species: a bird of prey, informed by a human courtly practice, uses an avian proverb employed by humans to say something about human morals, but which is here applied to a bird (although elsewhere in the poem humans are taken as proverbial subjects by which to compare avian perceptions [474–6]). Human lore, as in *The Owl and the Nightingale*, affects the ways in which birds are treated, even by other birds. In both poems, a skilful understanding and manipulation of literary bird species that do not successfully or entirely supersede their real-life counterparts produce a good deal of comedy, but also more sobering aspects that undermine the humour at critical moments.

Ethical issues of a slightly different sort may linger, too, in Gower's 'Tereus'. Birds' bodies are liberating in the final moments of the tale, but some readers might be disquieted by transformations which arguably diminish the heinous wrongs perpetrated upon Procne and Philomela and mask their powerlessness. Does metamorphosis function, that is, as an inadequate neutralisation of, or compensation for, the horrors of female suffering when the human tragedy is sublimated into an aetiological tale about the origins of bird species? What may seem like an anthropocentric quibble actually pertains to the ethics of depicting the nonhuman as much as the human. When we turn one into the other through metaphor, metamorphosis or simple correlation, what do we lose, overlook or misrepresent that exists irreducibly or fundamentally as part of one and cannot be transferred to another? Moments like these implicitly provoke speculation about just how far we can, or even should, take these comparative treatments.

Gower's avian–human conformations most overtly demonstrate that medieval conceptions of, and interactions with, the natural world could engage the nonhuman in human interests in ways that accentuate the desirable or necessary presence of the nonhuman. It does not seem to me that Gower's poetics risk diminishing the affective states of Philomela and Procne through idealised metamorphosis. Aerial escape does not resolve or dismiss human violation. The women continue to be haunted by their afflictions, and must tell of them, but Gower now entwines evolutionary paths so that the characters' psychological and physical states are recalibrated and intensified by radically avian bodies and ways of being. A human story multiplies its purposes so that it ends up telling parallel narratives about three avian species' existences, and the same human story is ultimately dependent upon the phenomena of these other beings.

These interests exist to some degree in all the poems I consider, where the human and the avian meet in numerous forms. Real birds never fully become 'the silent assumption', in Fudge's phrase, and it is their unique properties that engage predicaments of relation, representation and classification so remarkably.[6] Avian palpability persists as a significant component of each poem's artifice so that natural histories exist vitally as part of cultural formulations: in affective metaphors that envisage and theorise the tremendous importance of the soul's fate; in human actions against nonhuman species; in earnest debates about meaningful voices; and in alliances by which human legacies will be eternally translated and revealed through and in birds' diverse and transformative abilities.

[6] Ibid., p. 16.

GLOSSARY

OLD AND MIDDLE ENGLISH BIRD NAMES

This glossary records the genus and species names attested in Old and Middle English vocabularies. Names of domestic, foreign or mythical species are not included, apart from falconry birds. For ease of reference the list below is ordered alphabetically, rather than by conventional ornithological taxonomies. For further discussion of medieval bird names, see the recommendations listed after the glossary. Short references included in the glossary are to these works. Where particular species are discussed in the chapters of this book, page references are given at the end of each entry.

Barnacle goose **ME bernacle.** No recorded OE name, but the well-known peculiar myth of the species' genesis from mollusc shells attached to driftwood is apparent in Exeter Book Riddle 10. The Sherborne Missal (British Library, MS Add. 74326) depicts the species accurately, labelled *bornet*. For a description of this phenomenon, see Gerald of Wales, *Topographia hibernica*, I.xi.
See pp. 34, 70, 73–4

Bittern **OE raredumle. ME raredrumbel/bitour/miredromble.** OE probably meant something like 'reed-boomer' (cf. German *rohrdommel*), although Lacey suggests *rare* derives from *rarian* 'to roar' ('Birds and Words'). The suffix in both OE and ME may well function onomatopoeically. The bittern consistently glosses *onocratulus* (pelican) right across the Middle Ages; cf. Bartholomaeus Anglicus: 'The mirdrommel hatte *onacrocalus*' (Trevisa, XII.xxix; p. 635). For further discussion of this confusion, see below, s.v. *Pelican*.
See p. 41

Blackbird **OE osle. ME merule/osel/suswart/throstil.** In ME *suswart*, suffix *-swart* is cognate with OE *sweart* 'black'. The Sherborne Missal labels a male blackbird *throstil*.
See p. 93n

Black grouse **ME berkoc.** 'Birch-cock'. May be a generic term for grouse.

Blue tit **OE hicmase.** Probably refers specifically to blue tit, as suggested by a surviving West Country dialect term for the species, 'hickmal' (Lockwood). No recorded ME form.

Bullfinch **ME wop.** ME is attested in the Sherborne Missal, labelling what are clearly male bullfinches. If the name has OE roots, this might be germane to Hooke's suggestion that one charter landmark refers to an unidentified bird associated with a sloping wood (p. 277): *wopig hangran* (*wopig* is an adjective here, though – 'weepy' – so the reference is oblique). In any case, OE or ME *wop* 'cry, wail' may describe the characteristically subdued, melancholy 'pheew' of the species. West Country dialect 'mwope' is presumably related ('mawp' elsewhere); see Lockwood.

Bunting   **ME bunting.** *MED* specifies the corn bunting, but it may well be a generic term.

Buzzard   **OE putta/puttoc/tysca. ME busard.** OE *putta* and *puttoc* were probably general hawk terms, and may have covered kites, hawks and harriers. OE *bleripittel* 'bald-hawk (?)' is identified as hen-harrier by Kitson (ii), but I see no convincing evidence for this. OE *wrocc*, attested in place-names (e.g., Wroxhall), may also refer to the buzzard, or raptors in general.
See pp. 115, 138

Chaffinch   **OE ceaffinc. ME chaffinche.** OE term refers to 'bird associated with chaff'.
See p. 6

Chough   **OE ceo/cio. ME chough.** Onomatopoeic. See also below s.v. *Crow*.

Coal tit   **OE colmase. ME colmose.** OE *colmase* may refer to more than one type of dusky, coal-coloured tit, and it is possible that distinction was not drawn between the coal, marsh and willow tit. The Sherborne Missal depicts a colmose which could feasibly be any one of the three species. Strangely, ME *colmose* glosses *alcedo* (usually gull) in more than one ME text.

Cormorant   **OE scræf. ME cormeraunt/scarf.** If *scræf* derives from OE *scearfian* 'to scrape', there may be an onomatopoeic reference to the harsh guttural calls of the cormorant. Cf. surviving Scottish dialect 'scarf'.

Corncrake   **OE secgscara.** Literally 'sedge-shearer'. The emphasis on sound suggests this may well be the OE name for corncrake, describing the mechanical, rasping sound that would have been a distinctive summer noise across Britain in the Middle Ages, as it was for centuries afterwards. The term it glosses, *ortigometra*, is glossed *edischen* elsewhere, and often relates to the quail in ME texts, so it may also refer to this similarly skulking field bird.

Crane   **OE cran. ME crane.** Ancient origin; common Germanic. Onomatopoeic. Cognate to Lat. *grus*, which is also imitative.
See pp. 15, 16

Crow   **OE crawe. ME croue.** Onomatopoeic. The corvids are a good example of a bird family clearly defined according to sound in OE. The distinctions make it plausible that observers did separate species, but

Glossary of Bird Names

Lacey has cautioned against rigid identifications; see Lacey, 'When Is a Hroc not a Hroc?'.

See pp. 15, 41, 92n, 94, 108, 114, 132, 133, 210n

Cuckoo **OE geac. ME cokkou/gok.** *Geac* cognate with Germanic and Norse terms (Old Saxon *gok*), and with existing northern dialect terms (gowk, gawk) which must surely be onomatopoeic.

See pp. 15, 53, 55–6, 154, 161, 172, 173, 221

Curlew **OE huilpe. ME curleu.** *Huilpe* (from genitive *huilpan* in *The Seafarer*) may have referred to various large wader species, but surviving Scottish and northern dialect 'whaup' (Lockwood) and Dutch *wulp* make it plausible that this is a genuine term for the curlew – a large, distinctive-billed, and highly evocative-sounding coastal species. Also associated with *coturnix* (quail) in ME, but Bartholomaeus notes that the bird is so called because of its voice (Trevisa, XII.viii; p. 618), which would certainly match *curleu* well with *Numenius arquata* (rather than the trisyllabic quail's call).

See pp. 33n, 37–8, 46

Diver **OE dope/dopened/dopfugel/scealfor. ME dopper/domping.** There are various names for diving water birds generally, which presumably could refer to divers, grebes, ducks and the cormorant. OE *scealfor* glosses *Mergus* in some glossaries, the Lat. genus now applied to mergansers, but presumably referred to any number of diving seabirds and water birds.

See p. 98

Dove See below, s.v. *Pigeon, Turtle dove*.

Duck **OE duce/ened. ME doke/ende.** *Duce* presupposes OE **ducan* 'to dive'. *Ened* ancient in origin and the more common term.

See pp. 41n, 161n, 163, 166, 171n, 172, 173, 200n, 221

Dunlin **OE pur.** Name appears with different lemmata and OE terms in glosses, including bittern and snipe. Assumed to be a name for dunlin, on basis of surviving dialect term ('Purre'; Lockwood), but may have served as a general wader or wetland bird name.

Dunnock **OE hegesugge/dunnuc. ME sugge/heisugge/donek/pinnok.** OE *dunnuc* attested in place-names (e.g., Dunnockshaw). *Hegesugge* 'hedge-sucker' can be confidently assigned to hedge-sparrow through its continued use in ME, even if it may have referred to other small skulking birds as well. *Sugge* is sometimes applied to warblers; see Kitson (i) and Whitman. The 'sucking' description presumably refers to the arboreal creeping action of various small birds; the dunnock closely hugs the bottom of hedges, keeping hidden much of the time. OE *sweartling*, too, must refer to some sort of 'little brown job', but it is not clear which.

See pp. 41n, 132

Eagle   **OE earn. ME egle.** General term, but OE almost certainly referred to the white-tailed eagle which was widespread across the UK until relatively recently. Various eagle species, including the golden eagle, would have been known to falconers in the later Middle Ages.
See pp. 32n, 37–8, 49–50, 57n, 70n, 149, 166, 194, 195n

Fieldfare   **OE feldfara/feolufor. ME feldefare.** OE terms have proved tricky, but it is generally accepted that whatever the etymology of the extant terms, and to whichever birds these terms are applied in the glossaries, *feldfara* 'field-traveller' does apply to this species, as suggested by its survival in ME *feldfare* which is unquestionably *Turdus pilaris*. The Sherborne Missal labels an accurately depicted fieldfare (*vuelduare*). In one glossary, OE *feldfara* is accompanied by OE *clodhamer* – 'a type of bird associated with clod' – which may well describe the fieldfare, but may be a term for small farmland birds; *amer* is root of Modern English yellowhammer.
See pp. 171–3

Finch   **OE finc. ME finch/spink.** OE term imitative of typical call; e.g. chaffinch's note, rendered as 'fink!' in modern field guides. ME *spink* is imitative in same way.
See pp. 5, 41

Gannet   **OE ganot. ME ganet.** In OE, the name probably referred to a number of large sea or water birds, but was definitely applied to *Morus bassanus* by the later Middle Ages. The Sherborne Missal labels a juvenile gannet.
See pp. 33n, 34, 37–8, 46, 47, 60–1

Goldfinch   **OE goldfinc/þisteltwig. ME goldfinch.** Prefix of *þisteltwig* denotes the bird's favoured food. The suffix is less certain; popularly understood to mean 'tweaker' (OE *twiccian* 'to tweak'), but perhaps derived from *twige* 'twig', and thus simply transfers 'thistle-branch' to the bird that feeds upon it.
See pp. 41n, 132

Goose   **OE gos/ganra. ME gos.** Ancient origin; common Germanic. Names for particular species are not recorded, although late medieval manuscript illustrations do show distinction. Differences between domestic and wild species are clear to some extent: OE *hwit gos/græg gos/wildegos*; ME *wyld goos* (the Sherborne Missal depicts what might be a white-fronted goose).
See pp. 1, 78, 79, 161n, 163, 166, 172

Goshawk   **OE goshafoc. ME goshauk.** 'Goose-hawk'.
See pp. 120n, 138, 170, 192, 195–7, 200, 201, 203

Great bustard   **ME bustard.** French origin. Still a British breeding species in the medieval period.

Grey heron   **OE hragra. ME heiroun.** *Hragra* is probably onomatopoeic. ME *heiroun* is derived from French, but cognate with the OE term.

Glossary of Bird Names

See pp. 89, 170

Grey partridge   **ME patriche.** OE *erschen/edischen* may also have applied to partridge.

Grouse   **ME hethcok.** Grouse generally, but probably refers to the male red grouse.

ME morecok. Probably the male red grouse again, but see *morhen*.

ME morhen. Now applied to *Gallinule chloropus*, but presumably referred to either a female grouse specifically, or the female of various skulking marsh, moor or pasture birds: moorhen, coot, pheasant, quail. The Sherborne Missal portrays what is almost certainly a water rail, labelled *morcoc*.

Gull   **OE maew. ME meue/gulle.** OE maew onomatopoeic.

See pp. 14, 29n, 33, 37–8, 47, 48n, 78–9, 89

Hawk   **OE hafoc. ME hauk.** General term for hawk and falcon. Ancient name; common Germanic, from Indo-European root meaning 'seize'. Cognate with Lat. *capere* 'seize'. OE *mushafoc* 'mouse-hawk' might apply to a number of species. *Pipat* glossing *accipiter* in one glossary is likely a misunderstanding: *pipat* is the usual sound verb paired with *accipiter* in Lat. animal-sound word lists.

See pp. 78–9, 115, 120, 138. See also above, s.v. *Goshawk*.

Hoopoe   **ME houpere.** Old High German and Old Saxon consistently gloss *upupa* as *widehoppa* 'wood-hopper' (many variations), although this sounds more like a description of a woodpecker, or possibly golden oriole (sometimes confused and conflated with woodpecker in ME, and later, under *wodewale*). See, too, entry below for lapwing.

See pp. 179, 181, 215

House martin   **ME martinet.** French origin.

See p. 93n

House sparrow   **OE spearwe. ME sparwe.** Ancient name; common Germanic.

See pp. 25–7, 33, 37, 62, 153n

Ibis   **OE geolna.** Attested in one glossary. It is possible that ibises, like various other large water birds, may have bred in medieval Britain when there were much more extensive wetlands.

See p. 89

Jackdaw   **ME cadou/co/daue.** OE place-names may suggest onomatopoeic *ca* as the term for this species (e.g., Cabourne). See also above, s.v. *Crow*.

See pp. 15, 93n

Jay   **OE higera. ME jai.** One OE glossary adds *gagia* (etymon to ME *jai*) to *higera* in glossing *picus*.

See pp. 70, 72, 75, 78–84, 88, 153

Kestrel   **OE stangella. ME kesterell.** *Stangella* 'stone-yeller' is usually applied to the kestrel by scholars, based on later dialect terms for the

229

kestrel (from sixteenth century): *steingall*, *stanniel* and *stonegall*; see Lockwood. ME name is recorded in the 'Boke of St Albans' (fifteenth century).

Kingfisher **OE fiscere/isern. ME kingsfisher/kyngynsfystere.** Scholars have argued that *isern* 'ice-eagle' applies to kingfisher, on the basis that *isen* 'iron', via a process of conflation with *isern*, glosses variants of *alcyon* in one glossary, and possibly its similarity with German *eisvogel*; see Kitson (i).

Knot **ME knot.** Of late medieval origin. The spurious connection to Canute goes back centuries (hence Lat. *Calidris canutus*), but the name is usually now assumed to be imitative of the species' call.

Lapwing **OE hleapewinc. ME lapwinke.** Terms refer to *Vanellus vanellus*, but both are confused with other species. OE *hleapwinc* more than once glosses *cuculus* in glossaries, and ME *lapwinke* was associated with *upupa* (cf. Modern French *Vanneau huppé*). Whether this confusion resulted from an initial scribal error or as an intentional conflation because both species have crests is unclear.

See pp. 181, 188, 214, 215

Linnet **OE linetwige/linete. ME linet/lindetvigle.** Like the better known *pisteltwig* (goldfinch), OE terms refer to *carduelis* species noted for feeding on linseed. *Ragofinc* is also recorded in two glossaries, although not with *carduelis*. It suggests a finch that feeds on *ragu* (lichen/moss).

Long-tailed tit **ME tayl mose.** Depicted and labelled in the Sherborne Missal.

Magpie **OE agu. ME agas/pie.** OE term possibly imitative. OE *higera* 'jay' may also refer to the magpie. Cf. Kent dialect term 'haggister' (Lockwood).

See pp. 81, 82n, 114, 133, 151n, 153

Mallard **ME malard.** French origin.

Merlin **ME merlioun.** French origin.

See pp. 170, 173, 221

Night heron **OE nihtremn/nihtrefn. ME nihtfoul.** One of the best known and frequently recorded birds in OE, but *nycticorax* is a name fraught with identification difficulties throughout its usage, and this is no different in the medieval period. It is possible that *nihtrefn* did refer to a particular species, possibly even the night heron which now bears the scientific name *Nycticorax nycticorax*, a bird that probably did breed in England in the Middle Ages and is noted for its nocturnal activity and typically harsh 'corvid' call. More likely, though, given that the OE term frequently glosses owl species as well as *nycticorax*, it was a generic term for sinister-sounding night birds. The same goes for ME *nihtfoul* and its numerous variants.

See pp. 70n, 109–10, 114n, 128, 129n, 129–30, 141n

Glossary of Bird Names

Nightingale **OE nihtegale/hearpen. ME nightegale.** 'Night-singer'. *Hearpen* is speculative – it glosses what may be a corruption of Greek αηδόνες; see Whitman. If it is a genuine alternative to *nihtegale*, *hearpen* presumably compares the bird's voice to the sweetness of the harp, appropriately enough (cf. Exeter Riddle 8: *sceawendwisan* 'entertainer's song', 9b).
See pp. 17, 34n, 41, 70, 75–7, 106, 110, 111, 119,122, 127n, 128, 134–5, 179, 181, 194, 210–12, 214, 215

Nuthatch **OE rindeclifer. ME notehach.** OE term speculative – it nicely describes a nuthatch's feeding behaviour, but could also refer to treecreeper or woodpecker. ME term seems to refer to the bird's habit of caching nuts/seeds.

Owl **OE ule/ufe. ME oule.** Precisely whether, or how, medieval observers distinguished between British owl species in name is unclear, although the bestiaries show that they certainly recognised different species. On the possible distinction between *ufe/ule*, see Lacey, 'Birds and Words', pp. 88–93.
On owls generally, see Chapter Three of this book. On particular species identified in medieval bestiaries, see pp. 114n, 119n, 120n, 128, 129n, 130, 141–2n

Pelican **ME pellican.** One of the two Eurasian species; Dalmatians may have bred in England in the early Middle Ages. *Onocratulus*, the standard classical and medieval Lat. term for pelican, is usually glossed *raredumle* 'bittern', so whether glossators confused the species, or they applied *raredumle* consistently as an equivalent large British water bird to a species familiar to Mediterranean habitats, is difficult to say. OE *wanfota* 'dark-foot' glosses Lat. *pellicanus* in one instance, though why this would be the most distinctive aspect of a pelican's appearance is curious; nor are the feet distinctive in biblical references to the pelican. In the St Gall Leviticus glossary, *onocratulus* is described as like a small duck, so it seems safest to assume that the Lat. term was interpreted diversely in Anglo-Saxon England, loosely translated as any sort of water bird. Aldhelm's Enigma 59, however, describing *onocratulus* as a bird that swallows sea water and has white feathers, assumes at least some familiarity with what pelicans look like. Pliny, too, describes the bird accurately and was an important source for medieval writers (*NH*, X.lxvi).
See pp. 98, 108

Peregrine falcon **OE wealhafoc/fealcen. ME faucoun peregrine.** OE *wealhafoc* means literally 'foreign-hawk or -falcon', which suggests some correlation with Lat. *peregrinus*.
See pp. 35n, 114–15, 157, 170, 189, 193n

Pheasant **OE worhana. ME fesaunt.** Also, possibly, OE *reodmuða* 'red-mouth' and ME *wercok* (cf. OE *worhana*).

Pigeon/Dove **OE culfre/dufe. ME douve/colombe/pijoun.** *Culfre* ultimately derives from Lat. *columba*. *Dufe* is attested in OE place-names (e.g., Duffield) and is presumably cognate with OE *dufan* 'to dive', observing, perhaps, the wood pigeon's characteristic swoops following a wing clap. See also below, s.v. *Wood pigeon*.
See pp. 70n, 109, 171n, 195

Plover **OE hulfestra. ME plover.** Generic term for plover and, probably, plover-like species. *Hulfestra* glosses *pluvialis*. Plovers, like many water birds, were eaten in the Middle Ages.

Quail **OE erschen/edischen. ME quail.** The OE translates as 'park-hen', or, more fittingly, 'stubble-hen'.

Raven **OE hrefn/hremn. ME raven.** Onomatopoeic. See also above, s.v. *Crow*.
See pp. 39, 57n, 88, 130n, 171n

Red kite **OE glida/cyta. ME kite/glede/puttock.** OE derived from *glidan* 'to glide'. Term presumably referred most specifically to the native red kite. OE *frisca* also glosses *cyta* in one glossary.
See pp. 15, 41n, 76, 78–9, 138, 171n

Redshank **ME redshanke.** OE *pipere* is not recorded as a bird name in the glossaries or glosses, but its genitive plural form in place-names recommends a nonhuman subject for the term as well as usual 'pipe-player': Pepper Ness, Kent, particularly given its coastal location, may mean 'Piper Ness' (Kitson [ii] and Hough). Kitson associates the name specifically with sandpipers, but the conspicuous colours and 'piping' calls of the resident and common redshank and oystercatcher makes these species more likely possibilities.

Robin **OE rædda/rudduc/salthaga/sæltna/seltra. ME ruddock.** OE *salthaga* and variants on the prefix are presumed to derive from *saltian* 'to dance', perhaps indicating the flighty, twitching behaviour of the robin, or small birds like it. *Salthaga* 'hedge-dancer (?)' could describe the dunnock as well, although the term does specifically gloss Lat. *rubisca* along with *rudduc* in one glossary. It has always been stated that the current name for this species does not appear until early modern times, but the Sherborne Missal records *Rudduc robertus* along with *ruddok*, so the beginnings of the name change were already established by at least the end of the fourteenth century.
See pp. 41n, 171–2

Rook **OE hroc. ME roke.** Onomatopoeic. See also above, s.v. *Crow*.
See pp. 41, 132

Saker falcon **ME sacre.** French origin.

Sand martin **OE stæðswealwe.** Literally 'bank-swallow', probably referring to the characteristic breeding sites of sand martins in sand banks.

Shelduck **ME bergandir.** Recorded in the Sherborne Missal, labelling what is probably a shelduck.

Glossary of Bird Names

Shrike **ME wariangle.** No recorded OE term, but reconstructions have been suggested; see Kitson (i). The name's components may refer to OE *wearg* 'criminal, villain' (with *incel*, diminutive suffix), or, cognate with other Germanic terms, OE *angel* 'angel', or 'hook'. The favoured interpretation is 'strangling/suffocating angel', akin to German *würgengel*. The Sherborne Missal depicts a great grey shrike labelled *waryghanger*.

Skylark **OE lawerce. ME lark.** Ancient name, probably imitative. ME derives from OE term.
See pp. 155, 170, 194, 211n

Snipe **OE snite/hæferblæte. ME snite/snipe.** Probably ancient; common Germanic. *Hæferblæte* 'goat-bleater' surely refers to the bizarre winnowing noise made by air through the tail feathers of displaying male snipes, which does, indeed, sound very like a goat's bleat.
See p. 41

Sparrowhawk **OE spearhafoc.** 'Sparrow-hawk'.
See pp. 194, 211n

Spoonbill **ME popeler/shovelard.** *Shovelard* refers to the bird's bill shape. The name was presumably transferred in altered form to the shoveler (*Anas clypeata*) when 'spoonbill' succeeded the earlier name. A British breeding species in the medieval period.

Starling **OE stærling/stær. ME starling/stare.** Ancient name, perhaps onomatopoeic. It is tempting to assume a very early link to Proto-Germanic **sterzon* 'star' because of the species' spangled plumage, but there is no evidence for this. Both starling and star, though, likely derive from related meanings of Indo-European **ster*.
See pp. 171, 172

Stint **OE stint. ME stint.** OE probably generic term for small wader species. Recorded in place-names (e.g., Stinsford). Likely derived from *styntan* 'to blunten' (by extension, 'to make small').

Swallow **OE swalwe. ME swalwe.** Ancient name; common Germanic. It has been suggested that the name derives from OE *swelgan* 'to swallow', but this does not seem convincingly imitative to me. Lockwood recommends possible Proto-Germanic **swalwo* 'cleft stick'.
See pp. 34, 85–6, 92n, 93n, 94, 170, 171n, 179, 181, 212, 213n, 216

Swan **OE swan/ylfete. ME swan.** Ancient origin; common Germanic. OE terms possibly distinguish mute and whooper/Bewick's swan, respectively.
See pp. 15, 29n, 33n, 34, 37–8, 41, 47, 57n, 70, 73, 74, 80, 87, 92–3

Swift **OE swift.** Unattested but plausible that *Apus apus* is intended in a charter landmark in Gloucestershire: *swiftan beorh* 'the swift's hill'.
See p. 93

Teal **ME tel.** Origin possibly imitative.

Tern **OE stearn/tearn.** Names certainly refer to some sort of seabird. Possibly a general seabird term, applied later to genus *Sterna* (first attested in the sixteenth century), and surviving in dialect terms for tern species (e.g. 'stern').

See pp. 37–8, 49–50

Thrush   **OE scric/þrostle/þrysce. ME mavis/throstel/thrush.** For possible distinctions between *þrostle/þrysce* in relation to different thrush species, see Lacey, 'Birds and Words', pp. 93–8, and Kitson (i).

Tit   **OE mase. ME titmose.** OE *mase* may observe the mouse-like size and movements of these species. Although it is possible that *frecmase* 'greedy-titmouse', *spicmase* 'fat/lard-titmouse' and *cummase* (unknown root) refer to separate species, they cannot be positively identified and may be general titmouse names. Blue tits and great tits are depicted accurately in various late medieval manuscripts.

See pp. 32, 137

Turtle dove   **OE turtur/turtle. ME turtur/turtel.** In both cases onomatopoeic and derived directly from Lat. *turtur*.

See pp. 32, 108, 171n

Vulture   **OE earngeap. ME vulture.** OE may have referred to European vulture species encountered in literature (e.g. in Isidore of Seville), but may also have functioned as a generic term for large British raptors generally, particularly given the prefix *earn* 'eagle'. The suffix may refer to OE *geap* 'roomy, wide, spacious', relating to the bird's size and wing span. Another OE term, *herefong* 'army-seizer', has been assigned to vulture (and osprey), but it seems plausible that it could just be a general name for raptor carrion feeders.

Wagtail   **OE geoluwearte. ME wagstert.** *Geoluwearte*, if correct, refers specifically to the yellow (*geoluw*) wagtail; *earte* is usually assumed to have an Indo-European root referring to some kind of water bird, and possibly functioned as an OE term for wagtail generally. ME *sterte* means 'tail'. The Sherborne Missal depicts a pied wagtail labelled *waysterter*; another, even more accurate example is in Cambridge, Fitzwilliam Museum, MS 2–1954, f. 84b.

White stork   **OE storc. ME stork.** Ancient origin; common Germanic. Presumed to refer to the bird's long-legged 'stick' appearance, which likely goes back to Indo-European **ster* 'stiff'. British breeding species at times in the Middle Ages, as OE place-names suggest (e.g., Storrington).

See pp. 34, 35n, 90n, 171n

Woodcock   **OE wudusnite/wuducocc/holthana. ME wodecok.**

Woodpecker   **OE fina. ME heghwal/wodspek/wodehake/wodewale.** OE *fina* is perhaps supported by ME *fyne* recorded in the Sherborne Missal labelling what appears to be one of the spotted woodpecker species; *viuene* (finene?), labelling another possible spotted woodpecker, may also be cognate. Manuscript illuminations clearly portray different species, but the extant names do not clearly distinguish. *Wodewale* labels a green woodpecker in the Sherborne Missal, so most names presumably

refer to this species, which is the most vocally distinctive (cf. dialect term *hickwall*; Lockwood), or function generically. ME *wodspek* presupposes possible OE *speot*, suggested in some place-names (e.g., Spexhall). Cf. Old Saxon *ghronspeht* 'green woodpecker'.
See p. 78n

Wood pigeon **OE wuduculfre/cuscote. ME scuscote.** Root of OE *cuscote* unknown, but the prefix of the word, it seems to me, more likely derives from imitative 'cooing' typical of the bird's call, rather than OE *cu* 'cow', as sometimes suggested. Cf. Old Saxon *ring duva* (probably refers to the wood pigeon's distinctive white collar).

Wren **OE wrenna. ME wrenne.** Kitson suggests OE *irþling* as a possible synonym for *wrenna* on the strength of shared Lat. lemmata in the glossaries; Kitson (i). Meaning 'farmer or ploughman', though, the only thing we might confidently say about *irþling*, which glosses various different Lat. names, is that it probably describes some sort of small farmland bird.
See p. 32

Yellowhammer **OE amer.** Unattested in this form, but derived from corrupt *amore* in one glossary; cf. *clodhamer*. Etymon of the suffix surviving in yellowhammer, and may have referred specifically to this bright, noticeable farmland bird as well as bunting-type species generally. Origin unclear. Most commonly assumed to be some sort of reference to the bright plumage, but may derive from OE *omer* 'type of corn, spelt', defining the bird according to its favoured food in the same way as *linetwige, ragofinc*. Cf. German *ammer* 'bunting'. *Amer* may also be attested in some place-names (e.g., Amberley).

Sources and Further Reading

Birds in Old English Place-Names

Hooke, Della, 'Beasts, Birds and Other Creatures in Pre-Conquest Charters and Place-Names in England', in *Representing Beasts in Early Medieval England and Scandinavia*, ed. by Michael D. J. Bintley and Thomas J. T. Williams (Woodbridge: Boydell Press, 2015), pp. 253–82

Hough, Carole, 'Place-Name Evidence for Old English Bird-Names', *Journal of the English Place-Name Society*, 30 (1998), 60–9

Old English Bird Names and Taxonomies

Kitson, Peter, 'Old English Bird Names' (i), *English Sudies*, 78:6 (1997), 481–505

—— , 'Old English Bird Names' (ii), *English Studies*, 79:1 (1998), 2–22

Lacey, Eric, 'Birds and Words: Aurality, Semantics and Species in Anglo-Saxon England', in *Sensory Perception in the Medieval West*, ed. by Simon

C. Thomson and Michael D. J. Bintley (Turnhout: Brepols, 2016), pp. 75–98
——, 'When Is a Hroc not a Hroc? When It Is a Crawe or a Hrefn!: A Case-Study in Recovering Old English Folk-Taxonomies', in *The Art, Literature and Material Culture of the Medieval World*, ed. by M. Boulton, J. Hawkes and M. Herman (Dublin: Four Courts, 2015), pp. 138–52
Lockwood, W. B., *The Oxford Book of British Bird Names* (Oxford: Oxford University Press, 1984)
Whitman, Charles H., 'The Birds of Old English Literature', *Journal of Germanic Philology*, 2 (1898), 149–98

Germanic Bird Names

Steinmeyer, Elias, and Eduard Sievers, *Die althochdeutschen glossen* (Berlin: Weidmannsche Buchhandlung, 1895)
Suolahti, Hugo, *Die deutschen vogelnamen* (Strasbourg: Trübner, 1909)

BIBLIOGRAPHY

Classical and Medieval Primary Sources

Aelred of Rievaulx, *Dialogue on the Soul*, trans. by Charles H. Talbot (Kalamazoo, MI: Cistercian Publications, 1981)
Ælfric, *Ælfric's De Temporibus anni*, ed. by H. Henel, Early English Text Society OS, 213 (Oxford: Oxford University Press, 1942)
——, *Ælfrics Grammatik und Glossar*, ed. by Julius Zupitza (Berlin: Weidmannsche Buchhandlung, 1880)
——, *Ælfric's Lives of the Saints*, ed. by W. W. Skeat, 2 vols, Early English Text Society OS, 76, 82 (London: Trübner, 1881, 1885)
——, *Exameron Anglice or The Old English Hexameron*, ed. by Samuel J. Crawford, Bibliothek der angelsächsischen prosa, 10 (Hamburg: H. Grand, 1921)
Alan of Lille, *The Plaint of Nature*, trans. by James J. Sheridan (Toronto: Pontifical Institute of Medieval Studies, 1980)
Albertus Magnus, *On Animals: A Medieval Summa Zoologica*, trans. by K. F. Kitchell Jr. and I. M. Resnick, 2 vols (Baltimore, MD: John Hopkins University Press, 1999)
Aldhelm, *Aldhelm: The Poetic Works*, trans. by Michael Lapidge and James L. Rosier (1985; repr. Cambridge: D. S. Brewer, 2009)
——, *De metris et enigmatibus ac pedum regulis*, in *Monumenta germaniae historica*, ed. by Rudolf Ehwald, Auctores Antiquissimi, 15 (Berlin: Weidmann, 1919)
——, *Through a Gloss Darkly: Aldhelm's Riddles in the British Library MS Royal 12.C.xxiii*, ed. and trans. by Nancy Porter Stork (Toronto: Pontifical Institute of Medieval Studies, 1990)
Ancrene Wisse: A Corrected Edition of the Text in Cambridge, Corpus Christi College, MS 402 with Variants from Other Manuscripts, ed. by Bella Millet, Early English Text Society OS, 325, 326, 2 vols (Oxford: Oxford University Press, 2005, 2006)
The Anglo-Saxon Chronicles, ed. and trans. by Michael Swanton, rev. edn (London: Phoenix Press, 2000)
Aristotle, *The Complete Works of Aristotle*, ed. by Jonathan Barnes, 2 vols (Princeton, NJ: Princeton University Press, 1984)
Augustine, Saint, *Saint Augustine, City of God: Books VIII–XVI*, trans. by G. G. Walsh and G. Monahan, The Fathers of the Church: A New Translation, 14 (Washington, D.C.: Catholic University Press of America, 1952)

——, *Saint Augustine: Expositions on the Psalms*, trans. by Arthur Cleveland Coxe, Nicene and Post-Nicene Fathers, First Series, 8, ed. by Philip Schaff (1888; repr. Grand Rapids, MI: Eerdmans, 1984)

——, *The Immortality of the Soul, The Magnitude of the Soul, On Music, The Advantage of Believing, On Faith in Things Unseen*, ed. by Ludwig Schopp, The Fathers of the Church: A New Translation, 4 (Washington, D.C.: Catholic University of America Press, 1947)

Bartholomaeus Anglicus, *De genuinis rerum [De proprietatibus rerum]* (1601; repr. Frankfurt am Main: Minerva, 1964)

——, *On the Properties of Things: John Trevisa's Translation of Bartholomaeus Anglicus, De proprietatibus rerum*, ed. by M. C. Seymour and others, 3 vols (Oxford: Clarendon Press, 1975), vol. 1

Bayless, Martha, and Michael Lapidge, eds, *Collectanea Pseudo-Bedae*, Scriptores Latini Hiberniae, 14 (Dublin: School of Celtic Studies, Dublin Institute for Advanced Studies, 1998)

Bede, *Bede's Ecclesiastical History of the English People*, ed. and trans. by B. Colgrave and R. A. B. Mynors (Oxford: Clarendon Press, 1969)

Bestiary: Being an English Version of the Bodleian Library, Oxford, MS 764, trans. by Richard Barber (Woodbridge: Boydell Press, 1993)

The Book of Beasts: Being a Translation from a Latin Bestiary of the Twelfth Century, trans. by T. H. White (New York, NY: Dover Publications, 1984)

Buecheler, Franciscus, and Alexander Riese, eds, *Anthologia latina: sive poesis latinae supplementum*, 2 vols (Leipzig: B. G. Teubneri, 1869–94)

Cassiodorus, *Expositio Psalmorum LXXI–CL*, Corpus Christianorum Series Latina, 98, ed. by M. Adriaen (Turnhout: Brepols, 1958)

Charlemagne: An Anglo-Norman Poem of the Twelfth Century, ed. by Francisque Michel (London: William Pickering, 1836)

Chaucer, Geoffrey, *The Parlement of Foulys*, ed. by D. S. Brewer, 2nd edn (Manchester: Manchester University Press, 1972)

——, *The Riverside Chaucer*, gen. ed. Larry D. Benson, 3rd edn (Oxford: Oxford University Press, 1988)

Classen, E., and F. E. Harmer, eds, *An Anglo-Saxon Chronicle from the British Museum, Cotton MS., Tiberius B. IV* (Manchester: Manchester University Press, 1926)

Conlee, John, *Middle English Debate Poetry* (East Lansing, MI: Colleagues Press, 1991)

Dante Alighieri, *De vulgari eloquentia*, trans. by Stephen Botterill (Cambridge: Cambridge University Press, 1996)

Deschamps, Eustache, *Œuvres complètes d'Eustache Deschamps*, ed. by A. H. E. Marquis de Queux de St-Hilaire and Gaston Raynaud, 11 vols (Paris: Firmin Didot, 1878–1903), vol. 2

Donatus, *Ars grammatica*, ed. by Heinrich Keil (Leipzig: Teubner, 1864)

The Earliest Life of Gregory the Great by an Anonymous Monk of Whitby, trans. by Bertram Colgrave (Lawrence, KS: University of Kansas Press, 1968)

Bibliography

The Exeter DVD: The Exeter Anthology of Old English Poetry, ed. by Bernard J. Muir and programmed by Nick Kennedy (Exeter: University of Exeter Press, 2006)

Fein, Susanna Greer, ed., *Moral Love Songs and Laments*, TEAMS Middle English Text Series (Kalamazoo, MI: Medieval Institute Publications, 1998)

Frederick II, *The Art of Falconry*, trans. by Casey A. Wood and F. Marjorie Fyfe (Boston, MA: Charles T. Branford, 1955)

Gerald of Wales, *Topographia hibernica et expugnatio hibernica*, in *Giraldi Cambrensis opera*, Rolls Series, 8 vols, ed. by James F. Dimock (London, 1861–91), vol. 5

Glorie, Fr., ed., *Variae collectiones aenigmatum Merovingicae aetatis*, Corpus Christianorum Series Latina, vol. 133 (Turnhout: Brepols, 1968)

——, *Variae collectiones aenigmatum Merovingicae aetatis* (pars altera), Corpus Christianorum Series Latina, vol. 133a (Turnhout: Brepols, 1968)

Gower, John, *Confessio Amantis*, TEAMS Middle English Texts Series, ed. by Russell Peck and Latin trans. by Andrew Galloway, 3 vols (Kalamazoo, MI: Medieval Institute Publications, 2006)

——, *The Major Latin Works of John Gower*, trans. by Eric W. Stockton (Seattle, WA: University of Washington Press, 1962)

——, *The Works of John Gower*, ed. by G. C. Macaulay, 4 vols (Oxford: Clarendon Press, 1902)

Hessels, J. H., ed., *An Eighth-Century Latin–Anglo-Saxon Glossary, Preserved in the Library of Corpus Christi College, Cambridge* (Cambridge: Cambridge University Press, 1890)

Homer, *The Odyssey*, trans. by E. V. Rieu and D. C. H. Rieu, rev. edn (London: Penguin, 2003)

Hugh of Foilloy, *The Medieval Book of Birds: Hugh of Foilloy's Aviarium*, ed. and trans. by Willene B. Clark (Binghamton, NY: Center for Medieval and Early Renaissance Studies, 1992)

Isidore of Seville, *Etymologiarum sive originum*, ed. by W. N. Lindsay, 2 vols (Oxford: Clarendon Press, 1911)

——, *The Etymologies of Isidore of Seville*, ed. by Stephen A. Barney and others (Cambridge: Cambridge University Press, 2009)

John of Worcester, *The Chronicle of John of Worcester, Volume III: The Annals from 1067–1140*, ed. and trans. by P. McGurk (Oxford: Oxford University Press, 1995)

Krapp, G. P., and E. V. K. Dobbie, eds, *The Anglo-Saxon Poetic Records*, 6 vols (London: Routledge and Kegan Paul, 1931–1953)

Langland, William, *The Vision of Piers Plowman. A Critical Edition of the B-Text*, ed. by A. V. C. Schmidt (London: J. M. Dent, 1995)

Liber de ordine creaturarum: un anónimo irlandés del siglo VII, ed. by Manuel C. Díaz y Díaz (Santiago de Compostela: University Press of Santiago de Compostela, 1972)

Bibliography

Lindelöf, U., *Der Lambeth-Psalter: eine altenglische Interlinearversion des Psalters in der Hs 427 der erzbischoefliche Lambeth Palace Library; I, Text und Glossar; II, Beschreibung und Geschichte der Handschrift; Verhältnis der Glosse zu anderen Psalterversionen; Bemerkungen über die Sprache des Denkmals*, Acta Societatis Scientiarum Fennicae, 35.i and 43.iii, 2 vols (Helsinki: Druckerei der Finnischen Litteraturgesellschaft, 1909–1914)

Marie de France, *Lais Bretons (XII-XIII siècles): Marie de France et ses contemporains*, ed. by Nathalie Koble and Mireille Séguy (Paris: Champion, 2011)

——, *The Lais of Marie de France*, trans. by Glyn S. Burgess and Keith Busby, 2nd edn (London: Penguin, 1999)

Maurus, Hrabanus, *De rerum naturis*: Cod. Casin. 132, Archivio dell'Abbazia di Montecassino, ed. by Guglielmo Cavallo, 3 vols (Turin: Priuli & Verlucca, 1994)

A Medieval Book of Beasts: The Second-Family Bestiary, ed. and trans. by Willene B. Clark (Woodbridge: Boydell Press, 2006)

Miller, Thomas, ed., *The Old English Version of Bede's Ecclesiastical History of the English People*, Early English Text Society OS, 95, 96 (London: Trübner, 1890–91)

Neckam, Alexander, *De naturis rerum, libri duo, with the Poem of the Same Author, De laudibus sapientiae*, ed. by Thomas Wright (1863; repr. Cambridge: Cambridge University Press, 2012)

Odo of Cheriton, *The Fables of Odo of Cheriton*, trans. by John C. Jacobs (Syracuse, NY: Syracuse University Press, 1985)

Oliphant, R. T., ed., *Harley Latin-Old English, edited from British Museum MS Harley 3376* (The Hague: Mouton, 1966)

Ovid (P. Ovidi Nasonis), *Metamorphoses*, ed. by R. J. Tarrant (Oxford: Oxford University Press, 2004).

——, *Metamorphoses*, trans. by David Raeburn (London: Penguin, 2004).

Ovide moralisé; poème du commencement du quatorzième siècle, ed. by C. de Boer, 5 vols (Amsterdam: Johannes Müller, 1915–38)

The Owl and the Nightingale: Text and Translation, ed. by Neil Cartlidge (Exeter: Exeter University Press, 2001)

Le Petit Plet, Anglo-Norman Texts, 20, ed. by Brian S. Merrilees (Oxford: Oxford University Press, 1970)

Pheifer, J. D., ed., *Old English Glosses in the Épinal-Erfurt Glossary* (Oxford: Clarendon Press, 1974)

Philippe de Remi, *Jehan et Blonde, Poems, and Songs*, ed. and trans. by Barbara N. Sargent-Baur (Amsterdam and Atlanta, GA: Rodopi, 2001)

Physiologus: A Medieval Book of Nature Lore, trans. by Michael J. Curley (Chicago, IL and London: University of Chicago Press, 2009)

Pliny, *Natural History*, ed. by H. Rackham, 10 vols (Cambridge, MA: Harvard University Press, 1938–62)

Porter, David W., ed., *The Antwerp-London Glossaries: The Latin and Latin-Old English Vocabularies from Antwerp, Museum Plantin-Moretus 16.2 – London, British Library Add. 3224*, vol. 1 (Toronto: Pontifical Institute of Medieval Studies, 2011)

Probus, *Grammatici latini*, ed. by Heinrich Keil, 7 vols (Leipzig: Teubner, 1857–80)

Reynolds, W. D., 'The Ovidius moralizatus of Petrus Berchorius: An Introduction and Translation' (unpublished doctoral thesis, University of Illinois, 1971)

Quinn, J., 'The Minor Latin-Old English Glossaries in MS. Cotton Cleopatra A. III' (unpublished doctoral thesis, Stanford University, California, 1951)

The Seafarer, ed. by Ida Gordon, rev. edn (Exeter: University of Exeter Press, 1996)

Sir Gawain and the Green Knight in Poems of the Pearl Manuscript, ed. by Malcolm Andrew and Ronald Waldron, 4th edn (Exeter: Exeter University Press, 2002)

Thomas de Cantimpré, *Liber de natura rerum: Editio princeps secundum codices manuscriptos*, ed. by Helmut Boese (Berlin: W. de Gruyter, 1973)

Tupper, Frederick, ed., *The Riddles of the Exeter Book* (Boston, MA: Ginn and Company, 1910)

Vincent of Beauvais, *Speculum quadruplex, sive speculum maius*, 4 vols (1624, repr. Graz: Akademische Druck- u. Verlagsanstalt, 1964–5)

Williamson, Craig, ed., *The Old English Riddles of the Exeter Book* (Chapel Hill, NC: University of North Carolina Press, 1977)

Secondary and Post-Medieval Sources

Afros, Elena, 'Linguistic Ambiguities in Some Exeter Book Riddles', *Notes and Queries*, 52:4 (2005), 431–7

Amsler, Mark E., *Etymology and Grammatical Discourse in Late Antiquity and the Early Middle Ages* (Amsterdam: John Benjamins, 1989)

Archibald, Elizabeth, *Incest and the Medieval Imagination* (Oxford and New York, NY: Oxford University Press, 2001)

Archibald, Marion M., and Michael Dhenin, 'A Sceat of Offa of Mercia' <http://www.britnumsoc.org/publications/Digital%20BNJ/pdfs/2004_BNJ_74_4.pdf> [accessed 15 March 2016]

Arluke, Arnold, and Clinton R. Saunders, *Regarding Animals* (Philadelphia, PA: Temple University Press, 1996)

Armstrong, Edward A., *The Folklore of Birds: An Enquiry into the Origin and Distribution of some Magico-Religious Traditions* (London: Collins, 1958)

Avray, D. L., *The Preaching of the Friars: Sermons Diffused from Paris before 1300* (Oxford: Clarendon Press, 1985)

Backhouse, Janet, *Medieval Birds in the Sherborne Missal* (London: British Library, 2001)

Barley, Nigel F., 'Structural Aspects of the Anglo-Saxon Riddle', *Semiotica*, 10 (1974), 143–75

Barratt, Alexandra, 'Avian Self-Fashioning and Self-Doubt in *The Owl and the Nightingale*', in *Individuality and Achievement in Middle English Poetry*, ed. by O. S. Pickering (Cambridge: D. S. Brewer, 1997), pp. 1–18

Beer, Jeanette, ed., *Translation Theory and Practice in the Middle Ages*, Studies in Medieval Culture, 38 (Kalamazoo, MI: Medieval Institute Publications, 1997)

Bennett, Jane, *Vibrant Matter: A Political Ecology of Things* (Durham, NC and London: Duke University Press, 2010)

Bennett, J. A. W., *The Parlement of Foules* (Oxford: Oxford University Press, 1957)

Benson, David, 'Incest and Moral Poetry in Gower's *Confessio Amantis*', *Chaucer Review*, 19:2 (1984), 100–9

Berger, John, *About Looking* (1980; repr. London: Bloomsbury, 2009)

Bischoff, Bernhard, and Michael Lapidge, eds, *Biblical Commentaries from the Canterbury School of Theodore and Hadrian*, Cambridge Studies in Anglo-Saxon England, 10 (Cambridge: Cambridge University Press, 1994)

Bitterli, Dieter, *Say What I Am Called: The Old English Riddles of the Exeter Book and the Anglo-Latin Tradition* (Toronto, Buffalo, NY and London: University of Toronto Press, 2009)

Boswell, John, *Christianity, Social Tolerance, and Homosexuality* (Chicago, IL: University of Chicago Press, 1980)

Bosworth, James, *The Life of Samuel Johnson*, ed. by David Wormersley (London: Penguin, 2008)

Bosworth, Joseph, *An Anglo-Saxon Dictionary Based on the Manuscript Collection of the Late Joseph Bosworth*, ed. by T. Northcote Toller (1888–98; repr. London: Oxford University Press, 1954)

——, *An Anglo-Saxon Dictionary Based on the Manuscript Collection of the Late Joseph Bosworth, Supplement*, ed. by T. Northcote Toller (1921; repr. Oxford: Oxford University Press, 1955)

Braidotti, Rosi, 'Animals, Anomalies, and Inorganic Others', *Publications of the Modern Language Association of America*, 124:2 (2009), 526–32

Bruckner, Matilda Tomaryn, *Chrétien Continued: A Study of the* Conte du Graal *and Its Verse Continuations* (Oxford: Oxford University Press, 2009)

Bynum, Caroline Walker, *Metamorphosis and Identity* (New York, NY: Zone Books, 2005)

——, *The Resurrection of the Body in Western Christianity, 200–1336* (New York, NY: Columbia University Press, 1995)

——, 'Why All the Fuss about the Body? A Medievalist's Perspective', *Critical Enquiry*, 22:1 (1995), 1–33

Cameron, M. L., 'Aldhelm as Naturalist: a Re-Examination of Some of his *Enigmata*', *Peritia*, 4 (1985), 117–33

Camille, Michael, *Image on the Edge: The Margins of Medieval Art* (London: Reaktion Books, 1992)

Cannon, Christopher, *The Grounds of English Literature* (Oxford: Oxford University Press, 2007)

Cartlidge, Neil, 'The Date of *The Owl and the Nightingale*', *Medium Ævum*, 65 (1996), 230–47

——, 'Medieval Debate-Poetry and *The Owl and the Nightingale*', in *A Companion to Medieval Poetry*, ed. by Corinne Saunders (Oxford: Wiley-Blackwell, 2010), pp. 237–57

Clemoes, Peter, '*Mens absentia cogitans* in *The Seafarer* and *The Wanderer*', in *Medieval Literature and Civilization: Studies in Memory of G. N. Garmonsway*, ed. by D. A. Pearsall and R. A. Waldron (London: Athlone Press, 1969), pp. 62–77

Cocker, Mark, *Birds Britannica* (London: Chatto and Windus, 2005)

——, *Birds and People* (London: Jonathan Cape, 2013)

Cohen, Jeffrey Jerome, *Hybridity, Identity and Monstrosity in Medieval Britain: On Difficult Middles* (New York, NY: Palgrave Macmillan, 2006)

——, ed., *Inhuman Nature* (Washington, D.C.: Oliphaunt, 2014)

——, 'Inventing with Animals', in *Engaging with Nature: Essays on the Natural World in Medieval and Early Modern Europe*, ed. by Barbara A. Hanawalt and Lisa J. Kiser (Notre Dame, IN: University of Notre Dame Press, 2008), pp. 39–62

——, *Medieval Identity Machines* (Minneapolis, MN: University of Minnesota Press, 2003)

Conde Silvestre, Juan Camilo, and Juan Carlos Conde Silvestre, 'The Semiotics of Allegory in Early Medieval Hermeneutics and the Interpretation of *The Seafarer*', *Atlantis*, 16:1 (1994), 71–90

Coolman, B. T., *The Theology of Hugh of St. Victor* (Cambridge: Cambridge University Press, 2010)

Cramp, Stanley, gen. ed., *Birds of the Western Palearctic*, 9 vols (Oxford: Oxford University Press, 1977–94)

Crane, Susan, *Animal Encounters: Contacts and Concepts in Medieval Britain* (Philadelphia, PA: University of Pennsylvania Press, 2013)

——, 'For the Birds', *Studies in the Age of Chaucer*, 29 (2007), 23–41

——, 'Ritual Aspects of the Hunt à Force', in *Engaging with Nature: Essays on the Natural World in Medieval and Early Modern Europe*, ed. by Barbara A. Hanawalt and Lisa J. Kiser (Notre Dame, IN: University of Notre Dame, 2008), pp. 63–74

Cronon, William, 'The Trouble with Wilderness; or, Getting Back to the Wrong Nature', in *Uncommon Ground: Rethinking the Human Place in Nature*, ed. by William Cronon (New York, NY: W. W. Norton & Co., 1995), pp. 69–90

Dailey, Patricia, 'Riddles, Wonder and Responsiveness in Anglo-Saxon Literature', in *The Cambridge History of Early Medieval English Literature*, ed. by Clare A. Lees (Cambridge: Cambridge University Press, 2013), pp. 451–72

Davis, Rebecca, *Piers Plowman and the Books of Nature* (Oxford: Oxford University Press, 2016)

Deleuze, Gilles, and Félix Guattari, *A Thousand Plateaus*, trans. by Brian Massumi (London and New York, NY: Bloomsbury Academic, 2013)

Derrida, Jacques, *The Animal That Therefore I Am*, trans. by David Wills and ed. by Marie-Louise Mallet (New York, NY: Fordham University Press, 2008)

Diekstra, F. N. M., '*The Seafarer* 58–66a: The Flight of the Exiled Soul to Its Fatherland', *Neophilologus*, 55 (1971), 433–46

DiNapoli, Robert, 'In the Kingdom of the Blind, the One-Eyed Man is a Seller of Garlic: Depth-Perception and the Poet's Perspective in the Exeter Book Riddles', *English Studies*, 81 (2000), 422–55

Doane, A. N., 'Three Old English Implement Riddles: Reconsiderations of Numbers 4, 49 and 73', *Modern Philology*, 84 (1987), 243–57

Dobney, Keith, and Deborah Jaques, 'Avian Signatures for Identity and Status in Anglo-Saxon England', *Acta zoological cracoviensia*, 45 (2002), 7–21

Donovan, Mortimer J., 'The Owl as Religious Altruist in *The Owl and the Nightingale*', *Mediaeval Studies*, 18 (1956), 207–14

Eco, Umberto, *The Limits of Interpretation* (Bloomington and Indianapolis, IN: Indiana University Press, 1990)

Edwards, A. S. G., 'Bartholomaeus Anglicus' *De Proprietatibus Rerum* and Medieval English Literature', *Archiv für das Studium der neueren Sprachen und Literaturen*, 222 (1985), 121–8

Ellard, Donna Beth, 'Going Interspecies, Going Interlingual, and Flying Away with the *Phoenix*', *Exemplaria*, 23:3 (2011), 268–92

Elmes, Melissa Ridley, 'Species or Specious? Authorial Choices and *The Parliament of Fowls*', in *Rethinking Chaucerian Beasts*, ed. by Carolynn Van Dyke (New York, NY: Palgrave Macmillan, 2012), pp. 233–47

Estes, Heide, *Anglo-Saxon Literary Landscapes: Ecotheory and the Environmental Imagination* (Amsterdam: Amsterdam University Press, 2017)

Evans, Dafydd, 'The Nobility of Knight and Falcon', in *The Ideals and Practice of Medieval Knighthood III*, ed. by Christopher Harper-Bill and Ruth Harvey (Woodbridge: Boydell Press, 1990), pp. 79–99

Ferlampin-Acher, Christine, 'Le monstre dans les romans des XIIIe et XIVe siècles', in *Ecriture et modes de pensée au moyen âge (VIIIe-XVe siècle)*, ed. by Dominique Boutet and Laurence Harf-Lancner (Paris: Ecole Normale Supérieure, 1993), pp. 69–87

Fisher, James, *The Shell Book of Birds* (London: Ebury Press & Michael Joseph, 1966)

Fletcher, Alan J., 'Middle English Debate Literature', in *Readings in Medieval Texts: Interpreting Old and Middle English Literature*, ed. by David F. Johnson and Elaine Treharne (Oxford: Oxford University Press, 2005), pp. 241–56

Flora, Nona C., ed., *Animals of the Middle Ages* (New York, NY: Garland, 2000)

Forbes Irving, P. M. C., *Metamorphosis in Greek Myths* (Oxford: Oxford University Press, 1990)

Fry, Donald K., 'The Art of Bede: Edwin's Council', in *Saints, Scholars and Heroes: Studies in Medieval Culture in Honor of Charles W. Jones*, ed. by Margot H. King and Wesley M. Stevens, 2 vols (Collegeville, MN: St. John's Abbey and University, 1979), vol. 1, pp. 195–209

—— , 'Exeter Book Riddle Solutions', *Old English Newsletter*, 15:1 (1981), 22–33

Fudge, Erica, 'A Left-Handed Blow: Writing the History of Animals', in *Representing Animals*, ed. by Nigel Rothefels (Bloomington, IN: Indiana University Press, 2002) pp. 3–18

Gannon, Anna, *The Iconography of Early Anglo-Saxon Coinage: Sixth to Eighth Centuries* (Oxford: Oxford University Press, 2003)

Goldsmith, Margaret E., 'The *Seafarer* and the Birds', *Review of English Studies*, 5:19 (1954), 225–35

Gorst, Emma, 'Interspecies Mimicry: Birdsong in Chaucer's "Manciple's Tale" and *The Parlement of Fowles*', *New Medieval Literatures*, 12 (2010), 147–54

Griffin, Miranda, *Transforming Tales: Rewriting Metamorphosis in Medieval French Literature* (Oxford: Oxford University Press, 2015)

Gurney, J. H., *Early Annals of Ornithology* (London: H. F. & G. Witherby, 1921)

Ham, Jennifer, and Matthew Senior, eds, *Animal Acts: Configuring the Human in Western History* (London and New York, NY: Routledge, 1997)

Hansen, Elaine Tuttle, *The Solomon Complex: Reading Wisdom in Old English Poetry* (Toronto and London: University of Toronto Press, 1988)

Harbert, Bruce, 'The Myth of Tereus in Ovid and Gower', *Medium Aevum*, 41 (1972), 208–14

—— , 'Ovid and John Gower', in *Ovid Renewed: Ovidian Influences on Literature and Art from the Middle Ages to the Twentieth Century*, ed. by Charles Martindale (Cambridge: Cambridge University Press, 1988), pp. 83–97

Hayles, N. Katherine, *How We Became Posthuman: Virtual Bodies in Cybernetics, Literature and Informatics* (Chicago, IL and London: University of Chicago Press, 1999)

Hays, H. R., *Birds, Beasts and Men* (London: J. M. Dent and Sons, 1973)

Heaney, Seamus, *Seeing Things* (London: Faber and Faber, 1991)

—— , 'Small Fantasia for W.B.', *Times Literary Supplement* (27 January 1989)

Heron-Allen, Edward, *Barnacles in Nature and Myth* (Oxford: Oxford University Press, 1928)

Hiltner, Ken, *What Else Is Pastoral? Renaissance Literature and the Environment* (Ithaca, NY and London: Cornell University Press, 2011)

Hinckley, Henry Barrett, 'Science and Folklore in *The Owl and the Nightingale*', *Modern Language Association*, 47:2 (1932), 303–14

Holthausen, Ferdinand, 'Ein altenglisches rätsel', *Germanisch-Romanische Monatsschrift*, 15 (1927), 453–4

Holton, Frederick S., 'Old English Sea Imagery and the Interpretation of *The Seafarer*', *Yearbook of English Studies*, 12 (1982), 208–17

Hooke, Della, 'Beasts, Birds and Other Creatures in Pre-Conquest Charters and Place-Names in England', in *Representing Beasts in Early Medieval England and Scandinavia*, ed. by Michael D. J. Bintley and Thomas J. T. Williams (Woodbridge: Boydell Press, 2015), pp. 253–82

Hough, Carole, 'Place-Name Evidence for Old English Bird-Names', *Journal of the English Place-Name Society*, 30 (1998), 60–9

Howe, Nicholas, 'Aldhelm's *Enigmata* and Isidorian Etymology', *Anglo-Saxon England*, 14 (1985), 37–59

——, *Migration and Myth-Making in Anglo-Saxon England* (New Haven, CT: Yale University Press, 1989)

Hsy, Jonathan, 'Between Species: Animal-Human Bilingualism and Medieval Texts', in *Booldly Bot Meekly: Essays on the Theory and Practice of Translation in the Middle Ages in Honour of Roger Ellis*, The Medieval Translator, 14, ed. by Catherine Batt and René Tixier (Turnhout: Brepols, forthcoming)

Hultin, Neil, 'The External Soul in *The Seafarer* and *The Wanderer*', *Folklore*, 88:1 (1977), 39–45

Hume, Kathryn, 'The Concept of the Hall in Old English Poetry', *Anglo-Saxon England*, 3 (1974), 63–74

——, *The Owl and the Nightingale: The Poem and Its Critics* (Toronto and Buffalo, NY: University of Buffalo Press, 1975)

Ireland, C. A., 'Some Analogues of the O.E. *Seafarer* from Hiberno-Latin Sources', *Neuphilologische Mitteilungen*, 92 (1991), 1–14

Jacobs, Nicholas, 'Celtic Saga and the Contexts of Old English Elegiac Poetry', *Études celtiques*, 26 (1989), 95–142

——, '*The Seafarer* and the Birds: A Possible Irish Parallel', *Celtica*, 23 (1999), 125–31

——, 'Syntactical Connection and Logical Disconnection: The Case of *The Seafarer*', *Medium Ævum*, 58 (1989), 105–13

Jones, Richard, *The Medieval Natural World* (Harlow: Pearson, 2013)

Keller, Evelyn Fox, 'The Gender/Science System: or, Is Sex to Gender as Nature Is to Science?', in *Feminism and Science*, ed. by Nancy Tuana (Bloomington, IN: Indiana University Press, 1989), pp. 33–44

Kennedy, Charles W., *The Earliest English Poetry* (Oxford: Oxford University Press, 1943)

Kennedy, Ruth, '"A Bird in Bishopswood": Some Newly-Discovered Lines of Alliterative Verse from the Late Fourteenth Century', in *Medieval Literature and Antiquities: Studies in Honour of Basil Cottle*, ed. by Myra Stokes and T. L. Burton (Cambridge: D. S. Brewer, 1987), pp. 71–87

Kiernan, K. S., 'The Mysteries of the Sea-Eagle in Exeter Riddle 74', *Philological Quarterly*, 54 (1975), 518–22

Kiser, Lisa, 'Chaucer and the Politics of Nature', in *Beyond Nature Writing: Expanding the Boundaries of Ecocriticism*, ed. by Karla Armbruster and Kathleen R. Wallace (Charlottesville, VA: University Press of Virginia, 2001), pp. 41–56

Kitson, Peter, 'Old English Bird Names' (i), *English Sudies*, 78:6 (1997), 2–22

—— 'Old English Bird Names' (ii), *English Studies*, 79:1 (1998), 481–505

—— 'Swans and Geese in Old English Riddles', *Anglo-Saxon Studies in Archaeology and History*, 7 (1994), 79–84

Koff, Leonard Michael, '"Awak!" Chaucer Translates Bird Song', in *Traduire au Moyen Age, The Medieval Translator*, 5, ed. by Roger Ellis and René Tixier (Turnhout: Brepols, 1996), pp. 390–418

Kordecki, Lesley, *Ecofeminist Subjectivities: Chaucer's Talking Birds* (New York, NY: Palgrave Macmillan, 2011)

Kramer, Johanna, *Between Earth and Heaven: Liminality and the Ascension of Christ in Anglo-Saxon Literature* (Manchester: Manchester University Press, 2014)

Kull, Kalevi, and Peeter Torop, 'Biotranslation: Translation Between Umwelten', in *Translation Translation*, ed. by Susan Petrilli (Amsterdam: Rodopi, 2003), pp. 313–28

Kurath, Hans, and Robert E. Lewis, eds, *Middle English Dictionary* (Ann Arbor, MI: University of Michigan Press, 1999)

Lacey, Eric, 'Birds and Bird-Lore in the Literature of Anglo-Saxon England' (unpublished doctoral thesis, University College London, 2013)

—— 'Birds and Words: Aurality, Semantics and Species in Anglo-Saxon England', in *Sensory Perception in the Medieval West*, ed. by Simon C. Thomson and Michael D. J. Bintley (Turnhout: Brepols, 2016), pp. 75–98

—— 'When Is a Hroc not a Hroc? When It Is a Crawe or a Hrefn!: A Case-Study in Recovering Old English Folk-Taxonomies', in *The Art, Literature and Material Culture of the Medieval World*, ed. by M. Boulton, J. Hawkes and M. Herman (Dublin: Four Courts, 2015) pp. 138–52

Lawrence, Elizabeth, 'The Tamed Wild: Symbolic Bears in American Culture', in *Dominant Symbols in Popular Culture*, ed. by Ray Brown, Marshall Fishwick and Kevin Browne (Bowling Green, OH: Bowling Green State University Popular Press, 1990), pp. 140–53

Leach, Elizabeth Eva, *Sung Birds: Music, Nature, and Poetry in the Later Middle Ages* (Ithaca, NY and London: Cornell University Press, 2007)

Lendinara, Patrizia, 'Contextualized Lexicography', in *Latin Learning and English Lore: Studies in Anglo-Saxon Literature for Michael Lapidge*, ed. by Katherine O'Brien O'Keeffe and Andy Orchard, 2 vols (Toronto: University of Toronto Press, 2005), vol. 2, pp. 108–31
——, 'The World of Anglo-Saxon Learning', in *The Cambridge Companion to Old English Literature*, ed. by Malcolm Godden and Michael Lapidge (Cambridge: Cambridge University Press, 1991), pp. 264–81
Leslie, Roy F., 'The Editing of Old English Poetic Texts: Questions of Style', in *Old English Poetry: Essays on Style*, ed. by Daniel G. Calder (Berkeley, CA: University of California Press, 1979), pp. 111–25
Lévi-Strauss, Claude, *La Pensée sauvage* (Paris: Librairie Plon, 1962)
——, *The Savage Mind*, trans. by George Weidenfeld and Nicolson Ltd (London: Weidenfeld and Nicolson, 1966)
——, and Didier Eribon, *Conversations with Claude Lévi-Strauss*, trans. by Paula Wissing (Chicago, IL: University of Chicago Press, 1991)
Lewis, Suzanne, *The Art of Matthew Paris in* Chronica Majora (Berkeley and Los Angeles, CA: University of California Press, 1987)
Lingis, Alphonso, 'Understanding Avian Intelligence', in *Knowing Animals*, ed. by Laurence Simmons and Philip Armstrong (Leiden and Boston, MA: Brill, 2007), pp. 43–56
Lochrie, Karma, *Covert Operations: The Medieval Uses of Secrecy* (Philadelphia, PA: University of Pennsylvania Press, 1999)
Lockwood, W. B., *The Oxford Book of British Bird Names* (Oxford: Oxford University Press, 1984)
Low, Matt, '"Heard gripe hruson" (The hard grip of the earth): Ecopoetry and the Anglo-Saxon Elegy', *Mosaic*, 42:3 (2009), 1–18
MacNeice, Louis, *Selected Poems* (London: Faber and Faber, 1998)
Magennis, Hugh, 'Images of Laughter in Old English Poetry with Particular Reference to the "hleator wera" of *The Seafarer*', *English Studies*, 73:3 (1992), 193–204
Mainzer, C., 'John Gower's Use of the Medieval Ovid in the *Confessio Amantis*', *Medium Ævum*, 41 (1972), 215–29
Mann, Jill, *From Aesop to Reynard: Beast Literature in Medieval Britain* (Oxford: Oxford University Press, 2009)
Marenbon, J., 'Les sources du vocabulaire d'Aldhelm', *Bulletin du Cange*, 41 (1979), 75–90
Marsden, Richard, ed., *The Cambridge Old English Reader* (Cambridge: Cambridge University Press, 2004)
Matlock, Wendy, 'Talking Animals, Debating Beasts', in *Rethinking Chaucerian Beasts*, ed. by Carolynn Van Dyke (New York, NY: Palgrave Macmillan, 2012), pp. 217–32
Matthews, Paul, *The Revelation of Nature* (Aldershot and Burlington, VT: Ashgate Publishing, 2001)

McCracken, Peggy, *In the Skin of a Beast: Sovereignty and Animality in Medieval France* (Chicago, IL: University of Chicago Press, 2017)
—— , 'Translation and Animals in Marie de France's *Lais*', *Australian Journal of French Studies*, 46 (2009), 206–18
McFadden, Brian, 'Raiding, Reform, and Reaction: Wondrous Creatures in the Exeter Book Riddles', *Texas Studies in Literature and Language*, 50:4 (2008), 329–51
—— , 'Sweet Odours and Interpretative Authority in the Exeter Book *Physiologus* and *Phoenix*', *Papers on Language and Literature*, 42:2 (2006), 181–210
McFarland, Sarah E., 'Animal Studies, Literary Animals and Yann Martell's *Life of Pi*', in *The Cambridge Companion to Literature and the Environment*, ed. by Louise Westling (New York, NY: Cambridge University Press, 2014), pp. 152–65
McKinley, Kathryn L., 'Gower and Chaucer: Readings of Ovid in Late Medieval England', in *Ovid in the Middle Ages*, ed. by James G. Clark, Frank T. Coulson and Kathryn L. McKinley (Cambridge: Cambridge University Press, 2011), pp. 197–230
Meaney, Audrey L., 'Birds on the Stream of Consciousness: Riddles 7–10 of the Exeter Book', *Archaeological Review from Cambridge*, 18 (2002), 119–52
—— , 'Exeter Book Riddle 57 (55) – A Double Solution?" *Anglo-Saxon England*, 39 (1996), 187–200
Milovanović-Barham, Celica, 'Aldhelm's *Enigmata* and Byzantine Riddles', *Anglo-Saxon England*, 22 (1993), 51–64
Minnis, Alastair, *Fallible Authors: Chaucer's Pardoner and Wife of Bath* (Philadelphia, PA: University of Pennsylvania Press, 2008)
Mitchell, Bruce, and Fred C. Robinson, *A Guide to Old English*, 5th edn (Oxford: Blackwell, 1992)
Miyazaki, Mariko, 'Misericord Owls and Medieval Anti-Semitism', in *The Mark of the Beast: The Medieval Bestiary in Art, Life and Literature*, Garland Medieval Casebooks, 22, ed. by Debra Hassig (New York, NY and London: Garland, 1999), pp. 23–50
Morris, Desmond, *Owl* (London: Reaktion Books, 2009)
Morton, Jonathan, 'Wolves in Human Skin: Questions of Animal Appetite in Jean de Meun's *Roman de la Rose*', *Modern Language Review*, 105 (2010), 976–97
Moss, Stephen, *A Bird in the Bush: A Social History of Birdwatching* (London: Aurum, 2004)
Murphy, Patrick, *Unriddling the Exeter Riddles* (University Park, PA: Pennsylvania State University Press, 2011)
Mynott, Jeremy, *Birdscape: Birds in Imagination and Experience* (Princeton, NJ: Princeton University Press, 2009)
Neville, Jennifer, 'Fostering the Cuckoo: *Exeter Book* Riddle 9', *Review of English Studies*, New Series, 58 (2007), 431–46

——, '"None Shall Pass": Mental Barriers to Travel in Old English Poetry', in *Freedom of Movement in the Middle Ages: People, Ideas, Goods*, The Harlaxton Symposium, 2003, ed. by P. Horden (Donington: Shaun Tyas/ Paul Watkins, 2007), pp. 203–14

——, 'Precarious Insights into Wooden Artefacts', in *Trees and Timber in the Anglo-Saxon World*, ed. by Michael D. J. Bintley and Michael G. Shapland (Oxford: Oxford University Press, 2013), pp. 122–43

——, *Representations of the Natural World in Old English Poetry*, Cambridge Studies in Anglo-Saxon England, 27 (Cambridge: Cambridge University Press, 1999)

Newman, Barbara, *Medieval Crossover: Reading the Secular against the Sacred* (Notre Dame, IN: University of Notre Dame, 2013)

Nicholson, Adam, *The Seabird's Cry: The Lives and Loves of Puffins, Gannets and Other Ocean Voyagers* (London: William Collins, 2017)

Niles, John D., *Old English Enigmatic Poems and the Play of the Texts* (Turnhout: Brepols, 2006)

North, Richard, 'Heaven Ahoy! Sensory Perception in *The Seafarer*', in *Sensory Perception in the Medieval West*, ed. by Simon C. Thomson and Michael D. J. Bintley (Turnhout: Brepols, 2016), pp. 7–26

Oerlemans, Onno, 'The Animal in Allegory: From Chaucer to Gray', *Interdisciplinary Studies in Literature and Environment*, 20:2 (2013), 296–317

Olson, Paul, 'The *Parlement of Foules*: Aristotle's *Politics* and the Foundations of Human Society', *Studies in the Age of Chaucer*, 2 (1980), 53–69

Orchard, Andy, 'Enigma Variations: The Anglo-Saxon Riddle-Tradition', in *Latin Learning and English Lore: Studies in Anglo-Saxon Literature for Michael Lapidge*, ed. by Katherine O'Brien O'Keeffe and Andy Orchard, 2 vols (Toronto: University of Toronto Press, 2005), vol. 1, pp. 284–304

——, *The Poetic Art of Aldhelm*, Cambridge Studies in Anglo-Saxon England, 8 (Cambridge: Cambridge University Press, 1994)

Orton, P. R., 'Form and Structure of *The Seafarer*', *Studia Neophilologica*, 63 (1991), 37–55

——, 'The Seafarer 58–64a', *Neophilologus*, 66:3 (1982), 450–9

Osborn, Marijane, 'The Vanishing Seabirds in *The Wanderer*', *Folklore*, 85 (1974), 122–7

Pairet, Ana, 'Recasting the *Metamorphoses* in Fourteenth-Century France: The Challenges of the *Ovide moralisé*', in *Ovid in the Middle Ages*, ed. by James G. Clark, Frank T. Coulson and Kathryn L. McKinley (Cambridge: Cambridge University Press, 2011), pp. 83–107

Palmer Browne, Megan, 'Chaucer's Chauntecleer', in *Rethinking Chaucerian Beasts*, ed. by Carolynn Van Dyke (New York, NY: Palgrave Macmillan, 2012), pp. 203–15

Pascua, Esther, 'From Forest to Farm and Town: Domestic Animals from ca. 1000 to ca. 1450', in *A Cultural History of Animals in the Medieval Age*, ed. by Brigitte Resl (Oxford and New York, NY: Berg, 2007), pp. 81–102

Pfeffer, Wendy, 'Spring, Love, Birdsong: The Nightingale in Two Cultures', in *The Mark of the Beast: The Medieval Bestiary in Art, Life and Literature*, Garland Medieval Casebooks, 22, ed. by Debra Hassig (New York, NY and London: Garland, 1999), pp. 88–95

Poole, Kristopher, and Eric Lacey, 'Avian Aurality in Anglo-Saxon England', *World Archaeology*, 46:3 (2014), 400–15

Poole, Russell, *Old English Wisdom Poetry*, Annotated Bibliographies of Old and Middle English, 5 (Cambridge: D. S. Brewer, 1998)

Pope, John C., 'Second Thoughts on the Interpretation of *The Seafarer*', *Anglo-Saxon England*, 3 (1974), 75–86

Potkay, Monica Brzezinski, 'Natural Law in *The Owl and the Nightingale*', *Chaucer Review*, 28:4 (1994), 368–83

Pratt, Rebekah L., 'From Animals to Meat: Illuminating the Medieval Ritual of Unmaking', *eHumanista*, 25 (2013), 17–30

Price, Helen, 'Human and Nonhuman in Anglo-Saxon and British Postwar Poetry: Reshaping Literary Ecology' (unpublished doctoral thesis, University of Leeds, 2013)

Ramirez, Janina Sara, 'The Symbolic Life of Birds in Anglo-Saxon England' (unpublished doctoral thesis, University of York, 2006)

Rothschild, Victoria, '*The Parliament of Fowls*: Chaucer's Mirror up to Nature?', *English Studies*, 35 (1984), 164–84

Rowland, Beryl, *Birds with Human Souls: A Guide to Bird Symbolism* (Knoxville, TN: University of Tennessee Press, 1978)

—— , *Blind Beasts: Chaucer's Animal World* (Kent, OH: Kent State University Press, 1971)

Rudd, Gillian, *Greenery: Ecocritical Readings of Late Medieval English Literature* (Manchester: Manchester University Press, 2007)

Russell, Jeffrey Burton, *Witchcraft in the Middle Ages* (Ithaca, NY and London: Cornell University Press, 1972)

Salisbury, Joyce E., *The Beast Within: Animals in the Middle Ages*, 2nd edn (Abingdon and New York, NY: Routledge, 2011)

—— , 'Human Beasts and Bestial Humans in the Middle Ages', in *Animal Acts: Configuring the Human in Western History*, ed. by Jennifer Ham and Matthew Senior (New York, NY and London: Routledge, 1997), pp. 9–22

Salmon, Vivian, '"The Wanderer" and "The Seafarer", and the Old English Conception of the Soul', *Modern Language Review*, 55:1 (1960), 1–10

Salter, David, *Holy and Noble Beasts: Encounters with Animals in Medieval Literature* (Cambridge: D. S. Brewer, 2001)

Salvador-Bello, Mercedes, *Isidorian Perceptions of Order: The Exeter Book Riddles and Medieval Latin Enigmata*, Medieval European Studies Series, 17 (Morgantown, WV: West Virginia University Press, 2015)

Sanmark, Alexander, 'Living On: Ancestors and the Soul', in *Signals of Belief in Early England: Anglo-Saxon Paganism Revisited*, ed. by M. Carver, A. Sanmark and S. Semple (Oxford: Oxbow, 2010), pp. 162–84

Schichler, Robert L., 'From "Whale-Road" to "Gannet's Bath": Images of Foreign Relations and Exchange in *Beowulf*', *Reading Medieval Studies*, 28 (1999), 59–86

Shakespeare, William, *The Oxford Shakespeare*, gen. eds Stanley Wells and Gary Taylor, 2nd edn (Oxford: Oxford University Press, 2005)

Shaw, Philip A., 'Telling a Hawk from an *Herodio*: On the Origins and Development of the Old English Word *Wealhhafoc* and Its Relatives', *Medium Ævum*, 82:1 (2013), 1–22

Shepard, Paul, *The Others* (Washington, D.C.: Island Press, 1996)

Shipley, Joseph T., *The Origins of English Words: A Discursive Dictionary of Indo-European Roots* (Baltimore, MD: Johns Hopkins University Press, 1984)

Sieper, Ernst, *Die altenglische elegie* (Strasbourg: Trübner 1915)

Simpson, J. A., and E. S. C. Weiner, eds, *The Oxford English Dictionary*, 20 vols, 2nd edn (Oxford: Oxford University Press, 1989)

Slavin, Philip, 'Chicken Husbandry in Late-Medieval Eastern England: c. 1250–1400', *Anthropozoologica*, 44:2 (2009), 35–56

——, 'Goose Management and Reading in Late Medieval Eastern England, c. 1250–1400', *Agricultural History Review*, 58:1 (2010), 1–29

Smithers, G. V., 'The Meaning of *The Seafarer* and *The Wanderer*', *Medium Ævum*, 26:3 (1957), 137–53

——, 'The Meaning of *The Seafarer* and *The Wanderer* (continued)', *Medium Ævum*, 28:1 (1959), 1–22

Southmayd, David E., 'Chaucer and the Medieval Conventions of Bird Imagery' (unpublished doctoral thesis, McGill University, Montreal, Canada, 1980)

Spearing, A. C., *Medieval Dream Poetry* (Cambridge: Cambridge University Press, 1976)

Srivastava, Anila, '"Mean, Dangerous and Uncontrollable Beasts": Medieval Animal Trials', *Mosaic*, 40:1 (2007), 127–43

Stanley, E. G., 'Old English Poetic Diction and the Interpretation of *The Wanderer*, *The Seafarer* and *The Penitent's Prayer*', *Anglia*, 73 (1955), 413–66

Stanton, Robert, 'Mimicry, Subjectivity and the Embodied Voice in Anglo-Saxon Bird Riddles', in *Voice and Voicelessness in Medieval Europe*, ed. by Irit Ruth Kleiman (New York, NY: Palgrave Macmillan, 2015), pp. 29–46

Steel, Karl, *How To Make a Human: Animals and Violence in the Middle Ages* (Columbus, OH: Ohio State University, 2011)

Steinmeyer, Elias, and Eduard Sievers, *Die althochdeutschen glossen* (Berlin: Weidmannsche Buchhandlung, 1895)

Strickland, Debra Higgs, 'The Jews, Leviticus, and the Unclean', in *Beyond the Yellow Badge: Anti-Judaism and Antisemitism in Medieval and Early*

Modern Visual Culture, ed. by Mitchell B. Merback (Leiden: Brill, 2007), pp. 203–32

Stone, Louise W., ed., *Anglo-Norman Dictionary*, 7 vols (London: Modern Humanities Research Association, 1983)

Suolahti, Hugo, *Die deutschen vogelnamen* (Strasbourg: Trübner, 1909)

Svensson, Lars, Killian Mullarney and Dan Zetterström, *Collins Bird Guide*, 2nd edn (London: Collins, 2009)

Tate, Peter, *Flights of Fancy: Birds in Myth, Legend and Superstition* (London: Random House, 2007)

Thomas, Keith, *Man and the Natural World: Changing Attitudes in England, 1500–1800* (London: Penguin, 1984)

Timmer, B. J., 'Irony in Old English Poetry', *English Studies*, 24 (1942), 171–5

Toswell, M. J., 'Bede's Sparrow and the Psalter in Anglo-Saxon England', *American Notes and Queries*, 13:1 (2000), 7–12

Travis, Peter W., 'Thirteen Ways of Listening to a Fart: Noise in Chaucer's *Summoner's Tale*', *Exemplaria*, 16 (2004), 323–48

Van Dyke, Carolynn, *Chaucer's Agents: Cause and Representation in Chaucerian Narrative* (Madison, WI: Fairleigh Dickinson University Press, 2005)

——, 'Names of the Beasts: Tracking the *Animot* in the Medieval Texts', *Studies in the Age of Chaucer*, 34 (2012), 1–51

——, 'That Which Chargeth Not to Say: Animal Imagery in *Troilus and Criseyde*', in *Rethinking Chaucerian Beasts*, ed. by Carolynn Van Dyke (New York, NY: Palgrave Macmillan, 2012), pp. 101–12

——, 'Touched by an Owl: An Essay in Vernacular Ethology', *Postmedieval: A Journal of Medieval Cultural Studies*, 7:2 (2016), 304–27

Van Fleteren, Frederick, 'Principles of Augustine's Hermeneutic: An Overview', in *Augustine: Biblical Exegete*, ed. by Frederick Van Fleteren and Joseph C. Schnaubelt, Order of Saint Augustine (New York, NY: Peter Lang, 2001), pp. 1–32

Wallace, David, *Geoffrey Chaucer: A New Introduction* (Oxford: Oxford University Press, 2017)

Watt, Diane, 'Gender and Sexuality in *Confessio Amantis*', in *A Companion to Gower*, ed. by Siân Echard (Cambridge: D. S. Brewer, 2004), pp. 197–214

——, 'Sins of Omission: Transgressive Genders, Subversive Sexualities, and Confessional Silences in John Gower's *Confessio Amantis*', *Exemplaria*, 13:2 (2001), 529–51

Wells, Richard, 'The Old English Riddles and Their Ornithological Content', *Lore and Language*, 2 (1978), 57–66

Welsh, Andrew, *Roots of Lyric: Primitive Poetry and Modern Poetics* (Princeton, NJ: Princeton University Press, 1987)

——, 'Swallows Name Themselves: Exeter Book Riddle 55', *American Notes and Queries*, 3:2 (1990), 90–3

Wheeler, Wendy, '"Tongues I'll Hang on Every Tree": Biosemiotics and the Book of Nature', in *The Cambridge Companion to Literature and the Environment*, ed. by Louise Westling (New York, NY: Cambridge University Press, 2014), pp. 121–35

White, Hugh, *Nature, Sex, and Goodness in a Medieval Literary Tradition* (Oxford: Oxford University Press, 2000)

Whitehouse, Andrew, 'Listening to Birds in the Anthropocene: The Anxious Semiotics of Sound in a Human-Dominated World', *Environmental Humanities*, 6 (2015), 53–71

Whitelock, Dorothy, 'The Interpretation of *The Seafarer*', in *Early Cultures of Northwest Europe*, ed. by Cyril Fox and Bruce Dickins (Cambridge: Cambridge University Press, 1950), pp. 261–72

Whitman, Charles H., 'The Birds of Old English Literature', *Journal of Germanic Philology*, 2 (1898), 149–98

Wright, Thomas, and Richard Paul Wülcker, *Anglo-Saxon and Old English Vocabularies*, 2 vols (London: Trübner and Co., 1884), vol. 1

Yalden, D. W., and U. Albarella, *The History of British Birds* (Oxford: Oxford University Press, 2009)

Yamamoto, Dorothy, *The Boundaries of the Human in Medieval English Literature* (Oxford: Oxford University Press, 2000)

Yapp, Brunsdon, *Birds in Medieval Manuscripts* (London: British Library, 1981)

Yeager, R. F., *John Gower's Poetics: The Search for a New Arion* (Cambridge: D. S. Brewer, 1990)

INDEX

Abelard of Bath: *De avibus tractatus* 197 n.37
Aelred of Rievaulx: *Dialogue on the Soul* 153
Ælfric
  De temporibus anni 93 n.64
  Exameron Anglice 93 n.64
  Grammar 79 n.35, 83, 90, 92, 94 n.69
  Lives of the Saints 26
Alan of Lille
  Book of Nature metaphor (*De incarnatione christi*) 107
  De planctu naturae 153, 155, 169 n.52, 171 n.56, 196 n.36
Albertus Magnus: *On Animals* 155 n.21
Aldhelm
  De pedum regulis 48 n.66, 79 n.35, 90 n.61
  Enigmata 70 n.16, 84, 85, 86, 92 n.63; Enigma 22: 34 n.26; Enigma 29: 98 n.75; Enigma 34: 70 n.16; Enigma 41: 70 n.16; Enigma 46: 34 n.26, 85–6; Enigma 57: 70 n.16; Enigma 59: 98, 99, 100, 231; Enigma 64: 70 n.16
Allegory
  alternative perceptions of 21–2, 168–77
  Augustinian 63, 175
  complications with when representing the nonhuman 7–10, 21–2, 147, 149, 150–2
  conflicting or combined literal and metaphorical treatments in 8–9, 10, 36, 52, 54, 168–77
  ethics of 150, 174, 221–2
  in *Parliament of Fowls* see under Chaucer
  traditional examples of or approaches to 7–8, 9–10, 25, 106–7, 109–10, 130–1, 143, 150–2, 186–7
Ancrene Wisse 27 n.8, 109–10, 130
Anglo-Latin riddle tradition 65–6, 86, 87, 91–2, 95, 98–9
  Bern Riddle 8 77 n.33
  Boniface 85 n.47
  Pseudo-Bede: Riddle 79 86 n.51
  See also Aldhelm, Eusebius, Symphosius *and* Tatwine
Anglo-Norman debate-poems 103–4
Anglo-Saxon Chronicles 61
Anglo-Saxon ornithology 31–5
Animal legal trials 138
Animal studies 2–3, 112, 150, 183, 219–20
Aristotle 13, 34, 130 n.49
  De interpretatione 154 n.17
  Historia animalium 129–30 n.48, 152 n.10, 169, 213, 214 n.72
  On the Soul 152 n.10, 154 n.14
  Progression of Animals 11 n.29
Augustine, Saint 175
  allegory 63, 175
  De civitate dei 26
  De dialectica 63
  Exposition of Psalms 7–8, 26, 33
  On Music 151 n.5

Babewyns 180, 185
Bartholomaeus Anglicus: *De proprietatibus rerum* see Trevisa
Bede: *Historia ecclesiastica* 25–6, 27 n.9, 28, 33, 37, 59, 63 n.90

255

Index

Beowulf 34, 47 n.61, 61
Berger, John: *About Looking* 156
Bersuire, Pierre (Petrus Berchorius):
   Ovidius moralizatus 187, 208
Bestiaries
  birds in 2, 4, 108–9, 110, 113, 126,
    137 n.60, 141 n.70, 172, 213–14 n.72
  owls in 113, 114, 118–19, 126, 128–30,
    143
  sources for, and as sources for
    poems 86 n.48, 107 n.6, 169, 170,
    172, 213–14 n.72
  traditional representations of
    nonhuman in 2, 8, 104, 108–9, 111,
    169, 170, 172
Biotranslation 150, 164–5
Birds
  bipedality 11–12
  chickens 1, 2
  coins depicting 32 n.21
  debate-poems featuring 8, 20–2,
    103–4, 150; see also *Owl and*
    Nightingale and *Parliament of Fowls*
  flight of 15, 28–30, 51–63, 73–4, 92–3,
    208–9
  in glosses and glossaries 31, 39–40,
    88–92
  in Greek myths and poems 29 n.13,
    181–2 n.5, 213
  medieval philosophy on 11–18
  medieval vocabulary for 1
  migration of 15, 29–30, 33–4, 55–63,
    73, 213 n.72
  mobbing behaviour of 136–7
  modern philosophy on 6–7, 11
  mythical species 4, 171
  naming 39–41, 67, 87–92, 212–16
  particular species *see* Isidore,
    Trevisa *and also* the Glossary
  place-names and 31–2; *see also* the
    Glossary
  seabirds 25–63, especially at 29–30,
    32–5, 58–63
  song and voice 15–17, 40–1,
    45–51,75–7, 81–4, 93, 106, 111,
    122, 124, 128, 147–50, 152–68, 174,
    176–7, 209–12; *see also* Vox
  souls and   *see Seafarer* under *Exeter*
    Book
  transforming and transformative
    bodies of 57–8, 61–3, 72–4,
    189–201, 206–12
  translating song of 45–51, 81–3,
    155–68, 212
  writing and 1, 20, 96–101
'Bird in Bishopswood, A' 9 n.25
'Bird with Four Feathers, The' 9–10,
    18, 162
Bishopstone (Sussex) 32, 40
Boccaccio:
  Filicolo 193 n.32
  Teseida 176
Boethius: *De consolatione*
    philosophiae 11–12 n.30
Book of Nature, The 105–10, 119, 120,
    122, 123, 124

Cassiodorus 130 n.49
Chaucer, Geoffrey
  Adam 161 n.33
  Boece 11 n.30
  Book of Duchess, The 208 n.62
  House of Fame, The 166, 176
  Legend of Good Women, The 195, 208
  Manciple's Tale, The 154 n.16, 161
  Mars 10
  Merchant's Tale, The 211 n.68
  Nun's Priest's Tale, The 157, 166, 189
  Parliament of Fowls, The 10, 20, 21–2,
    147–77, 189, 196–7, 210, 212,
    221; allegory in, 150–52, 168–77;
    catalogue of birds, 169–73; critical
    tradition of, 150–2, 167–8, 169;
    rime royal, 176; use of French in,
    176–7
  Squire's Tale, The 157, 158, 159, 166,
    174, 189, 193 n.28
  Summoner's Tale, The 148
  Troilus and Criseyde 10, 163 n.36,
    193–4, 195, 206 n.60, 210, 211 n.67
    and 68, 212 n.69
  Wife of Bath (character) 163
Clerk and the Nightingale, The 8 n.23
Confessio Amantis, see Gower

Index

Cuckoo and the Nightingale, The 8 n.23, 104 n.2

'Debate of the Carpenter's Tools' 104 n.2
'Debate of the Horse, Goose and Sheep' 104 n.2
'De cantibus avium' 16 n.50, 55 n.79, 90–1
'De filomela' 17 n.51
Deleuze, Gilles 6
Derrida, Jacques 14
De scala natura (Chain of Being) 125–6
Deschamps, Eustache 176 n.69
Donatus: *Ars grammatica* 72

Ecocriticism 2–3, 36
Eco, Umberto 154, 156
Elene 61
Ethics of representing the nonhuman 150, 168–9, 119, 122, 126–8, 134–44, 174, 177, 219–23
Etymologies, The see Isidore of Seville
Eusebius 85 n.47
 Enigma 38, 77 n.33
Exeter Book, The 18
 Christ II 33 n.25
 didactic purpose of 65–6, 91–2
 Husband's Message, The 33
 Panther, The 35
 Phoenix, The 27–8, 35 n.30, 67–8, 76
 Physiologus 67–8
 Riddles 14, 19–20, 41, 47–8, 65–101, 219, 221; Riddle 2: 95; Riddle 7: 34, 41, 70, 73, 74, 80, 87, 92; Riddle 8: 73, 75–7, 78, 92, 97, 231; Riddle 9: 70, 73, 74, 77, 80; Riddle 10: 34, 73, 74, 92, 225; Riddle 24: 41, 72, 73, 76, 78–84, 154 n.16; Riddle 26: 99; Riddle 29: 100; Riddle 31: 72–3; Riddle 42: 88, 95; Riddle 43: 58n; Riddle 47: 80, 95; Riddle 51: 73, 96–101; Riddle 57: 70 n.16, 73, 92–6, 97–8; Riddle 74: 70 n.16; Riddle 93: 99 n.77; Riddle 95: 100
 Wonder in 67–71

Seafarer, The 8, 10, 18–19, 22, 25–63, 71, 76, 80, 119, 175, 220; the *anfloga*/bird-soul: 29, 30 n.16, 51–8, 59, 62–3
Wanderer, The 8–9, 29, 38–9, 42 n.46, 49, 50–1, 52–3, 54, 55, 61

Falconry 1–2, 31, 195–6
Fifteen Signs tradition 165
Foreignness (Anglo-Saxon ideas of) 60–1
Foulness Island (Essex) 32
Frederick II, Holy Emperor 2 n.4, 195 n.35

Genesis B 62
Gerald of Wales: *Topographia hibernica* 140 n.69, 183 n.6, 185 n.14, 225
Gervase of Tilbury 183 n.6
Gower, John
 Confessio Amantis 14, 22, 30, 180 n.1, 181, 186, 188, 195, 197–8, 200, 201–2; Amans, 181, 187, 197, 198, 206; ambiguous morality in, 201–6; 'Calistona', 197; 'Canace and Machaire', 198 n.40; 'Ceix and Alceone', 181 n.4, 186, 187, 189–92, 200, 206 n.60; 'Neptune and Cornix', 181 n.4, 193, 197, 209 n.63, 210 n.66; 'Phebus and Cornide', 181 n.4; 'Tale of Tereus' 11, 22–3, 179–217, 222; avian transformations in, 189–201, 206–12; mutilation in, 202–6; Philomela, 17, 22, 192–201, 203–4, 207–8, 209–12, 214–17, 222; Procne, 22, 205, 207, 209–12, 214–17, 222; Tereus, 22, 192–206, 214–17
 Vox Clamantis 188, 197
Gregory the Great 25 n.4, 57 n.83
Guattari, Félix 6
Guthlac A 42, 43

Heaney, Seamus: 'Small Fantasia for W. B.' 25, 28–9, 58–9

Index

Hugh of Foilloy: *Avarium* 108–9, 120 n.39, 129 n.47, 130
Hugh of Saint Victor 107 n.7

Isidore of Seville: *Etymologiae*
  animals in 106–7, 49
  birds' voices in 15–16, 41 n.44
  introduction to birds in 14, 34, 55–6, 73, 90, 101
  as source or analogue 11 n.30, 15, 77 n.33, 78 n.34, 120 n.39; 129 n.48; 171 n.56; 196 n.36; 214 n.72
  specific bird species in crane, 16 and 171 n.56; swallow, 34 and 213 n.72; stork, 34; magpie, 81, 82 n.40, 153; peacock, 88; raven, 88 and 171 n.56; *nycticorax*, 130 n.49; parrot, 153 and 171 n.56; duck, 171 n.56; goose, 171 n.56; kite, 171 n.56; goshawk, 196 n.36
  subject of etymology in 85–6

Jehan et Blonde 157 n.28
John of Worcester 5
Johnson, Samuel 213 n.72
Judgement, Day of 18, 58 n.84

Lambeth Psalter 28 n.11
Langland, William: *Piers Plowman* 8 n.23
Leiden Glossary 89–90
Lévi-Strauss, Claude
  Conversations with Claude Lévi-Strauss 167
  Savage Mind, The 6–8, 10, 17, 148,
Leviticus (unclean creatures) 106, 114–15 n.27
Liber de ordine creaturarum 73 n.24

MacNeice, Louis 25, 28
Marie de France 183 n.6, 185 n.15; *Yonec*, 196–7, 200
  See also under *Owl and the Nightingale*
Matthew of Paris 5 n.13
Maurus, Hrabanus: *De rerum naturis* 15 n.44, 129 n.47

Metamorphosis
  medieval responses to 183–9
  see also Ovid
Metaphor (involving birds)
  in bestiaries and other sources 2, 108–10, 137
  ethics of 219–23
  in fables 108, 115–19
  goshawk metaphor in 'Tale of Tereus' 192–201
  in Lévi-Strauss 6–8
  literal qualities as part of 7–8, 8–10, 51, 116–19, 173–4, 175
  in Old English Riddles 77, 79–81, 84
  seabird-soul metaphor 8–9; see also *The Seafarer* under *Exeter Book*
  sparrow metaphor 25–7
  workings of 7–8, 79–81, 217, 219–223
  see also Allegory
Merle and the Nightingale, The 8n
Metres of Boethius 76

Names for birds *See under* Birds
Neckham, Alexander: *De naturis rerum* 15 n.44, 138, 169 n.52, 171 n.56, 172 n.59
Nonhuman (use of term) 3
Norwich cathedral (owls) 142

Odo of Cheriton: fables 108, 115
Odyssey, The 29 n.13
Olaus Magnus, archbishop 213 n.72
Ornithology (medieval) 11–18 and 31–5
Ovid
  Metamorphoses 22, 119 n.36, 181, 187, 188, 190, 191, 192, 195, 199, 202, 203, 208, 209, 211, 214, 215
  Ovidian transformation 14, 181, 185–8, 204
Ovide moralisé, L' 179–80, 186–7, 195 n.34, 196, 213
Owl and the Nightingale, The 10, 20–1, 103–44, 147, 221–2
  bestiary sources for owl *see* Hugh of Foilloy *and under* Bestiary
  date of 107 n.8

258

Index

fables in 108, 114–19, 134–5
King Alfred 116, 129
Marie de France: 'De l'ostur e del huan' 115, 116; *Laüstic*, 134–5
mistreatment of human social groups 138–41
mistreatment of Jews 141–43
Nicholas of Guildford 116
nightingale 106, 110 n.17, 119, 122, 128, 134–5
rustic life in 132–3

Parliament of Fowls see under Chaucer
Peter Damien 3
Petit Plet, Le 139
Philomena *see under* Gower
Physiologus 4, 119 n.36, 141 n.70
  See under Exeter Book for Old English *Physiologus*
Pilgrimage (*peregrinatio*) 26–8, 43, 52–8
Place-names *see under* Birds
Pliny the Elder: *Naturalis historia* 34, 35 n.29, 56 n.80, 76, 77 n.31, 86 n.48, 120 n.38, 169 n.52, 213–14 n.72, 231
Priscian 153–4, 155, 162
Probus 153–4
Procne *see under* Gower
Properties of Things, The see Trevisa
Psalms 26–7

Riddles *see under* Anglo-Latin riddle tradition *and* Exeter Book
Roman de la Rose 201

Seafarer, The see under Exeter Book
Shakespeare, William
  Comedy of Errors 214 n.73
  Macbeth 136 n.59
  Measure for Measure 214 n.73
  Much Ado about Nothing 214 n.73
Sherborne Missal 5, 38, 172 n.57, 225, 226, 228, 230, 232, 234
Sir Gawain and the Green Knight 204 n.57

Solomon and Saturn 67 n.4
Soul and Body poems 58 n.84
Symphosius 85 n.47
  Enigma 14 77 n.33
  Enigma 26 99

'Tale of Tereus', *see under* Gower
Tatwine 85 n.47
  Enigma 6, 99
Tereus *see under* Gower
Thomas de Cantimpré: *Liber de natura rerum* 152 n.10
Thomas of Chobham 132
Thrush and the Nightingale, The 8n, 104 n.2
Translating nonhuman voices 45–51, 81–3, 147–77, 212
Trevisa, John: *The Properties of Things*
  as source or analogue 169 n.52; 171 n.56; 214 n.72
  categorisation of birds in 12–13
  introduction to birds in 14–15, 96, 173, 175, 219
  specific bird species in bittern, 225; curlew, 227; lapwing, 215 n.74; goshawk, 195–6, 197, 201; gull (*larus*), 14, 33; owl (*ulula*), 129 n.48; swallow, 213 n.72

Uexküll, Jakob von: *Umwelt* 164, 166 n.43

Vincent of Beauvais: *Speculum naturale* 169 n.52, 171 n.56, 172 n.59, 200 n.44
Voces animantium 16, 79, 90
Vox (medieval grammar theories of) 16–17, 48, 83, 152–6, 158–9, 161–2, 163 n.36

Wanderer, The see under Exeter Book
White, Gilbert 213 n.72
William of Malmesbury 183 n.6

www.ingramcontent.com/pod-product-compliance
Lightning Source LLC
Chambersburg PA
CBHW051607230426
43668CB00013B/2018